U
Lotus

ALSO AVAILABLE

(By the same author)

BP232 A Concise Introduction to MS-DOS

BP243 BBC-BASIC86 on Amstrad PCs & IBM Compatibles
Book 1 - Language#1

BP244 BBC-BASIC86 on Amstrad PCs & IBM Compatibles
Book 2 - Graphics and Disk Files#1

BP250 Programming in FORTRAN 77

BP258 Learning to Program in C

BP259 A Concise Introduction to UNIX

BP260 A Concise Introduction to OS/2

BP261 A Concise Introduction to Lotus 1-2-3

BP264 A Concise Advanced User's Guide to MS-DOS

BP274 A Concise Introduction to SuperCalc5

BP270 A Concise Introduction to Symphony#2

BP279 A Concise Introduction to Excel

BP283 A Concise Introduction to SmartWare II#3

BP284 Programming in QuickBASIC

BP288 A Concise Introduction to Windows 3.0

BP294 A Concise Introduction to Microsoft Works#2

BP302 A Concise User's Guide to Lotus 1-2-3 Release 3.1#2

BP306 A Concise Introduction to Ami Pro 3#2

BP314 A Concise Introduction to Quattro Pro 3.0

BP318 A Concise User's Guide to MS-DOS 5

BP319 Making MS-DOS Work for You#2

BP325 A Concise User's Guide to Windows 3.1

#1co-author Keith Thompson
#2co-author Phil Oliver
#3co-author Steve Cant

A Concise User's Guide to Lotus 1-2-3 Release 2.4

by

Noel Kantaris

BERNARD BABANI (publishing) LTD.
THE GRAMPIANS
SHEPHERDS BUSH ROAD
LONDON W6 7NF
ENGLAND

PLEASE NOTE

Although every care has been taken with the production of this book to ensure that any projects, designs, modifications and/or programs, etc., contained herewith, operate in a correct and safe manner and also that any components specified are normally available in Great Britain, the Publishers and Author(s) do not accept responsibility in any way for the failure (including fault in design) of any project, design, modification or program to work correctly or to cause damage to any equipment that it may be connected to or used in conjunction with, or in respect of any other damage or injury that may be so caused, nor do the Publishers accept responsibility in any way for the failure to obtain specified components.

Notice is also given that if equipment that is still under warranty is modified in any way or used or connected with home-built equipment then that warranty may be void.

First Published - March 1993

British Library Cataloguing in Publication Data:

Kantaris, Noel
Concise User's Guide to Lotus 1-2-3
Release 2.4
I. Title
005.369

ISBN 0 85934 330 8

Printed and Bound in Great Britain by Cox & Wyman Ltd, Reading

ABOUT THIS BOOK

This Concise User's Guide to Lotus 1-2-3 was written to help the beginner. The book deals mainly with the Lotus 1-2-3 Release 2.4, but it can also be used with earlier 2.x Releases. Users of Release 3.0 and 3.1 could use the book as an introduction to spreadsheet concepts, but must bear in mind that the more advanced facilities of multi-dimensionality, or multi-file display, available in Release 3.0, or windowing, available in Release 3.1, are not covered here, but can be found in a separate book entitled 'A Concise User's Guide to Lotus 1-2-3 Release 3.1, also published by BERNARD BABANI (publishing) LTD.

The material in this book is presented on the "what you need to know first, appears first" basis, although the underlying structure of the book is such that you don't have to start at the beginning and go right through to the end. The more experienced user can start from any section, as the sections have been designed to be self contained.

Lotus 1-2-3 is an integrated package containing three major types of applications; spreadsheets, graphics and data management. The package is operated by selecting commands from menus or by writing special 'macros' which utilise the Lotus Command Language to chain together menu commands. Each method of accessing the package is discussed separately, but the emphasis is mostly in the area of menu-driven command selection.

Below we list the major enhancements found in Release 2.4 over earlier releases of the package. These are:

- The inclusion of the SmartIcon add-in which allows the user to create and display 'icons' which when selected perform 1-2-3 or Wysiwyg functions.

- The inclusion of the Backsolver add-in that allows the creation of a formula to achieve a desired result by changing one or more variables that affect the result of the formula

- The inclusion of SmartPics library which contains graphics objects that can be included in a worksheet.

- The ability to print in landscape mode on all supported printers.
- The ability to print to encapsulated PostScript files.
- The inclusion in the Translate utility of the ability to convert .WK1 and .FMT files for use in programs that do not support such file structure.

In addition to the above new features, Release 2.4 supports all the functionality built into Release 2.3, such as

- The ability to link files, and use minimal recalculation.
- The inclusion of a better graphing facility than previous versions of the program (including printing of graphs from within the worksheet).
- The inclusion of the undo mode, macro learn mode, and search and replace facility.
- The inclusion of an add-in manager, and support of the Wysiwyg graphical interface add-in which provides for spreadsheet publishing and allows WYSIWYG display.

Most features of the package (old and new) will be discussed using simple examples that the user is encouraged to type in, save, and modify as more advanced features are introduced.

This book was written with the busy person in mind. You don't need to read hundreds of pages to find out most there is to know about the subject, when a few pages can do the same thing quite adequately!

ABOUT THE AUTHOR

Graduated in Electrical Engineering at Bristol University and after spending three years in the Electronics Industry in London, took up a Tutorship in Physics at the University of Queensland. Research interests in Ionospheric Physics, led to the degrees of M.E. in Electronics and Ph.D. in Physics. On return to the UK, he took up a Post-Doctoral Research Fellowship in Radio Physics at the University of Leicester, and in 1973 a Senior Lectureship in Engineering at The Camborne School of Mines, Cornwall, where since 1978 he has also assumed the responsibility of Head of Computing.

ACKNOWLEDGEMENTS

I would like to thank colleagues at the Camborne School of Mines for the helpful tips and suggestions which assisted me in the writing of this book.

TRADEMARKS

HP LaserJet and **HP DeskJet 500** are registered trademarks of Hewlett Packard Corporation

IBM and **PC-DOS** are registered trademarks of International Business Machines Corporation

Intel is a registered trademark of Intel Corporation

Microsoft and **MS-DOS** are registered trademarks of Microsoft Corporation

Lotus 1-2-3 and **Wysiwyg** are registered trademarks of Lotus Development Corporation

PostScript is a registered trademark of Adobe Systems, Inc.

CONTENTS

1. INTRODUCTION

Lotus 1-2-3 is a powerful versatile software package that, over the last few years, has proved its usefulness, not only in the business world, but with scientific and engineering users as well. The program's power lies in its ability to emulate everything that can be done with pencil, paper and a calculator, and is, therefore, called an 'electronic spreadsheet' or simply a 'spreadsheet', a name also used to describe this and other similar products. Its power is derived from the power of the computer it is running on, and the flexibility and accuracy with which it can deal with the solution of the various applications it has been programmed to manage. These can vary from budgeting to forecasting to the solution of scientific and engineering problems.

Lotus 1-2-3 comes in several flavours; Version 2.x (the subject of this book), incorporating Release 2.0, 2.01, 2.2, 2.3 and 2.4, running mainly on IBM XTs and compatibles (computers equipped with Intel's 8086 or 8088 processor). Then, there is Version 3.x (the subject of another, more advanced book) encompassing Releases 3.0, 3.1 and 3.4, that require a more powerful computer as a platform, such as an IBM AT, PS/2 or compatible (a computer equipped with Intel's superior 80286, 80386 or 80486 processor). Versions 3.x make use of certain programmable aspects of the 80286 and 80386 processors and, therefore, cannot run on computers with the less powerful processors, but there is nothing to stop you from running any of the versions 2.x on any IBM compatible computer, irrespective of the type of processor. All the above versions run under the DOS operating system, while another version of the program, 1-2-3/W, requires the advanced processing power of computers equipped with at least the 286 processor, running under DOS, but with the Windows front-end graphical interface. Last but not least, there is Lotus 1-2-3/G, the Presentation Manager version, using a graphical interface front-end, but running under the OS/2 operating system.

This book deals with Lotus 1-2-3 Version 2.x. As releases within this version are downward compatible, Release 2.4 will be used as the main platform for discussion, but variations between it and earlier releases of the package will be pointed out whenever they occur.

Release 2.4 Features

In general, it is worth upgrading to Release 2.4, which offers several options not found in earlier releases. These are:

- The inclusion of the SmartIcon add-in which allows the user to create and display 'icons' which when selected perform 1-2-3 or Wysiwyg functions.
- The inclusion of the Backsolver add-in that allows the creation of a formula to achieve a desired result by changing one or more variables that affect the result of the formula.
- The inclusion of SmartPics library which contains graphics objects that can be included in a worksheet.
- The ability to print in landscape mode on all supported printers.
- The ability to print to encapsulated PostScript files.
- The inclusion in the Translate utility of the ability to convert .WK1 and .FMT files for use in programs that do not support such file structures.

In addition, the package also supports all the features found in Release 2.3, such as:

- The use of the Undo option.
- The use of the Search and Replace option.
- The ability to use minimal recalculation.
- The ability to set the width of a range of columns.
- The ability to link files on disc.
- The use of 'printer settings' sheet.
- The ability to print text and graphics on the same page.
- The support for PostScript laser printers.
- The ability to save printer information and use background printing.
- The ability to use Quickgraph for groups of data.

- The use of 'graph settings' sheet.
- The ability to use improved graph appearance and new graph types, including 3D effects.
- The ability to access the built-in Manager from the main menus.
- The use of WYSIWYG display & spreadsheet publishing capability.
- The use of a macro library manager, menu macro commands, macro debugging step mode, learn mode for macros with 11 new macro commands and macro run key with unlimited macro names.
- The availability of server and node packs, network file locking, network printing, and support for IBM, NOVELL and 3COM networks.
- The use of dialogue boxes and preselection of ranges.
- Mouse support.
- The use of a context sensitive help system.
- The ability to view the contents of files on disc.

Releases 2.2, 2.3 & 2.4 allow you to improve the overall looks of your charts and reports, the very medium used to communicate information to others. The former is achieved through substantial changes and improvements to the charting and graphing capabilities of the package, while the latter is achieved with either the Allways spreadsheet add-in in the case of Release 2.2, or the Wysiwyg module in the case of Releases 2.3 & 2.4, which are supplied with the package. These allow you complete formatting control over the appearance of your reports, with the capability of producing professional-looking business forms or financial reports which can include both numerical and graphical information on the same page.

Installing 1-2-3

It is assumed here that for releases earlier than Release 2.4 of Lotus 1-2-3, you have followed the instructions accompanying the software, relating to its installation on the hard disc of your computer, or its installation and use from a floppy drive.

To install Release 2.4, first make sure that you have at least 5MB of free space on your hard disc (more if the available free space is fragmented), insert the 'Install' disc in the A: drive, type A: to log onto it, then type

install

and press the <Enter> key.

Lotus 1-2-3 will display a screen in which you are asked to enter your name and your company's name, after which you are presented with the 'Install' screen, shown below.

```
                                 Lotus
     Lotus                  Install Program
                              Release 2.4

    Install     Copyright 1990, 1991, 1992 Lotus Development Corp.
                               All Rights Reserved.

                The Install program sets up 1-2-3 Release 2.4 on
                your system.  The Install program lets you

                * Record your name and organization name on your
                  copy of 1-2-3 Release 2.4.
                * Create a 1-2-3 Release 2.4 directory and transfer
                  the 1-2-3 Release 2.4 files to this directory.
                * Specify equipment to use with 1-2-3 Release 2.4.


                Use, duplication, or sale of this software, except
                as described in the Lotus License Agreement, is
                strictly prohibited.  Violators may be prosecuted.

                Press ENTER to begin.
                                                                NUM
```

Pressing <Enter> causes the screen shown on the next page to be displayed which informs you which files, corresponding to the listed programs, will be transferred on to your hard disc, if you continue. To perform a complete installation, use the cursor keys to highlight, in turn, first the 'PrintGraph' and then the 'Translate' programs and pressing the <Space Bar> to add them to the installation.

```
 Lotus    TRANSFERRING 1-2-3 RELEASE 2.4 AND ITS COMPANION PROGRAMS

          Install transfers the programs with check marks beside
 Install  their names to your hard disk.  To add or remove a check
          mark, press ↑ and ↓ to move the highlight to the program
          name and press the space bar.

          √ 1-2-3 and SmartIcons    ┌──1-2-3 and SmartIcons──────────┐
          √ Wysiwyg                 │1-2-3 and SmartIcons combine    │
          √ Add-Ins                 │spreadsheet, graphics, and      │
          √ 1-2-3-Go!               │database management functions.  │
          √ Wysiwyg-Go!             │                                │
            PrintGraph              │Space required: 2000000 bytes   │
            Translate               └────────────────────────────────┘

          Press ENTER to continue
 ─────────────────────────────────────────────────────────────────────
          ↑ and ↓ move highlight     SPACE BAR adds/removes √
          F1 displays Help           ESC ends Install
                                                                   NUM
```

To continue, press <Enter>. You are now offered the C:\123r24 as the default drive and subdirectory on which 1-2-3 could be installed, but you could change this to one of your choice. On pressing <Enter> the named subdirectory is created and the appropriate files are transferred to it, provided there is enough space on your hard disc. After all the files have been copied, the program displays a screen headed with the message 'File Transfer Successful' and then displays the 'Main Menu' screen, as follows, from which you can specify your equipment.

```
                             MAIN MENU
 ─────────────────────────────────────────────────────────────────────
 Select an option:

   Select Your Equipment            ┌──Select Your Equipment─────────┐
   Change Selected Equipment        │Use Select Your Equipment to    │
   Specify Wysiwyg Options          │select drivers for your screen  │
   End Install                      │display cards and printers      │
                                    │so 1-2-3 will work correctly    │
                                    │with them.                      │
                                    │                                │
                                    │If you plan to use Wysiwyg,     │
                                    │Select Your Equipment also lets │
                                    │you generate font sizes.        │
                                    └────────────────────────────────┘

 ─────────────────────────────────────────────────────────────────────
 ↓  and  ↑  move menu pointer          F1  displays a Help screen
 ENTER selects highlighted choice      F10 displays current selections
                                                                   NUM
```

From the 'Main Menu' screen, choose the 'Select Your Equipment' option, which provides you with step-by-step instructions for completing the installation procedure. It is here that you specify the type of screen adaptor, text printers and graphics printers you intend to use (you can specify more than one printer). At a later stage, you can return to the 'Install' program from the "1-2-3 Access System" to change the selected equipment or specify the Wysiwyg options.

For the present, proceed with the installation by selecting the 'No' option from the 'Saving the Driver Set' screen, and proceed with the installation of the fonts (for use with Wysiwyg), by selecting the 'Basic' option. After a short time, the program displays the 'successful installation' message and returns to the DOS prompt.

Upgrading Other 1-2-3 Add-In Programs:

Most Release 2.0, 2.01, 2.2 & 2.3 add-in programs will work with Releases 2.4. However, some programs were not developed using the Lotus Developer Tools and, if that is the case, will not work correctly with Release 2.4. If you have difficulty in running any of your add-in programs, contact the original manufacturer for a possible upgrade to run with Release 2.4.

Before you can use a Release 2.x add-in program with Release 2.4, you must repeat the installation instructions that came with the add-in program. If such an add-in program installs a copy of the 'Add-In Manager' in your 1-2-3 set, you should remove it as it can save up to 21K of memory. To remove the 'Add-In Manager' from the 1-2-3 driver set, log onto the subdirectory containing your Release 2.4 program by typing **cd\123r24** (if that is its name), and type

```
del_mgr 123.set
```

if you have allowed the program to use the filename **123.set** for your driver set. Otherwise use the name you gave it.

Loading the 1-2-3 Program

If your are using an already installed package on hard disc, then it is most likely that the files which make up the complete package will be found in a subdirectory of your computer's hard disc, and that the actual program can be invoked by typing **Lotus** or **123** at the root directory's prompt. An appropriately written batch file would then locate the subdirectory in which the program's files reside and load the "1-2-3 Access System" into memory.

If you have just installed the package in your computer's hard disc and in the suggested subdirectory, then use **Edit** or a similar editor to produce an appropriate batch file, call it **lotus.bat**, which could contain the following commands:

```
@echo off
cls
cd\123r24
lotus
cd\
```

If your system is correctly implemented, typing

```
lotus
```

should display the "1-2-3 Access System" menu, as follows:

```
Create worksheets, graphs, and databases
1-2-3     PrintGraph     Translate     Install     Exit

                         Lotus
                  1-2-3 Access Menu
                     Release 2.4

     Copyright 1990, 1991, 1992 Lotus Development Corporation
                  All Rights Reserved.

To select a program to start, do one of the following:

   * Use ←, →, HOME, or END to move the menu pointer
     to the program you want and then press ENTER.

   * Type the first character of the program's name.

Press F1 (HELP) for more information.
                                                      NUM
```

The second line of the "1-2-3 Access System" menu displays the options available to you, while the top line is the description line of the highlighted option. It describes what will happen if the highlighted option is selected. In the case of Release 2.2, this is the other way round; the top line displays the Lotus menu while the second line is the description line.

Note that to start with, the "1-2-3" option is highlighted and that the highlighted bar can be moved by pressing the <Right> arrow, <Left> arrow or <Spacebar> (the latter might not work with the older releases of the program). As the highlighted bar moves, the description line changes. Selection of an option can also be made by typing the first character of an option given in the menu. Releases 2.0, 2.01 & 2.2 of the program, include an additional 'View' option in the "1-2-3 Access System" menu which allows the user to choose between three options; an 'Introduction' to the worksheet, graphs, and database, 'A Sample Session' in which you evaluate alternative business strategies, and 'New Features in Release 2'.

Releases 2.3 & 2.4 include a new online tutorial to learning 1-2-3 and Wysiwyg. The appropriate programs are called 1-2-3-Go! and Wysiwyg-Go!, respectively. These tutorials can either be started from DOS (for less experienced users), or (for more experienced users) from a 1-2-3 worksheet, by selecting the **/Add-In Attach** command (more about command selection later), then choose the TUTOR.ADN, select the key you would like to start 1-2-3-Go!, choose **Invoke**, and select TUTOR. However, TUTOR cannot be invoked unless all add-ins are detached. As you can see, the latter method requires you to know your way around 1-2-3, before you can invoke the tutorials to learn how to do it!

Thus, if you want to use the 1-2-3 tutorial or the Wysiwyg tutorial, change to the 1-2-3 program subdirectory and type

learn123

or

learnwis

depending on your learning needs. Typing these commands displays the following two screens, respectively.

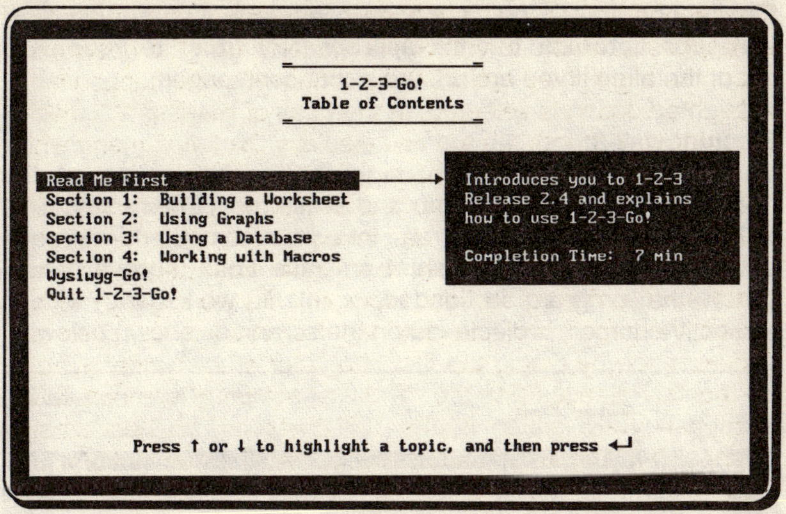

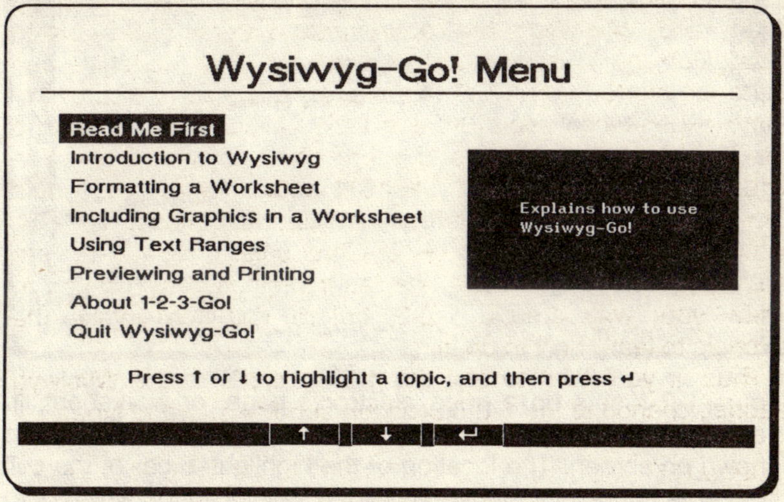

Loading the "1-2-3 Access System" menu takes up some of your computer's memory because it remains resident. You can start 1-2-3 or any of its utilities by typing **123** (to load 1-2-3), **pgraph** (to load PrintGraph), **install** (to load Install), or **trans** (to load Translate) while logged in the Lotus 1-2-3 subdirectory, or by writing appropriate batch files.

Finally, Lotus 1-2-3 only supports code page 437, so you must edit your **autoexec.bat** file appropriately (refer to your DOS documentation if you are unsure about code pages).

Running 1-2-3:
To load the 1-2-3 program, highlight the first option on the "1-2-3 Access System" menu and press the <Enter> key. This will load the relevant program into your computer's memory, after first displaying for a short time the Lotus licence notice. When the program is loaded, a blank worksheet, with a distinctive border, is displayed on the screen as shown below:

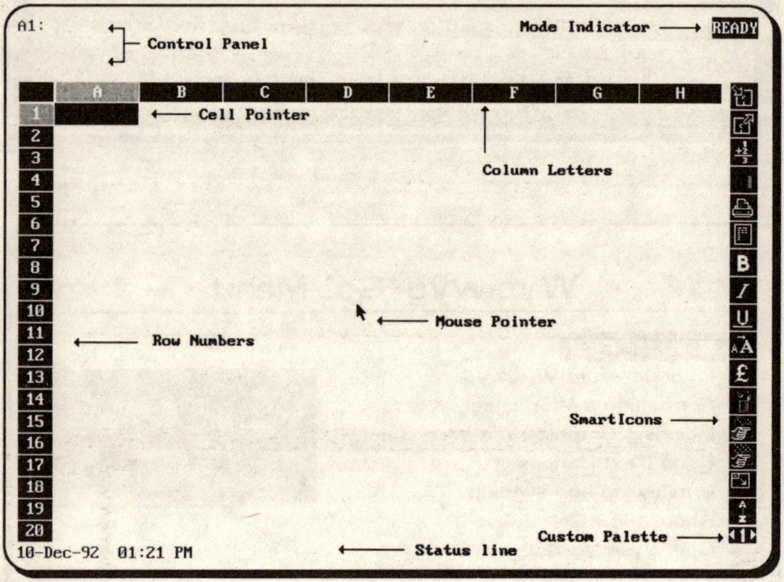

Lotus 1-2-3 sets up a huge electronic page, or worksheet, in your computer's memory, many times larger than the small part shown on screen. The location of the highlighted bar of the cell pointer is constantly monitored by the 'cell indicator' which is to be found on the top left-hand corner of the screen. As the highlighted bar is moved, this indicator displays its cell address.

Your screen is divided into several areas; the area within which you can move the highlighted bar is referred to as the working area, while the letters and numbers in the highlighted border form the reference points. The highlighted bar cannot be moved into these border areas. If you try it, the speaker bleeps.

Finally, the very top and bottom lines of the screen are reserved for displaying certain 'control information'. For example, on the very top right-hand corner of the screen, the 'mode indicator' displays the word READY in inverse video and, if you are using a recent release of Lotus 1-2-3, the date and time appears on the last line of the screen. Release 2.2 also displays the word UNDO to the right of the date and time. In the case of Releases 2.3 & 2.4, the UNDO feature is disabled to start with, and to use it you must first enable it, as discussed under the 'Undo Feature' section which is to be found towards the end of this chapter. For a list of both 'mode' and 'status' indicators, refer to Appendix A.

In the case of Release 2.3, the screen has five icons at the extreme right-hand side of the display, under the READY mode indicator, while in Release 2.4, the first 16 of a total of 77 SmartIcons are displayed. You can use the mouse to point to and click (by pressing the left mouse button) at any of these icons to activate a required operation. Clicking on the question mark (?) of Release 2.3 or pressing **F1** in Release 2.4, displays a help screen as shown below. Note that doing this changes the mode indicator from READY to HELP.

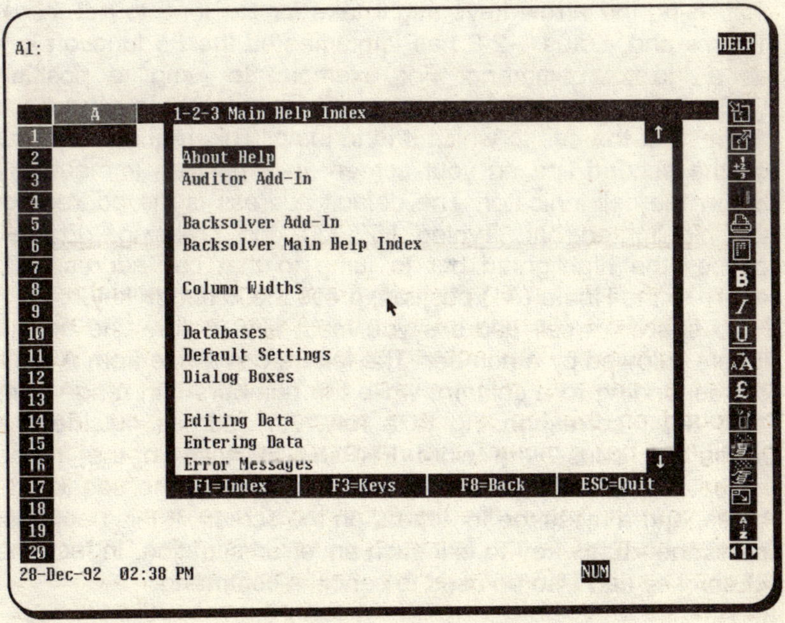

Worksheet Navigation

Navigation around the spreadsheet is achieved by use of the four arrow cursor keys. Each time one of these keys is pressed, the highlighted bar moves one position right, down, left or up, depending on which arrow key was pressed. The <PgDn> and <PgUp> keys can also be used to move vertically 20 rows at a time. A spreadsheet can be thought of as a two-dimensional table made up of rows and columns. The point where a row and column intersect is called a cell.

When you have finished navigating around the spreadsheet, press the <Home> key which will bring you to the Home cell position, (A1), which is the top left-hand corner of the spreadsheet. Individual cells are identified by column and row location (in that order), with present size extending to 256 columns and 8192 rows. The columns are labelled from A to Z, followed by AA to AZ, BA to BZ, and so on, to IV, while the rows are numbered from 1 to 8192. The reference points of a cell are known as the cell address.

The GOTO Command:

Sometimes it is necessary to move to a specific address in the spreadsheet which, however, is so far from our present position that using the arrow keys might take far too long to get there. To this end, Lotus 1-2-3 has implemented the **F5** function key as a 'go to' command. For example, to jump to position HZ5000, press the **F5** key, which will cause 1-2-3 to ask for the address of the cell to which it is to jump. This request appears on the second line on your screen, in a position immediately below the cell indicator. The default address is the address of the highlighted bar. Typing HZ5000 and pressing <Enter>, causes the highlighted bar to jump to that cell address. To return to the Home (A1) position, press the <Home> key.

To specify a cell address you must always key one or two letters followed by a number. The letters can range from A to IV corresponding to a column, while the numbers can range from 1 to 8192 corresponding to a row. An address outside this range will cause the word ERROR to flash in the 'mode indicator' (top right-hand corner of the screen), the speaker to bleep, and a message to appear on the screen. If this happens, press the <Esc> key to exit such an 'error' situation. In fact, the <Esc> key can also be used to cancel a command.

Entering Basic Information

We will now investigate how information can be entered into a worksheet. But first, return to the Home (A1) position by pressing the <Home> key, then type the words:

PROJECT ANALYSIS

As you type, the characters appear in the control area of the worksheet under the cell indicator. If you make a mistake, press the <BkSp> key to erase the previous letter or the <Esc> key to start again. When you have finished, press <Enter>.

Note that what you have typed now appears in cell A1, even though part of the word ANALYSIS appears to be in cell B1. Thus, typing any letter at the beginning of a cell entry causes 1-2-3 to accept the entry as a 'label', automatically preceding it with the apostrophe (') character. Pressing <Enter> inserts the information as a 'label' into the highlighted cell. If the length of a label is longer than the width of a cell, it will continue into the next cell, provided that cell is empty, otherwise the label will be truncated. Now move the highlighted bar to cell B3, type

Jan

and press <Enter>. Use the <Right> arrow key to move to the next cell (C3), type

Feb

and this time press the <Right> arrow key. The arrow keys can be used to both enter information into a cell and move to the next cell. Now move to cell A4, type

\=

and press <Enter>. Note that typing the backslash (\) and then following it with any character it replicates that character and fills the entire cell with it. Repeat this last entry in cells B4 and C4 so that a double line appears, extending the full width of cells A4..C4. Finally, move the cell pointer to A5 and type

Consult:

then, enter the numbers 14000 and 15000 in cells B5 and C5. What you should have on your screen now is the following:

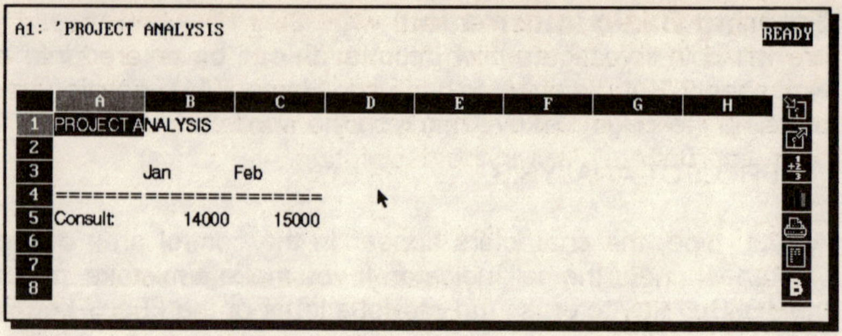

Note how the labels 'Jan' and 'Feb' do not appear above the numbers 14000 and 15000. This is because by default, labels are left justified, while numbers are right justified.

The EDIT Command:

One way of correcting the looks of this spreadsheet is to also right-justify the labels 'Jan' and 'Feb' within their respective cells. To do this, move the cell pointer to B3 and press the **F2** function key which changes the mode indicator to EDIT and allows you to edit the contents of the cell. The cursor is now moved into the control area below the cell indicator. What you see is:

B3: 'Jan

with the cursor at the end of the label. Use the <Left> arrow key to move the cursor under the apostrophe (') and delete it with the <Del> key. Then type the double quote (") character which will be inserted to take the place of the deleted apostrophe. On pressing the <Enter> key, the label is now right justified within its cell and the mode indicator changes back to READY.

To cancel any changes made to the worksheet since 1-2-3 was last in READY mode, press the **Alt+F4** keystroke (hold the **Alt** key down and while holding it down, press the **F4** function key). Pressing again the **Alt+F4** keystroke, restores the changes. The UNDO mode is only available in Releases 2.2 and higher.

Using Function Keys

Each function key, with the exception of **F6**, performs two operations; one when pressed by itself, and another when pressed while the **Alt** key is held down.

The function keys, together with what they do when pressed, are listed in the table which follows. Six of these are new to Releases 2.2 and higher, or have additional built-in functionality to earlier releases, and are marked by a superscript asterisk (*) at an appropriate place in the description.

Key	*Mode*	*Description*
F1	HELP	Displays a 1-2-3 Help screen.
F2	EDIT	Enters EDIT mode and displays the current cell contents in the control panel.
F3	NAME	Displays a full screen of filenames when in FILES mode, or a menu of range names when in POINT mode. * When entering a formula, pressing **F3** after an arithmetic operator or a parenthesis displays a list of range names which can then be included in the formula.
F4	ABS	Toggles a cell or a range of cells between relative, absolute, and mixed addressing.
F5	GOTO	Moves the cell pointer to a specified location.
F6	WINDOW	Moves the cell pointer between two windows. * When in MENU mode, press **F6** to toggle the display of setting sheets between on/off.
F7	QUERY	Repeats most recent **/Data, Query** operation.
F8	TABLE	Repeats most recent **/Data, Table** operation.
F9	CALC	Recalculates all formulae (READY mode only). Converts formula to its value (VALUE and EDIT modes).
F10	GRAPH	Draws a graph using the current graph settings.
Alt+F1	COMPOSE	When used with alphanumeric keys, creates characters you can't enter directly from the keyboard.

Alt+F2	STEP	Allows macro execution one step at a time, which facilitates debugging.
Alt+F3	RUN	* Allows selection of a macro name from a display of named worksheet ranges. Pressing <Esc> switches to POINT mode so you can highlight the range containing the macro instructions you want to run.
Alt+F4	UNDO	*Cancels any changes made to the worksheet since 1-2-3 was last in READY mode. Press again to restore the changes.
Alt+F5	LEARN	* Turns LEARN mode on and records keystrokes. Press again to turn off the feature.
Alt+F7	APP1	*Activates add-in program assigned to key, if any.
Alt+F8	APP2	*Activates add-in program assigned to key, if any.
Alt+F9	APP3	*Activates add-in program assigned to key, if any.
Alt+F10	APP4	Displays add-in menu, if key has not been assigned to an add-in program. *Otherwise, it activates the add-in program assigned to the key.

The detailed use of these function keys will be discussed as and when needed.

It is worth noting that should you need help, at any stage, pressing the function key **F1** will produce the required effect. The first help screen, when the mode indicator is on READY, is a 1-2-3 Help Index. Try it now. Any topic can be selected from the displayed list on your screen by simply moving the highlighted bar to the require choice and pressing the <Enter> key. Furthermore, the help command is context sensitive which means that pressing the **F1** function key while in a particular mode, or in the middle of entering a command, brings up the help screens relevant to the mode you are in, or the command being entered.

The File Commands

To activate the menu system provided by 1-2-3, either move the mouse pointer into the area above the column letters, or press the forward slash key (/) which is found on the query (?) key. The forward slash (/) must not be confused with the backslash (\) which has a totally different meaning.

On moving the mouse into the area above the column letters, or pressing /, a horizontal menu in the 'Lotus' style appears on the second line of the screen, as shown below.

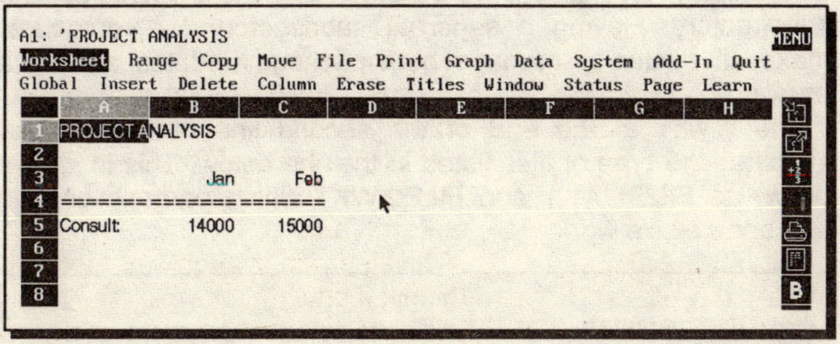

The line below the menu describes the option that is currently highlighted by the bar. This menu operates in the same manner as the menu we came across when we first loaded the "1-2-3 Access System".

The highlighted bar can be moved by using the <Right> or <Left> arrows, the <Home> key or the <Spacebar>. Note that the 'mode indicator' at the top right-hand corner of the screen now reads MENU.

To make a menu selection, say **F** (for File), we can either highlight the option and press <Enter>, or simply press the first letter of the command (**F** in this case). We shall use this last method to select 'File' - indeed, from now on, we will always use the first letter method as it is quicker. If you make a mistake, simply press the <Esc> key and try again. On selection of 'File', a sub-menu of options appears on the screen.

Saving a Worksheet:

Now, let us assume that we would like to stop at this point, but would like to save the work entered so far, before leaving the program. First, let us return to the Home position by pressing the <Home> key, then press

/	to reveal the menus
F	to select **File**
S	to select **Save.**

On pressing **S** (for Save), the mode indicator on the top right-hand corner of the screen changes to FILES and 1-2-3 asks you to name a file into which your work is to be saved. The message appears on the second line of your screen, and the default subdirectory to which such data files will be saved is also displayed. This should be preferably the c:\lot123v2\data subdirectory. Having a separate subdirectory for your data, makes it easier to manage both package updates and data back-ups.

The *.wk1 at the end of the second line of the display, indicates the type of files listed in the line below. This is shown below as FILE1.WK1 and FILE2.WK1 which perhaps contain someone else's work.

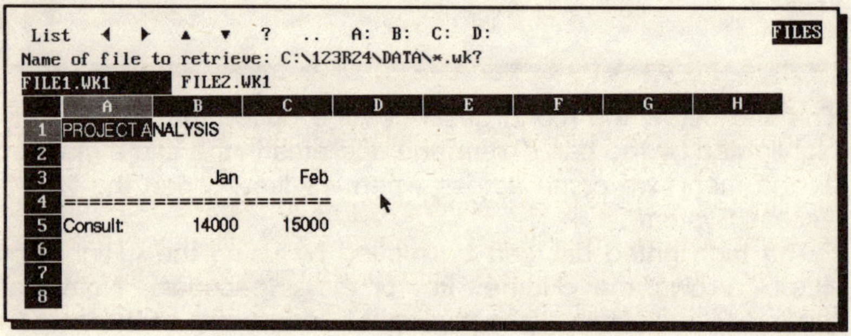

If you are the first person to be using the package, it is more likely that there will not be any filenames of previously saved work. If this is not the case with the data path, and you still want to save your files on your hard disc, it is imperative to change the default data file path (see next section), so as to save the files you create into a separate directory from that in which Lotus 1-2-3 program files are kept.

To save the present contents of memory to a file you must either highlight an existing filename with the help of the cursor keys or type a new filename. If you choose to save your work under an existing filename, you will be asked whether you would like the contents of the file on disc to be 'Replaced' by the contents of the current memory. If you do, type **R** to confirm your decision. If, on the other hand, you choose to save your work under a new filename, then the moment you start typing its name, the menu of existing filenames disappears and what you type replaces the *.wk1 at the end of the data path. To end this session, type

PROJECT1

and press the <Enter> key.

The name of the file can be composed of a mixture of letters and numbers, but must not be longer than 8 characters. The extension .WK1 will be added automatically by the program.

Summarising:- To save worksheet files, first, make sure that the mode indicator is on READY. If not, press the <Esc> key as many times as necessary to achieve it, then press

/	to reveal the menus
F	to select **File**
S	to select **Save**.

Lotus 1-2-3 asks for a filename to save under. If your current work has not been saved before, and there are other data files in the specified drive\path, an alphabetical list of these files appears on the third line of your display with the first file highlighted. Selecting an existing filename causes 1-2-3 to ask for replacement confirmation. Typing a new filename replaces the *wk1 at the end of the data path. You can type a filename in either lower-case letters or uppercase letters, but 1-2-3 displays filenames in uppercase letters only.

If you have just edited a previously saved worksheet and you want to save your work again, on selecting **Save**, the previously specified name is offered as a default filename. Pressing <Enter> causes 1-2-3 to ask for confirmation. If, on the other hand, you would like to edit the default filename, then you must first press the space-bar (which adds a space at the end of the existing filename) before you can use the cursor keys, <BkSp> key, or <Del> key. However, before beginning to edit the default drive\path\filename, use the <BkSp> key to remove the added space, otherwise 1-2-3 will not accept your efforts as a valid filename. You *must* delete the added space.

Changing the Default Data Drive/Path:
Assuming you want to change the default drive/path to which your data is to be saved, do the following:

First, make sure that the mode indicator is on READY. If not, press the <Esc> key as many times as necessary to achieve it, then press

/	to reveal the menus
W	to select **Worksheet**
G	to select **Global**
D	to select **Default**
D	to select **Directory**

On the second line, the current directory for data is displayed. To change this to, say, the A: drive, press <Esc>, then type A: and press <Enter>.

If, on the other hand you wanted to save your work on the C: drive, then provided a \data subdirectory to the main 1-2-3 directory already exists, type c:\lot123v2\data and press <Enter>.

If you want to make this change permanent, then press

U	to select **Update**

From now on data will be saved and retrieved from the newly 'Updated' drive\path. Finally, press the <Esc> key to return to the READY mode. Each time <Esc> is pressed, 1-2-3 returns to the previous sub-menu. Repeating the process will eventually return you to the READY mode.

Retrieving a Worksheet:
An already saved worksheet file can be retrieved by pressing

/	to reveal the menus
F	to select **File**
R	to select **Retrieve**.

Lotus 1-2-3 asks for a filename to load. The first data file saved in the specified drive\path is highlighted. Pressing <Enter>, retrieves the highlighted file or pressing the <Right> arrow cursor key highlights the next file. Pressing NAME (**F3**) displays filenames in full screen mode. When a file is loaded in memory in this manner it replaces what was currently held there. Therefore, you don't have to erase the memory before retrieving a new worksheet.

Since you will be working with a lot of different files, it is useful to know which file is loaded in memory at any given time. Lotus allows you to replace the Date & Time indicator with the Filename indicator. To do this, type the following commands from the READY mode

/	to reveal the menus
W	to select **Worksheet**
G	to select **Global**
D	to select **Default**
O	to select **Other**
C	to select **Clock**
F	to select **Filename**

If you want to make this change permanent, then press

U	to select **Update**
Q	to select **Quit**

From now on the filename of the retrieved file will appear at the bottom left of your display in place of the Date & Time indicator.

Lotus 1-2-3 provides a facility whereby files can be merged in various ways. This facility can be reached from the READY mode by pressing

/	to reveal the menus
F	to select **File**
C	to select **Combine**

which reveals a sub-menu with **Copy, Add** & **Subtract** options.

The Undo Feature

A very useful feature Lotus have added to their 1-2-3 Release 2.2 and higher, is the ability to cancel the most recent operations that have changed your worksheet data and/or settings. Pressing the UNDO key (Alt+**F4**), causes 1-2-3 to automatically restore worksheet data or settings which existed the last time 1-2-3 was in READY mode. In addition, if you use the UNDO feature and then change your mind, pressing UNDO again, restores your work to the latest changes.

By default, the first time you use 1-2-3, the UNDO feature is on in the case of Release 2.2 and off in the case of Releases 2.3 & 2.4. It is easy to tell if this is so, by looking for the UNDO indicator on the status line at the bottom of your screen which, however, only appears after a file has been retrieved into memory. If the UNDO indicator is not displayed, first erase the current worksheet from memory (see beginning of next chapter on how to do this), then enable it by pressing

/	to reveal the menus
W	to select **Worksheet**
G	to select **Global**
D	to select **Default**
O	to select **Other**
U	to select **Undo**
E	to select **Enable**
U	to select **Update**

If you attempt to issue the above commands while a worksheet is in memory, 1-2-3 will tell you that it cannot enable the undo feature, because the memory it requires to do so is otherwise in use.

Because the UNDO facility creates a temporary back-up copy of all the data and settings affected by the current operation, it uses computer memory that may otherwise be needed to run the program. Unless your computer is fitted with a large amount of RAM, you may find you have to disable UNDO frequently, especially if you work with large macros or spreadsheets.

Quitting 1-2-3

To quit the program, make sure that 1-2-3 is in READY mode. If it is not, press the <Esc> key as many times as it is necessary for the mode indicator to change to READY, then press

/	to reveal the menus
Q	to select **Quit**

which asks for confirmation, because if you quit a session without saving your worksheet you will lose any changes made. Pressing **Y** (for Yes) ends the 1-2-3 session.

2. FILLING IN A WORKSHEET

We will use, as an example on how a worksheet can be built up, the few entries on 'Project Analysis' which we used in the Introduction to Lotus 1-2-3. If you haven't saved the PROJECT1 example, don't worry as you could just as easily start afresh. However, if you have a worksheet with unwanted entries in it, clear it from memory (see below) before you start creating a new worksheet.

Erasing a Worksheet:
To erase a worksheet from memory, which also clears the screen (make sure you have saved your work first), press

/	to reveal the menus
W	to select **Worksheet**
E	to select **Erase**
Y	for 'Yes', to confirm command.

Always use this command to clear memory and screen of unwanted information before starting with a new worksheet. Never switch off your computer in order to clear its memory of unwanted work! Computers are best left running for the entire working period, as switching them on and off too many times in a day can cause hardware failure.

Editing a Worksheet

If you have saved PROJECT1, then enter 1-2-3 and at the READY mode, press

/	to reveal the menus
F	to select **File**
R	to select **Retrieve**.

If there are a lot of files with the .WK1 extension on disc, you could force their display on more than one line, by pressing the **F3** function key.

Next, highlight PROJECT1 and press <Enter> to display the worksheet on screen. Then, use the **F2** function key to 'Edit' existing entries or simply re-type the contents of cells so that you end up with the worksheet shown overleaf.

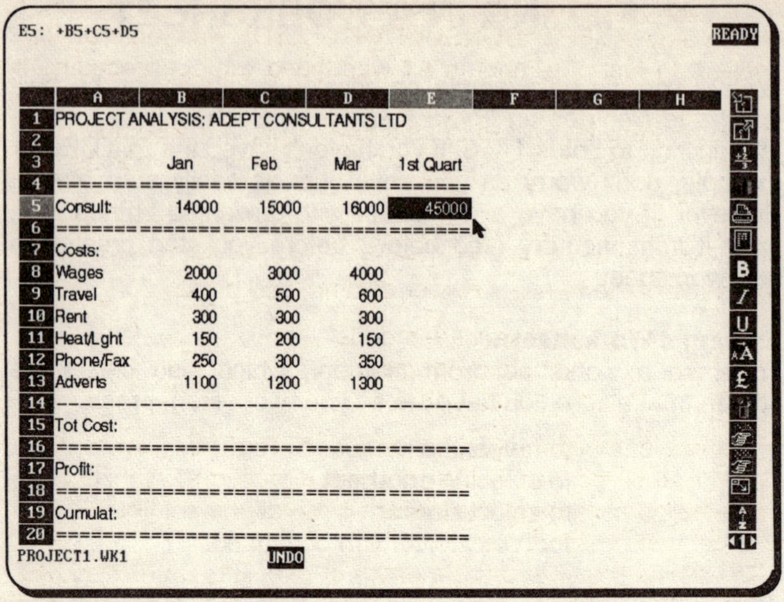

Label Prefixes:

Label prefixes allow you to control the way labels are aligned within their cell. The five available label prefixes are:

Prefix	*Purpose*
'	(apostrophe) is used to left justify the label within a cell.
"	(quotation marks) is used to right justify a label within a cell.
^	(caret) is used to centre a label within a cell.
\	(backslash) is used to fill a cell with the repeated character(s) that follow it.
|	(appears as a split vertical bar on the keyboard) is used to embed set-up strings. If it is located at the beginning of a row, the data in that row will not be printed. If it is located anywhere else in a row, the data in that row is printed. To print the actual split vertical line (|), prefix it with an apostrophe (').

With these in mind, the information in cell A1 (PROJECT ANALYSIS: ADEPT CONSULTANTS LTD) was entered left justified. In fact, the label in A1 was typed without preceding it with the apostrophe. Similarly, all the labels appearing in column A were just typed in as shown. This is the default entry mode for labels, with Lotus 1-2-3 automatically adding the apostrophe.

If you have several rows or columns of labels whose alignment you would like to change, move the cell pointer to the beginning of the relevant row or column, and press

/	to reveal the menus
R	to select **Range**
L	to select **Label**

select one of the displayed options, **Left, Right** or **Centre**, then move the cell pointer in the required direction to highlight the whole range containing the labels whose alignment you want to change, and press <Enter>.

The labels relating to the months in cells B3, C3, D3 and E3 were centre justified within their respective cell. Note that had we attempted to just type

1st Quart

in cell E3, on pressing <Enter> 1-2-3 would have bleeped and refused to accept the information into the cell. This is because the label starts with the numeral 1 which causes 1-2-3 to expect a number. However, what follows is not a number, therefore the objection.

Repeated information, like the double line stretching from A4 to E4 was entered by first highlighting cell A4 and typing

\=

On pressing <Enter> the equals (=) character fills the entire cell.

The /Copy Command:

To replicate information into other cells we could repeat the above procedure (in this particular case entering the \= characters) within each cell, or we could use the **/C** (for Copy) command which is by far the quickest and easiest method of copying information from one cell (or a range of cells) to a range of other cells.

The copy command is not restricted only to repeated character-type information, but can equally well be used with numbers or formulae. When copying a formula in this way, references to cells within the formula are adjusted relative to their new position.

To copy the contents of cell A4 to the cell range B4 through E4, ensure that you are in the READY mode (press <Esc> until you are), then move the cell pointer to A4, and press

/	to reveal the menus
C	to select **Copy**.

At this point, you'll be asked for the range to copy from. In this case, the cell pointer (note that the mode indicator has changed to POINT) is at the cell we want to start copying from and the entire copy range is highlighted (i.e. the range is given by A4 to A4), therefore press

<Enter>	to confirm the range

which will cause 1-2-3 to ask you to enter the range to copy to. Now press

<→>	arrow key to move to the starting location of the range
<.>	(period) to anchor the first target cell
<→>	to select and highlight target cell range
<Enter>	to confirm target range.

If you make any mistakes and copy information into cells you did not mean to, then use the **E** (for Erase) command, as discussed below.

The /Range Erase Command:
To erase a range, or block of adjacent cells, highlight the first cell of the range or one corner cell of the block, and press

/	to reveal the menus
R	to select **Range**
E	to select **Erase**

then press the <→>, <←>, <↑> or <↓> arrow keys as many times as needed to highlight the range of cells, or block of cells, you want to erase, and press

<Enter> to confirm range or block selection.

If you make a mistake in highlighting the wrong starting cell of a range of cells or a block of cells, press <Esc> to release the automatic anchorage, use the arrow keys to move to the required cell, press <.> (period) to anchor the newly selected cell, and carry on as before.

Entering Numbers and Formulae:

When numbers are entered into a cell, or reference is made to the contents of a cell by preceding the cell address with an arithmetic operator, or a Lotus 1-2-3 function (which is preceded by the @ sign) is entered into a cell, then the mode indicator changes from READY to VALUE.

Returning to our example of PROJECT ANALYSIS, move the cell pointer to B5 and start entering the 'consultancy' income of the company. As soon as the first number is typed into the line below the cell indicator (the number 1 of the 14000), the mode indicator changes to VALUE and when the complete amount is typed in, pressing <Enter> inserts it into the specified cell, right justifying the number within the cell width. Now complete typing in the rest of the amounts into cells C5 and D5.

We can find the 1st quarter total income from consultancy, by highlighting cell E5 and typing

+B5+C5+D5

and on pressing <Enter> the total first quarter consultancy income is added from the above formula and the result placed in cell E5. Notice that the above formula is preceded by a plus (+) sign. Had we not typed this first '+' sign into the formula, 1-2-3 would have mistaken the formula for a label and no calculation would have resulted.

Now complete the insertion into the worksheet of the various amounts under 'costs' and then save the result into the file PROJECT2 before going on any further. Remember that saving your work on disc often enough is a good thing to get used to, as even the shortest power cut can cause the loss of hours of hard work!

Order of Precedence in Formulae:
The table shown on the next page, lists the arithmetic, logical, and string operators available in 1-2-3, with their associated order of precedence. What we mean by precedence is the priority order in which 1-2-3 evaluates a formula. The lower the priority number, the earlier 1-2-3 performs the operation. Operations with the same priority number are performed sequentially from left to right. A precedence order can be overridden by enclosing an operation in parentheses; 1-2-3 will perform the operations inside the parentheses first.

Operator	*Function*	*Priority*
( )	Parenthesized operation	1
^	Exponentiation	2
* or /	Multiplication or division	3
+ or –	Addition or subtraction	4
= or <>	Equal-to or not-equal-to	5
< or >	Less-than or greater-than	5
<=	Less-than-or-equal-to	5
>=	Greater-than-or-equal-to	5
#NOT#	Logical NOT	6
#AND#	Logical AND	7
#OR#	Logical OR	7
&	String concatenation	7

Using Functions

In our example, writing a formula that adds the contents of three columns is not too difficult or lengthy a task. But imagine having to add 20 columns! For this reason 1-2-3 has an inbuilt summation function (for others see Appendix B) in the form of @SUM( ) which can be used to add any number of cells.

To illustrate how this function can be used, move the cell pointer to E5 and type

@SUM(

which changes the mode indicator to VALUE, then use the arrow keys to move the cell pointer (note that pressing an arrow key changes the mode indicator to POINT) to the start of the summation range (B5 in this case), press

<.> (period) to anchor the starting point of the range

and use the arrow keys to move the cell pointer to the end of the summation range (in this case D5). What appears under the cell indicator is the entry

@SUM(B5..D5

which has to be completed by typing the closing bracket ')' and pressing <Enter>.

Now use the 'Copy' command to replicate the function from cell E5 into the target range E8 through E13. To achieve this move the cell pointer to E5 and press

/	to reveal the menus
C	to select **Copy**
<Enter>	to confirm highlighted copy range
<↓>	to move to beginning of target range
<.>	to anchor the first target cell
<↓>	to select and highlight target range
<Enter>	to confirm target range.

Immediately this command is confirmed, its execution causes the actual sums of the 'relative' columns to appear on the target area. Notice that when the cell pointer is on E5 the function target range is B5..D5, while when the cell pointer is moved to E8 the function target range changes to B8..D8 which indicates that copying formulae with this method causes the 'relative' target range to be copied. Had the 'absolute' target range been copied instead, the result of the various summations would have been wrong.

Using the SmartIcon to Sum a Range:
Any range of rows or columns can be added up by simply highlighting the range and including one empty cell (on the right of the range for summing rows, or at the bottom of the range for summing columns), and then pointing and clicking the left mouse button at the '1+2=3' SmartIcon (the 3rd on palete 1) on the right edge of the Lotus 1-2-3 screen.

To highlight a range with the mouse, simply move the mouse pointer to the beginning of the range, press the left mouse button, and while holding it pressed, drag the mouse in the required direction to highlight the complete range, then release the mouse button. Pressing <Esc> or clicking the right mouse button, cancels the highlighting process.

Next, complete the insertion of functions and formulae in the rest of the worksheet, noting that 'Total Cost' is the summation of rows 8 through 13, 'Profit' is the subtraction of 'Total Cost' from 'Consultancy', and that 'Cumulat' in row 19 refers to cumulative profit. Then, add another column to your worksheet to calculate (and place in column F) the average monthly values of earnings, costs, and profit, using the @AVG() function. The worksheet should be saved as PROJECT2 should look as shown below:

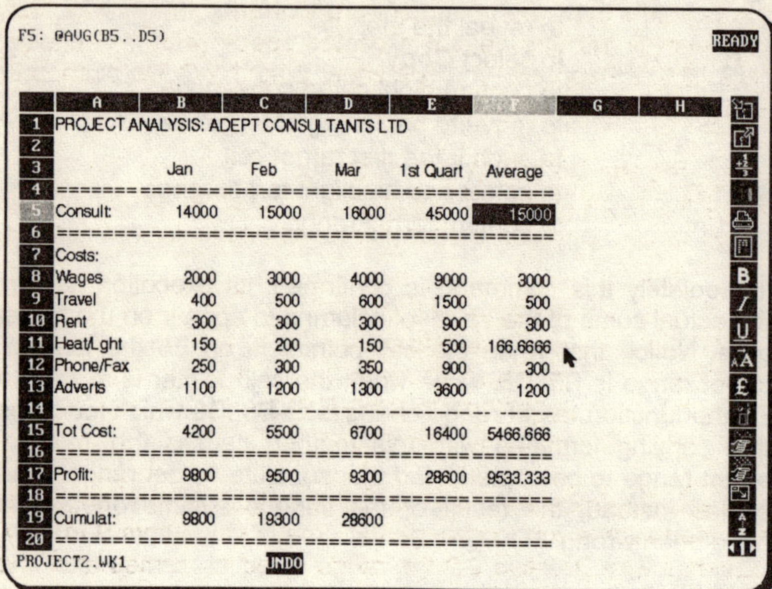
F5: @AVG(B5..D5) READY

	A	B	C	D	E	F	G	H
1	PROJECT ANALYSIS: ADEPT CONSULTANTS LTD							
2								
3		Jan	Feb	Mar	1st Quart	Average		
4	=======	======	======	======	======	=======		
5	Consult:	14000	15000	16000	45000	15000		
6	=======	======	======	======	======	=======		
7	Costs:							
8	Wages	2000	3000	4000	9000	3000		
9	Travel	400	500	600	1500	500		
10	Rent	300	300	300	900	300		
11	Heat/Lght	150	200	150	500	166.6666		
12	Phone/Fax	250	300	350	900	300		
13	Adverts	1100	1200	1300	3600	1200		
14	-------	------	------	------	------	-----		
15	Tot Cost:	4200	5500	6700	16400	5466.666		
16	=======	======	======	======	======	=======		
17	Profit:	9800	9500	9300	28600	9533.333		
18	=======	======	======	======	======	=======		
19	Cumulat:	9800	19300	28600				
20	=======	======	======	======	======	=======		

PROJECT2.WK1 UNDO

Formatting Numbers:

Note the contents of F11, F15 and F17, under the 'Average' column, are no longer whole numbers. Furthermore, the number of digits after the decimal point is variable and depends on the available space - the width of the appropriate field.

To make our present worksheet more presentable, we need to format specific cells so that we are in control of what is printed out. To format the contents of a numeric cell or block of cells, highlight the starting target cell (in our example, F5) and press

/	to reveal the menus
R	to select **Range**
F	to select **Format**
F	to select **Fixed** number of decimal points - the default value is two decimal places
<Enter>	to select the default value
<↓>	to highlight target range (F5..F17 for this example)
<Enter>	to confirm target range.

It is possible that when numbers are formatted in this way, they might not fit into the default allocated space (width) of chosen cells. If that happens, you will know it as 1-2-3 fills such cells with asterisks (*).

Changing the Default Width of Cells:
To change the width of columns (in order to accommodate either large numbers or numbers expressed in the form of currency, press

/	to reveal the menus
W	to select **Worksheet**
C	to select **Column**
C	to select **Column-Range**
S	to select **Set-Width**

Release 2.3 & 2.4 asks you to highlight the column range first and then allows you to change the default value from 9 to, say, 12, while with Release 2.2 the range selection comes after the width choice. If you are changing the width of a single column, highlight the column and repeat the above commands, but miss out the **Column-Range** command. This command is new to Releases 2.2 and higher. Users of earlier releases will have to change the width of each column separately by recycling through the commands.

When the worksheet is 'Saved', the new column-width display format will be saved with it.

Changing Default Currency & Date Formats:

What follows is only relevant to earlier versions than Release 2.2 of Lotus 1-2-3. Later releases are already configured for the UK currency prefix and the European date format.

To change the default formats of currency and date of earlier than Release 2.2, from $ and MM-DD-YY to UK's £ and DD/MM/YY, press

/	to reveal the menus
W	to select **Worksheet**
G	to select **Global**
D	to select **Default**
O	to select **Other**
I	to select **International**
C	to select **Currency**. At this point the **$** sign will be displayed. Backspace, and press
£	to select UK currency symbol
<Enter>	to confirm selection
P	to select **Prefix** so that the currency symbol prefixes numbers displayed in 'Currency' (£xxxxx.xx) format.
D	to select **Date**
B	to select option **B**.

To make these options permanent, return to a previous menu by pressing the <Esc> key once, and then press

U	to select and execute **Update**
Q	to **Quit**.

Dialogue Boxes:

If you are using Release 2.3 or 2.4, you can change settings using dialogue boxes rather than use the previous menu commands. These replace the settings screens of Release 2.2. One such dialogue box, which is displayed on your screen while selecting the **/Worksheet, Global, Default** commands, is shown on the next page.

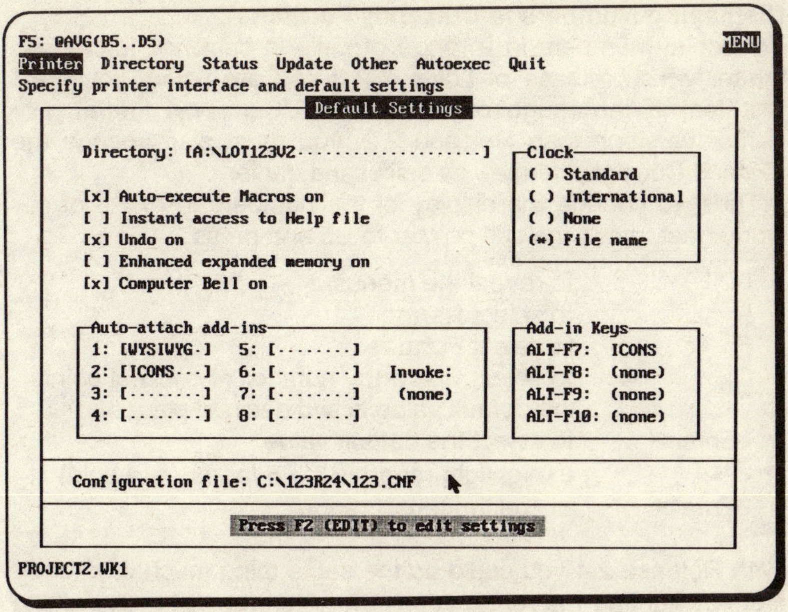

A dialogue box shows the current settings for a particular task. These settings can be changed with either the keyboard or the mouse, or you can select commands from the menu above the dialogue box.

Dialogue boxes offer you the following facilities for selecting settings:

- Option buttons - you can select one option button from a group of option buttons by using the mouse to click it. A selected button is marked with an asterisk (*) next to the option.
- Check boxes - you can select one or more options (or none) from a group of option check boxes. A selected check box is marked with an x next to the option.
- Text boxes - you type entries in text boxes which can include numbers, range names, or text, depending on what the command requires.

Displaying Numbers in Currency Format:
To display numbers in a range of cells in currency format, no matter which release of Lotus 1-2-3 you are using, you must first format the range of cells to the 'Currency' format. For earlier versions than Release 2.2, you must also change the 'Default Currency' format, as discussed earlier.

Thus, to change the display of the numbers in row 5 of our worksheet, move the cell pointer to B5 and press

/	to reveal the menus
R	to select **Range**
F	to select **Format**
C	to select **Currency** number of decimal points - the default value is two decimal places
<Enter>	to select the default value
<→>	to highlight range (B5..F5 for this example)
<Enter>	to confirm target range.

With Release 2.4 you could do the same thing much quicker by first highlighting the range you want to format and then clicking at the '£' SmartIcon (the 11th on palette 1).

Printing a Worksheet

To print a worksheet, make sure that the printer is switched on and that the cell pointer is in the 'Home' position and the worksheet mode is on READY. Then, press

/	to reveal the menus
P	to select **Print**
P	to select **Printer**
R	to select **Range**
<Esc>	to deselect previous range selection (or automatic range selection in the case of Release 2.2 and higher)
<.>	to anchor range from required position
<Arrows>	to move cell pointer to the bottom right-hand corner of the rectangle you wish to print
<Enter>	to confirm selection
G	to select **Go**

which should start printing. It is assumed here that you have configured your system to your printer. If not, (see next section) your printer might not respond to your print commands.

With Release 2.4 you could highlight the range you wish to print and then click at the 'Printer' SmartIcon (the 5th on palette 1).

On completion of the printout, press

Q	to select **Quit**

and return to the READY mode.

A request to print again, will automatically remember the previous range. If you require a different range, then when the highlighted rectangular area appears on screen, as a result of selecting the **Range** command, cancel the current range by pressing the <Esc> key, then move the cell pointer to the required starting position (top left-hand corner) of target area, and press

<.>	to anchor top left hand corner of rectangle
<Arrows>	to move the cell pointer to the bottom right-hand corner of rectangle you require to print
<Enter>	to confirm selection

Carry out the suggested formatting changes to column F of worksheet PROJECT2, then, save the resultant worksheet, shown below, as PROJECT3.

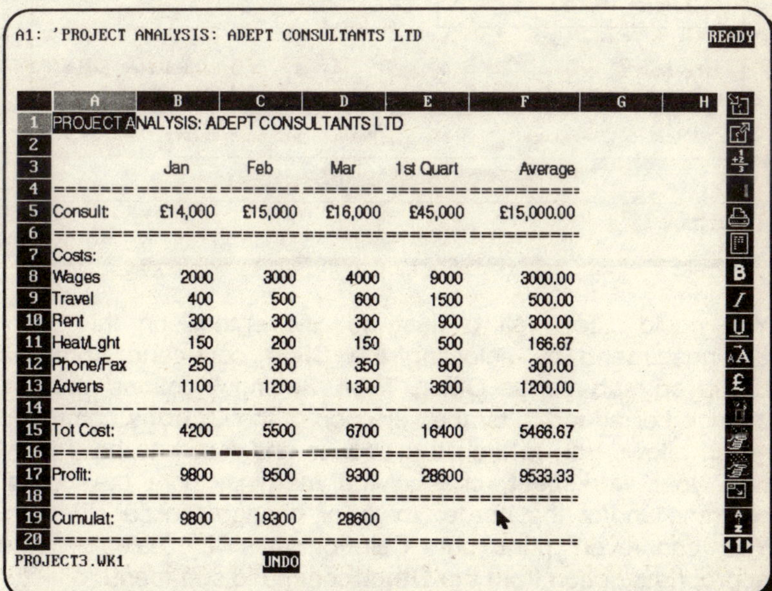

A1: 'PROJECT ANALYSIS: ADEPT CONSULTANTS LTD READY

	A	B	C	D	E	F	G	H
1	PROJECT ANALYSIS: ADEPT CONSULTANTS LTD							
2								
3		Jan	Feb	Mar	1st Quart	Average		
4	=========	=========	=========	=========	=========	==========		
5	Consult:	£14,000	£15,000	£16,000	£45,000	£15,000.00		
6	=========	=========	=========	=========	=========	==========		
7	Costs:							
8	Wages	2000	3000	4000	9000	3000.00		
9	Travel	400	500	600	1500	500.00		
10	Rent	300	300	300	900	300.00		
11	Heat/Lght	150	200	150	500	166.67		
12	Phone/Fax	250	300	350	900	300.00		
13	Adverts	1100	1200	1300	3600	1200.00		
14	---------	---------	---------	---------	---------	----------		
15	Tot Cost:	4200	5500	6700	16400	5466.67		
16	=========	=========	=========	=========	=========	==========		
17	Profit:	9800	9500	9300	28600	9533.33		
18	=========	=========	=========	=========	=========	==========		
19	Cumulat:	9800	19300	28600				
20	=========	=========	=========	=========	=========	==========		

PROJECT3.WK1 UNDO

The Print Settings Menu:
If you are using Release 2.2 or higher, then the program automatically sets the printer range when you select the

/Print, Printer

command, to what it can print on the predefined size paper, which is what can be displayed on your screen. This information is displayed in the 'Print Settings' menu, as shown below (in Release 2.2 the displayed screen is slightly different to the one shown here).

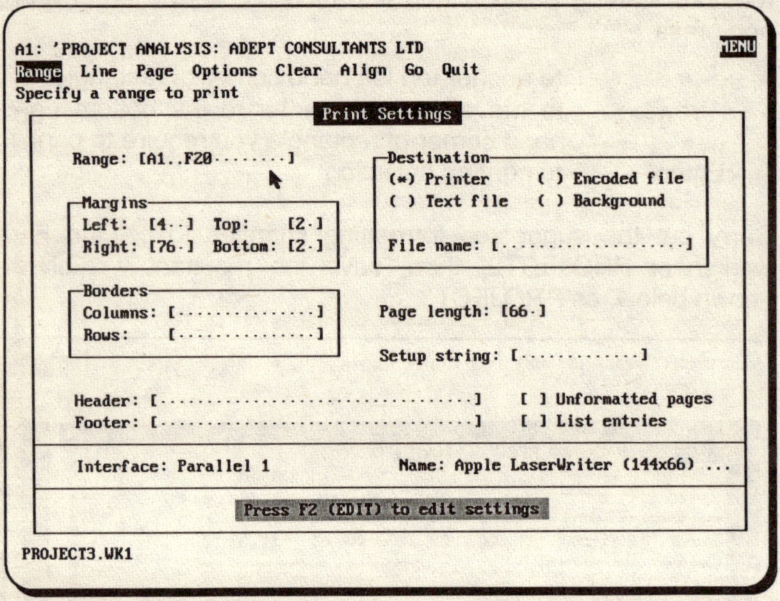

You could 'Clear' all or just specific entries on this 'Print Settings' menu by selecting the **Clear** command from the displayed sub-menu. Other 'Print Settings' options can be changed or added to by the selection of the **Options** command which allows you to type the header and footer to be printed with your worksheet, change the margins, print the border columns and/or the border rows, or change the page length. You can even print out 'Cell-Formulas' by selecting the appropriate option from the **Other** command sub-menu.

Use your printer to print out the rectangle A1 to F20. If your worksheet is too wide for your printer, you might consider printing it in condensed mode. To do this, use the **\Print, Printer, Options, Setup** command, type the set-up string **\015** and press <Enter>. The set-up string now appears on the 'Print Settings' display. In addition, you will have to change the page margins by selecting the **Margins** command from the **Options** sub-menu and changing the right margin to 132 for portrait page orientation, or 200 for landscape. If your worksheet is wider than even this, it will be printed out in two rectangular strips which you can then glue together.

Printing in Landscape Mode:

Lotus 1-2-3, Release 2.4 also allows you to print to a laser or dot-matrix printer in *landscape mode* which prints along the length of the paper. The mode, 'Portrait' of 'Landscape' can be selected by using the Wysiwyg **:Print, Config, Orientation** command, which displays the following dialogue box.

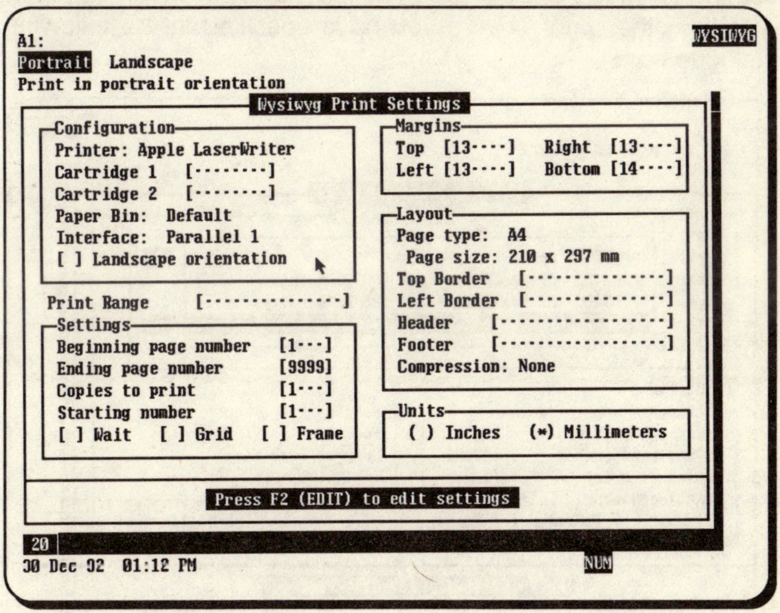

Printing to an Encapsulated PostScript File:

Lotus 1-2-3 Release 2.4 includes a driver that allows you to print to an *encapsulated PostScript file* (an .EPS file) which can contain both text and graphics. Such a file can then be used by other programs, such as a word processing or a desktop publishing program.

However, before you can print to an .EPS file, you must install the encapsulated PostScript file driver. If you have not done so already, use the 'Install' option from the Lotus 1-2-3 Access menu and select the 'Change Selected Equipment' option from the Main menu. Now, choose 'Modify the Current Driver Set', then 'Graphics Printer' and select 'PostScript', and from the two options displayed, choose 'Encapsulated PS file'. Save your changes by returning to the previous menu and selecting 'Sve the Current Driver Set' and accepting the default drive/path and filename by pressing <Enter>.

You can check that the encapsulated PostScript file driver is safely installed by using the Wysiwyg **:Print, Config, Printer** command which should then list the required driver, together with the other print drivers you have specified in the following dialogue box.

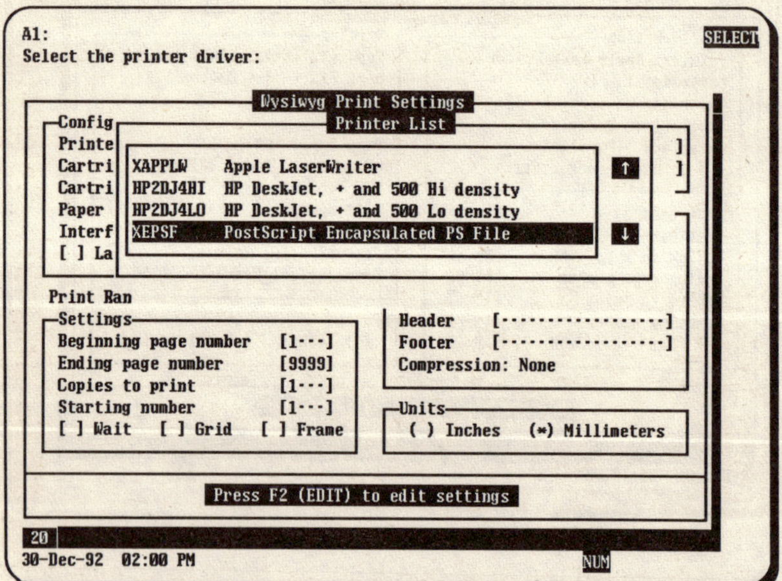

3. ADDING WORKSHEET SKILLS

We will now use the worksheet saved under PROJECT3 (see end of previous chapter) to show how we can add to it, rearrange information in it and freeze titles in order to make entries easier, before going on to discuss more advanced topics. If you haven't saved PROJECT3 on disc, it will be necessary for you to enter the information shown below into 1-2-3 so that you can benefit from what is to be introduced at this point. Having done this, do save it under PROJECT3 before going on with the suggested alterations.

If you have saved PROJECT3, then enter 1-2-3 and when the mode indicator reads READY, press

/	to reveal the menus
F	to select **File**
R	to select **Retrieve**

and highlight PROJECT3. On pressing <Enter>, the worksheet is displayed on the screen as shown below.

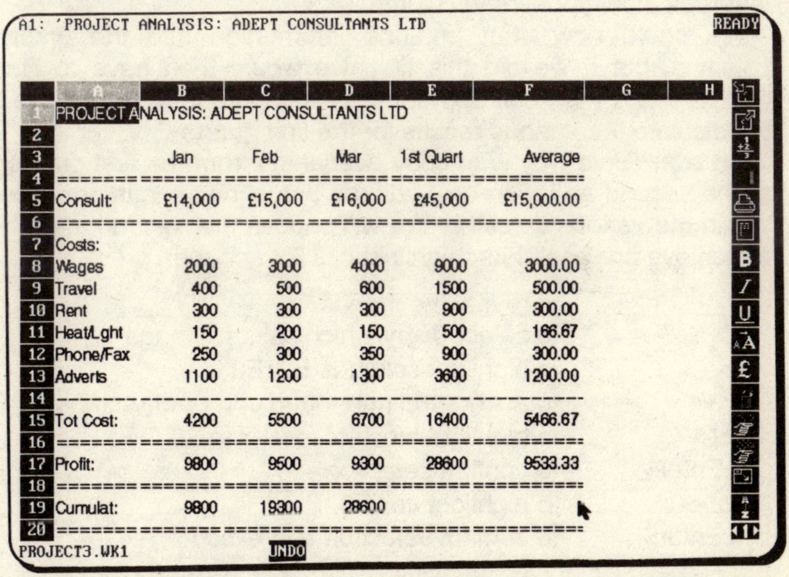
A1: 'PROJECT ANALYSIS: ADEPT CONSULTANTS LTD READY

	A	B	C	D	E	F	G	H
1	PROJECT ANALYSIS: ADEPT CONSULTANTS LTD							
2								
3		Jan	Feb	Mar	1st Quart	Average		
4	=========	=========	=========	=========	=========	=========		
5	Consult:	£14,000	£15,000	£16,000	£45,000	£15,000.00		
6	=========	=========	=========	=========	=========	=========		
7	Costs:							
8	Wages	2000	3000	4000	9000	3000.00		
9	Travel	400	500	600	1500	500.00		
10	Rent	300	300	300	900	300.00		
11	Heat/Lght	150	200	150	500	166.67		
12	Phone/Fax	250	300	350	900	300.00		
13	Adverts	1100	1200	1300	3600	1200.00		
14	---------	---------	---------	---------	---------	---------		
15	Tot Cost:	4200	5500	6700	16400	5466.67		
16	=========	=========	=========	=========	=========	=========		
17	Profit:	9800	9500	9300	28600	9533.33		
18	=========	=========	=========	=========	=========	=========		
19	Cumulat:	9800	19300	28600				
20	=========	=========	=========	=========	=========	=========		

PROJECT3.WK1 UNDO

What we would like to do now is to add some more information to the worksheet with the insertion of another quarter's figures in columns between E and F.

Controlling Cell Contents

In general, you can insert or delete columns and rows in a worksheet, copy cell contents (including formulae) from one part of the worksheet to another, and freeze titles in order to make entries into cells easier.

The /Worksheet Insert Command:

To insert columns into a worksheet, move the cell pointer into the column where insertion is required (in this case F1) and press

/	to reveal the menus
W	to select **Worksheet**
I	to select **Insert**
C	to select **Column** which asks for range
<→>	arrow key to highlight range F1..I1
<Enter>	to confirm range selection and execute.

On execution, empty cells are inserted into the worksheet in the requested range, and in this particular case, the column headed 'Average' now appears in column J.

We could now start entering information into the empty columns, but if we did this first, we would then have to first replicate and then edit appropriately the various formulae used to calculate the various results for the first quarter.

An alternative way is to copy everything from the first quarter to the second and then only edit the actual numeric information within the various columns. We will choose this second method to achieve our goal. First highlight cell B3 and then press

/	to reveal the menus
C	to select **Copy** which asks for range
<→>	to highlight columns B3..E3
<.>	to anchor top right-hand corner of rectangle
<↓>	to highlight block of rows 3 to 20
<Enter>	to confirm selection
<→>	to highlight cell F3
<Enter>	to confirm selection and execute.

Now edit the copied headings 'Jan', 'Feb', 'Mar', and '1st Quart' to 'Apr', 'May', 'Jun', and '2nd Quart'.

Note that by the time the highlighted bar is moved to column I, the 'titles' in column A have scrolled to the left and are outside the viewing screen area. This will make editing of numeric information very difficult if we can't see what refers to what. Therefore, before we attempt any further editing, it would be a good idea to use the 'Title' command ability of 1-2-3 to freeze the titles in column A of our present worksheet.

Freezing Titles on Screen:

To freeze column (or row) headings on a worksheet, move the cell pointer a cell to the right (or below) the column (or row) which you want to freeze the titles on the screen, and press

/	to reveal the menus
W	to select **Worksheet**
T	to select **Titles**
V (or **H**)	to select **Vertical** (or **Horizontal**)

which will automatically set the headings to the left (or above) the cell pointer's current position. Moving around the worksheet, leaves the headings frozen on the screen. Any attempt to enter the frozen area causes the speaker to bleep.

Now implement the above changes and change the numeric entries on your worksheet into what is shown below.

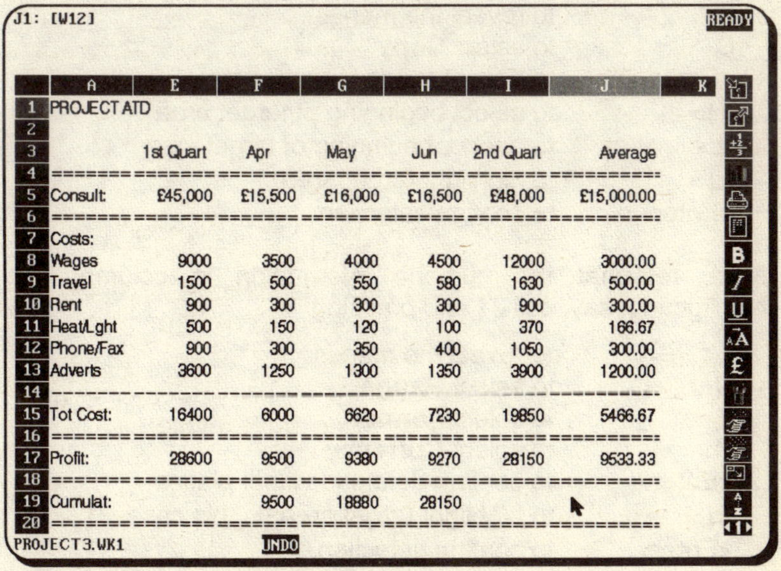
J1: [W12] READY

	A	E	F	G	H	I	J	K
1	PROJECT ATD							
2								
3		1st Quart	Apr	May	Jun	2nd Quart	Average	
4	======	======	======	======	======	======	=========	
5	Consult:	£45,000	£15,500	£16,000	£16,500	£48,000	£15,000.00	
6	======	======	======	======	======	======	=========	
7	Costs:							
8	Wages	9000	3500	4000	4500	12000	3000.00	
9	Travel	1500	500	550	580	1630	500.00	
10	Rent	900	300	300	300	900	300.00	
11	Heat/Lght	500	150	120	100	370	166.67	
12	Phone/Fax	900	300	350	400	1050	300.00	
13	Adverts	3600	1250	1300	1350	3900	1200.00	
14	------	------	------	------	------	------	---------	
15	Tot Cost:	16400	6000	6620	7230	19850	5466.67	
16	======	======	======	======	======	======	=========	
17	Profit:	28600	9500	9380	9270	28150	9533.33	
18	======	======	======	======	======	======	=========	
19	Cumulat:		9500	18880	28150			
20	======	======	======	======	======	======	=========	

PROJECT3.WK1 UNDO

Note: If you examine the previous worksheet carefully, you will notice that two errors have occurred; one of these has to do with the average calculation in column J, while the other has to do with the accumulated values in the second quarter.

Non-Contiguous Address Range:

The calculations of average values in column J of the previous worksheet are wrong because the range values in the formula are still those entered for the first quarter only. To correct these, highlight cell J5 and edit the formula shown in the control panel from

@AVG(B5..D5)

to

@AVG(B5..D5,F5..H5)

which on pressing <Enter> changes the value shown in cell J5. Note the way the argument of the function is written when non-contiguous address ranges are involved. Here we have two contiguous address ranges B5..D5 and F5..H5 which we separate with a comma.

Now replicate the formula to the J8..J13 cell range by highlighting cell J5 and pressing

/	to reveal the menus
C	to select **Copy**
<Enter>	to accept range to copy from
<↓>	to select beginning of target area
<.>	to anchor beginning of target area
<↓>	to highlight target area
<Enter>	to confirm selection.

Next, reformat the numeric information in column J by highlighting, say, cell J1 and pressing

/	to reveal the menus
R	to select **Range**
F	to select **Format**
C	to select **Currency**
<Enter>	to confirm default decimal places
<↓>	to highlight target area (in this case, J1..J21)
<Enter>	to confirm selection.

Relative and Absolute Cell Addresses:
Entering a mathematical expression into the worksheet, such as the formula in cell C19 which was

+B19+C17

causes 1-2-3 to interpret it as 'add the contents of cell one column to the left of the current position, to the contents of cell two rows above the current position'. In this way, when the formula was later replicated into cell address D19, the contents of the cell relative to the left position of D19 (i.e. C19) and the contents of the cell two rows above it (i.e. D17) are used, instead of the original cell addresses entered in C19. This is relative addressing.

To see the effect of relative versus absolute addressing, type in cell E19 the formula

+E5–E15

which will be interpreted as relative addressing. Now, add another row to your worksheet, namely 'Profit/Q:' in row 21 to calculate the profit per quarter. Before you are able to enter the new label, however, you must first unfreeze the titles by pressing

/	to reveal the menus
W	to select **Worksheet**
T	to select **Titles**
C	to select **Clear**.

Having entered the label in cell A21, copy the formula in cell E19 to cell E21, using the **/Copy** command. The displayed calculated value in E21 is, of course, wrong because the cell references in the copied formula are now given as

+E7–E17

as the references were copied relatively. Next, change the formula in E19 by editing it to

+$E$5–$E$15

which is interpreted as absolute addressing. Copying this into cell E21 calculates the correct result; the cell references in the formula in E21 have not changed from those of cell E19.

The $ sign must prefix both the column reference and the row reference. Mixed cell addressing is permitted; as for example when a column address reference is needed as absolute, while a row address reference is needed as relative. In such a case, only the column letter is prefixed by the $ sign.

Finally, correct the formula in cells F19 and I19 in order to obtain the correct results shown below.

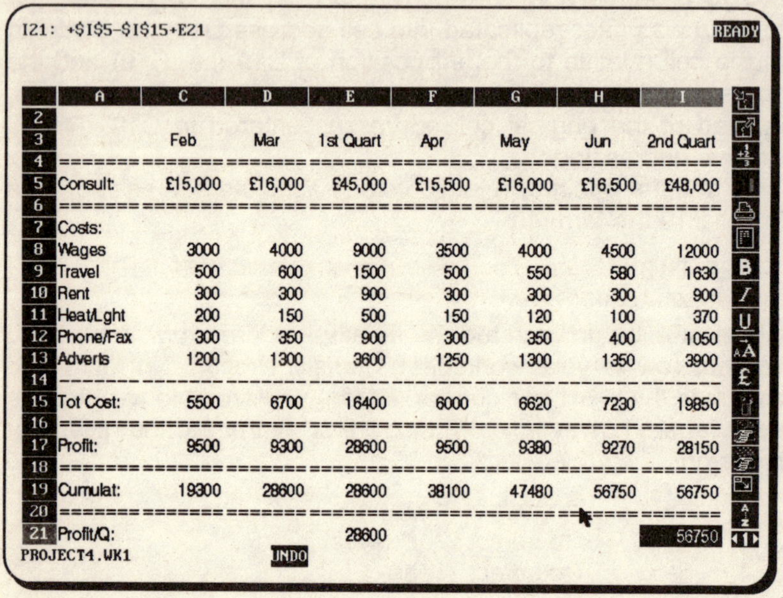

I21: +$I$5-$I$15+E21 READY

	A	C	D	E	F	G	H	I
2								
3		Feb	Mar	1st Quart	Apr	May	Jun	2nd Quart
4	=======	=======	=======	=======	=======	=======	=======	=======
5	Consult:	£15,000	£16,000	£45,000	£15,500	£16,000	£16,500	£48,000
6	=======	=======	=======	=======	=======	=======	=======	=======
7	Costs:							
8	Wages	3000	4000	9000	3500	4000	4500	12000
9	Travel	500	600	1500	500	550	580	1630
10	Rent	300	300	900	300	300	300	900
11	Heat/Lght	200	150	500	150	120	100	370
12	Phone/Fax	300	350	900	300	350	400	1050
13	Adverts	1200	1300	3600	1250	1300	1350	3900
14	-------	-------	-------	-------	-------	-------	-------	-------
15	Tot Cost:	5500	6700	16400	6000	6620	7230	19850
16	=======	=======	=======	=======	=======	=======	=======	=======
17	Profit:	9500	9300	28600	9500	9380	9270	28150
18	=======	=======	=======	=======	=======	=======	=======	=======
19	Cumulat:	19300	28600	28600	38100	47480	56750	56750
20	=======	=======	=======	=======	=======	=======	=======	=======
21	Profit/Q:			28600				56750

PROJECT4.WK1 UNDO

The /Move Command:

In order to improve the printed output of the example we have been discussing, we could move the caption to somewhere in the middle of the worksheet so that is centrally placed when we print it out. To do this, move the cell pointer to A1 and move the caption by pressing

/	to reveal the menus
M	to select **Move**
<Enter>	to select default range to move
<→>	to select target range (say D1..D1)
<Enter>	to confirm target range and execute.

Now freeze again the titles in column A, press the <Home> key and save the resultant worksheet as PROJECT4.

Working with SmartIcons

SmartIcons are provided in Release 2.4 with the use of an add-in. In all there are 77 icons organised in 7 palettes, depending on your screen display type (VGA, EGA, or CGA); a palette being a column of icons that appears on the extreme right-hand side of the 1-2-3 display. With a VGA or EGA screen, the icons appear as small clear pictures on your display, while with a CGA screen they appear mostly as a combination of text and line drawings. Which palette is currently displayed is indicated by the palette number that appears at the bottom of the column of icons.

The first palette (identified by the ←1→ at the bottom of the icons) can be customised to display the icons you most frequently use. The icons in the remaining palettes are fixed; you can copy them to the first palette, but you cannot move them or delete them. The last palette of icons (identified by U1 through to U12) are user icons to which you can assign macros.

To activate a SmartIcon, either use the mouse to point to it and click the left mouse button, or press Alt+F7 to highlight the first icon, then use the ↑ & ↓ arrow keys to highlight the required icon and press <Enter>. However, you might find that in most cases, you might be required to select a range of cells before activating a SmartIcon, which can be done with either the keyboard or the mouse. With the mouse, drag the cell pointer (by pressing the left mouse button and keeping it pressed while moving the mouse) to highlight the required range. With the keyboard, move the cell pointer to the first cell of the range, press **F4**, use the arrow keys to highlight the required range and press <Enter>.

To change palettes, with the mouse point to one of the arrows on either side of the palette number at the bottom of the column of icons and click the left mouse button to scroll forward or backward through the various palettes, while with the keyboard press **Alt+F7** and use the → & ← arrow keys.

To find out what each SmartIcon can do, either point to the required icon with the mouse pointer and hold down the right mouse button, or press **Alt+F7** to highlight the first icon in the current palette, then use the ↓ key to point to the required icon. In either case a brief message appears at the top left corner of the screen, describing the function of the chosen icon.

Working with Palettes:
The custom palette, palette 1, is the only one that you can customise. It should display the icons you use most often. SmartIcons can be added to, removed from or rearranged within the custom palette, with the use of three special SmartIcons which are to be found in palette 6. These icons are shown here as they would display in the Wysiwyg mode and have the following function:

Icon *Function*

The *Add icon* allows you to add a selected icon to your custom palette. You can select any icon from any other palette, which 1-2-3 then moves to the last position in the custom palette. If the custom palette is full, the last icon in the custom palette is replaced by the selected icon.

The *Del icon* allows you to delete a selected icon from your custom palette. When you select this icon, 1-2-3 displays the custom palette so that you can remove unwanted icons. Having done so, you can then add new icons.

The *Move icon* allows you to arrange the icons in your custom palette in the order you would like to see them. When you select this icon, 1-2-3 displays the custom palette and waits for you to select the icon you want to move, and indicate the position to which you want to move it. Moving an icon above its present position, forces all the icons below it to move down one position, while moving it below its present position, forces all the icons above it to move up one position.

Customising the User Icons:
If you have a unique set of tasks which are often repeated, and 1-2-3 hasn't a SmartIcon to do the job, then it is easy to set one of the 'user icons' to achieve your requirements. To do this, select the *User icon* (the last icon from palette 6 - which in the Wysiwyg mode looks as follows and has the following function:

Icon	*Function*
	The *User icon* allows you to write a set of instructions to carry out a given process, and attach it to one of the 'user icons' (to be found in palette 7).

Let us assume we would like to attach to the U1 user icon the **/Range, Erase** commands. On activating the *User icon*, 1-2-3 displays the following dialogue box:

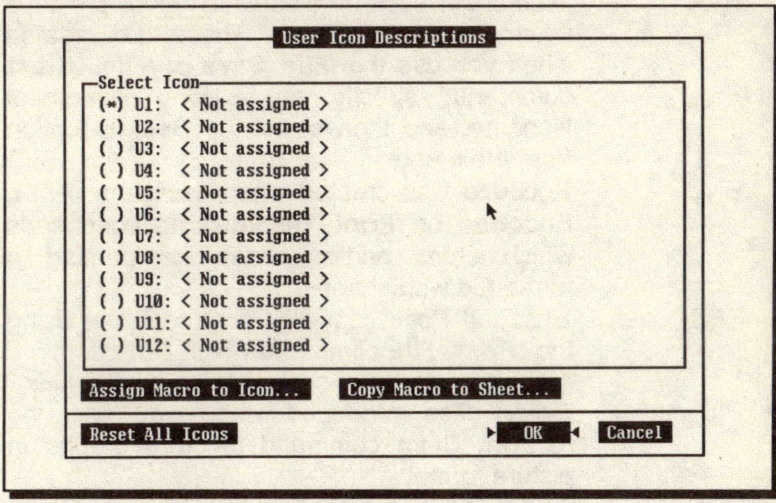

The asterisk next to the U1 icon means that the first user icon is selected. Select 'Assign Macro To Icon', then select 'Icon Description' in the further dialogue box and enter the name *Erase Range*. Then select the 'Macro Text' field and type

/RE

and click on the **OK** button (or press <Enter>) twice. To use the icon, highlight a range of worksheet cells and activate icon U1.

Working with Files

So far, we have discussed the **/File, Save** and **/File, Retrieve** commands which were used to respectively save to disc and load into memory worksheet files. Filenames were restricted to eight alphanumeric characters, with worksheet files having the three letter extension .WK1 automatically added to them. However, 1-2-3 can deal with lots of differently formatted files which are recognised by their different extensions.

Types of Files:

In addition to the worksheet files .WK1, 1-2-3 can create worksheet back-up , graph, and text files. Such files are created when you carry out certain processes. These are:

Extension	*Process*
.WK1	Worksheet files produced when you use the **/File, Save** or **/File, Xtract** command
.BAK	Worksheet back-up files which store previous versions of worksheets. These are created when you use the **/File, Save** or **/File, Xtract** command, specify an existing worksheet filename, and then select the **Backup** option from the menu
.ENC	Encoded files created when using the **/Print, Encoded** or **/Print, Background** commands which store printer codes for printing a formatted worksheet
.EPS	Encoded PostScript files created when using the **:Print, File** command which can contain a graphic image consisting of text and graphics
.PIC	Graph files produced when you use the **/Graph, Save** command to store graphs in picture format
.PRN	Text or print files produced when you use the **/Print, File** command which stores worksheet data in text or ASCII format on disc
.CNF	Configuration file created when using the **/Worksheet, Global, Default, Update** command which stores default settings.

If you want to find out what type of 1-2-3 files are held on the currently logged drive\directory, use the **/File, List** command. You can then select one of the following options:

Worksheet	Lists worksheet files (*.WKS, *.WK1, and *.WK3, corresponding to release 1A; release 2.0, 2.01, 2.2, 2.3 & 2.4; and release 3.0, 3.1 & 3.4, respectively) in the current directory.
Print	Lists print files (*.PRN) in the current directory.
Graph	Lists graph files (*.PIC) in the current directory.
Other	Lists all Files (*.*) in the current directory.
Linked	Lists all files on disc that are linked to the current worksheet.

Linking Files

A new feature of 1-2-3 Release 2.2 and higher, is file linking. This allows you to use values from cells in other worksheets (which have been saved on disc) into the current worksheet (the worksheet in memory). As the current file receives data, it is referred to as the target file, while the file that the formula refers to is called the source file.

File linking can save you the trouble of having to constantly update worksheets, such as a consolidation report which you might have built on a separate worksheet for the sake of security. Once files have been linked, 1-2-3 copies the value of the cell in the source file into the cell of the target file which is then automatically updated whenever the target file is retrieved or you issue the **Link-Refresh** command while working on the target file (more about this later).

As an example of linking files together we will work through an exercise to carry out a consolidation operation. The file we would like to construct is shown on the next page. But before you start typing information in order to create this new file, it might be worth considering whether you will save yourself some time by perhaps copying part of an existing file. How to do this is also explained on the next page.

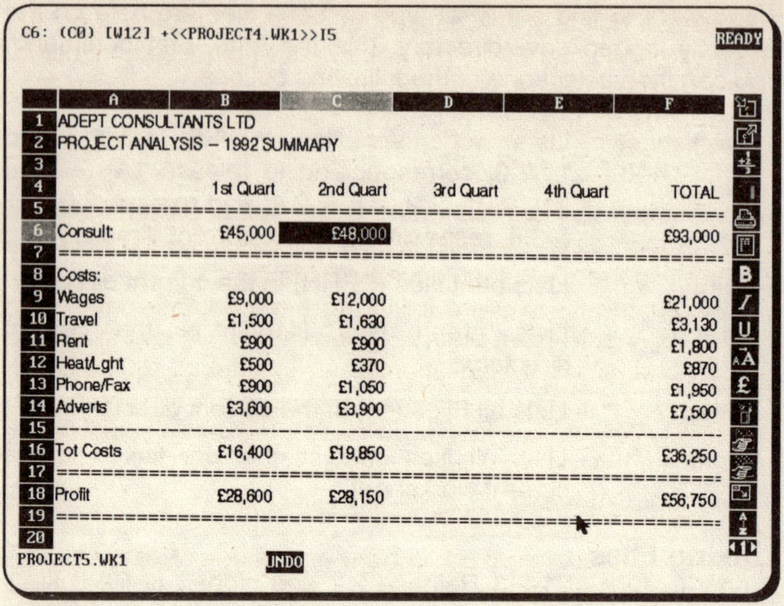

Copying a File into Memory:

Before you can copy a file into memory, use the **/Worksheet, Erase, Yes** command (discussed previously) to clear the computer's memory. Having done so, press

/	to reveal the menus
F	to select **File**
C	to select **Combine**
C	to select **Copy**
N	to select **Named/Specified-Range**

then specify range A1..A18, and type the filename PROJECT4. You could now type the missing label in cell A1 and the five column headings in row 4, then move the cell pointer into A2 and use the **/Worksheet, Insert** command to insert another row, so there is room for the additional label 'PROJECT ANALYSIS - 1990 SUMMARY'.

Format of Linking Formulae:

Cell references between different files are shown with the path and filename, included in double angular brackets (<<...>>), placed before the cell address.

The screen dump of the consolidation sheet displayed on the previous page shows how the linkage between files is effected. When the cell pointer is in C6 (the 2nd quarter's consultancy income), the formula is

+<<PROJECT4.WK1>>I5

indicating that this cell (C6 in the target file) has been linked to cell I5 of the source file PROJECT4 which is to be found on the disc in the currently logged drive and directory.

If the source file you are linking to is on another drive, then the full drive\path must also be given between the first double angular brackets and the filename. For example, to link a cell in the current (target) worksheet to, say, cell A1 in the source file, called 'myfile', to be found in the C: drive in subdirectory \lot123v2\data, you will have to type

+<<C:\lot123v3\data\myfile>>A1

in the highlighted cell of the current worksheet. Note that if you don't include the filename extension .WK1, 1-2-3 will add it for you.

Linked formulae can be edited, or copied from one part of the consolidation worksheet to another, just like ordinary formulae. Thus, after completing the entry, editing, and copying of linked formulae, save the consolidation worksheet under the filename PROJECT5.

Refreshing Linkages:

Whenever a target file that is linked to another file is retrieved into memory with the **/File, Retrieve** command, the formulae that contain the linkages are automatically 'updated'. However, if you are sharing files in a multi-user environment, other users might change the source files while you are viewing a target file. To make quite sure that the target file contains all the latest changes, select the **/File, Admin, Link-Refresh** command. This command recalculates formulae in active files that include references to other files on disk.

Note: When attempting to link files, try to observe the following restrictions and suggestions:

- Do not include a linking formula in another formula.

- Always include a path as part of the file reference, because should you change the current directory, 1-2-3 will not be able to find the source file and will display ERR in the target cell.

- Remember not to erase or rename the source file, or a referenced range name, otherwise 1-2-3 will display ERR in the target cell.

- Always use a range name (see next chapter) as the cell reference in a linking formula rather than making direct reference to a cell address, because if you move the source cell to a different location within the source worksheet, 1-2-3 will not be able to locate the new cell address and will display ERR in the target cell.

Finally, if you have more than two files linked, remember that the order in which you retrieve these files is important in correctly refreshing their links. For example, if worksheet A depends on worksheet B, which in turn depends on worksheet C, changing data in worksheet C will not be reflected in worksheet A, unless you first retrieve and save worksheet B.

4. SPREADSHEET GRAPHS

Lotus 1-2-3 allows you to represent information in graphical form which makes data more accessible to non-Lotus users who might not be familiar with the spreadsheet format. In any case, the well known saying 'a picture is worth a thousand words', applies equally well to graphs and figures.

Types of Charts

Lotus 1-2-3 Release 2.2 allows five different types of charts to be drawn, each illustrating up to six separate ranges of data. Release 2.3 & 2.4 adds two more main types, and also allows for special effects, like plotting bars sideways or adding a 3D-effect, which increases quite considerably the overall number of charts available to the user. You can display dots, lines or bars, and you can add titles, legends, labels, and a grid. These charts (you can have several per worksheet) can be displayed on the screen or can be saved separately on disc so that they can be sent to the printer later. The types of charts, or graphs, available are:

Release 2.2

Line	Bar	XY	Stack-Bar	Pie

Release 2.3 & 2.4

As above, plus	HLCO	Mixed	Features

On selecting one of these, 1-2-3 expects you to define the X data range, followed by up to six (A - F) y-axis data ranges. The five graph-types are normally used when we would like to describe the following relationships between data:

Line	for showing changes in data over time - up to six sets, A - F, can be drawn against an x-axis range of labels.
Bar	for comparing differences in data - up to six sets, A - F, can be drawn against an x-axis range of labels.
XY	for showing scatter relationships between X and Y - up to six points on the chart (using the A - F data range) can be plotted against an x-axis range of values.

Stack-Bar	for comparing cumulative data - up to six sets, A - F, can be drawn against an x-axis range labels. The data in the A range appear at the bottom of the stack with data in the F range appearing at the very top.
Pie	for comparing parts with the whole. Use the X range for pie-slice labels, the A range for the pie-slice values, and the B range for allocating colour or hatch patterns to the slices.
HLCO	for showing the extreme high and low fluctuations of data values with time, together with their corresponding closing and opening values during that period. The X data range is used to specify the x-axis labels, with ranges A, B, C and D being used for the sets of high, low, close, and open values, respectively. The E range can be used as a set of bars below the HLCO area, while the F range can be used as a line in the HLCO area. This type of chart is useful for describing opening and closing trading figures of shares in the stock market.
Mixed	for showing different types of data on the same graph; they are combinations of bar and line graphs. The X data range is used for the x-axis labels, while ranges A, B, and C are used as sets of bars, and ranges D, E, and F are used as sets of lines.

The Features option of the **/Graph, Type** command, offers the following five charting capabilities:

Vertical	Displays a horizontal x-axis across the bottom of the graph, with a vertical y-axis along the left edge. This is the default choice.
Horizontal	Displays the chart rotated by 90 degrees, with the x-axis vertical and the y-axis horizontal.
Stacked	Displays corresponding data-range values in stacked form. This feature can be used with line, bar, XY and mixed charts.

Frame	Controls how much of the graph 1-2-3 surrounds by a frame, adds or removes gutters, or adds or removes zero lines.
3D-Effect	Adds a three-dimensional effect on your bar, stacked bar, and mixed graphs.

Graphs can not be displayed at the same time as the worksheet (unless you use the Allways add-in or Wysiwyg module) because graphs use the graphics mode of your computer while worksheets use the text mode. Nevertheless, once the preliminary definition of data and selection of the type of graph you would like to see is made, viewing graphs is quite easy; simply press the **F10** key. As graphs are dynamic, any changes made to the data on the worksheet are automatically reflected on the already defined graphs.

Preparing for a Line Graph:
In order to illustrate some of the graphing capabilities of 1-2-3, we will now plot the 'Profit' from consultancies graph of the PROJECT4 worksheet. First we need to define the type of graph to be displayed followed by the range of the data we want to graph. However, the specified range of data to be graphed must be contiguous for each graph. But in our example, the range of data is split into two areas; Jan-Mar (occupying cell positions B3..D3), and Apr-Jun (occupying cell positions F3..H3), with the corresponding profit values in cells B17..D17 and F17..H17. Thus, to create an appropriate contiguous data range, we must first replicate the labels and values of these two range areas in another area of the worksheet (say, beginning in cell B21 for the actual month labels and B22 for the values of the corresponding profit).

To do this, use **/Worksheet, Titles, Clear** command to unfreeze the titles in column A, then select **/Range, Erase** to erase the contents of row 21 so that all cells of interest are visible on the screen at once. Labels can be copied in the usual way with the **/Copy** command. However, before you start copying the profit row, stop and consider what will happen if you do so. As these cells contain formulae, using the **/Copy** command would cause the relative cell addresses to adjust to the new locations and each formula will then recalculate a new value for each cell, which will give wrong results.

The /Range Value Command:

This command copies only the value in a cell and not its underlying formula which calculated this value. To do this, make sure that PROJECT4 is your current worksheet and that the mode indicator is on READY, then highlight cell B17 and press

/	to reveal the menus
R	to select **Range**
V	to select **Value**
<→>	to highlight the columns corresponding to the Jan-Mar range
<Enter>	to confirm range selection, at which point you'll be asked to enter range to copy to
<↓>	to move and highlight the beginning of the range to copy data values to (B22 in this case)
<Enter>	to confirm and execute the copy of data.

Now repeat the same procedure for the profit data in the Apr-Jun range, but copy them into E22 to form a contiguous data range. Finally, add labels for 'Months' and 'Profit' in cells A21 and A22, as shown below, and save the resultant worksheet under the filename PROJECT6.

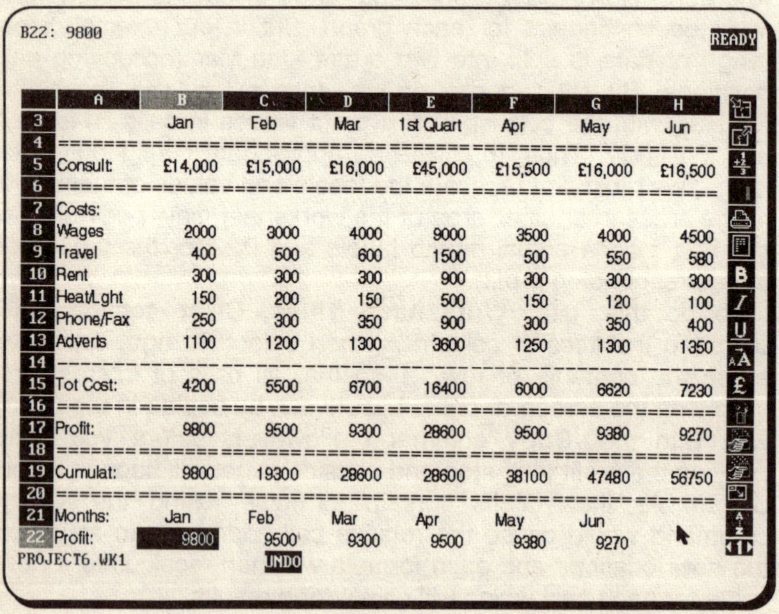

B22: 9800 READY

	A	B	C	D	E	F	G	H
3		Jan	Feb	Mar	1st Quart	Apr	May	Jun
4	======	======	======	======	======	======	======	======
5	Consult	£14,000	£15,000	£16,000	£45,000	£15,500	£16,000	£16,500
6	======	======	======	======	======	======	======	======
7	Costs:							
8	Wages	2000	3000	4000	9000	3500	4000	4500
9	Travel	400	500	600	1500	500	550	580
10	Rent	300	300	300	900	300	300	300
11	Heat/Lght	150	200	150	500	150	120	100
12	Phone/Fax	250	300	350	900	300	350	400
13	Adverts	1100	1200	1300	3600	1250	1300	1350
14	------	------	------	------	------	------	------	------
15	Tot Cost:	4200	5500	6700	16400	6000	6620	7230
16	======	======	======	======	======	======	======	======
17	Profit:	9800	9500	9300	28600	9500	9380	9270
18	======	======	======	======	======	======	======	======
19	Cumulat:	9800	19300	28600	28600	38100	47480	56750
20	======	======	======	======	======	======	======	======
21	Months:	Jan	Feb	Mar	Apr	May	Jun	
22	Profit:	9800	9500	9300	9500	9380	9270	

PROJECT6.WK1 UNDO

The /Graph Command:

We can now proceed with the definition of the type of graph to be drawn. To do this, make sure that the mode indicator is on READY and press

/	to reveal the menus
G	to select **Graph** and display the 'Type' sub-menu. With Release 2.2 or higher, the Graph Settings screen will also be displayed
T	to select **Type**
L	to select **Line** graph.

The Graph menu then reappears so that you can first select the X (horizontal) range, and then up to 6 vertical ranges (A through F) in a single graph. In this case, we only need to select one vertical range as we are dealing with the profit from consultancies only. Thus, first define the X range by pressing

X	to select the X-range
<Arrows>	to highlight the beginning of the range
<.>	to anchor the beginning of the X range
<Arrows>	to highlight entire range (B21..G21)
<Enter>	to confirm range selection
A	to select the first Y range
<Arrows>	to highlight the beginning of the A range
<.>	to anchor the beginning of the A range
<Arrows>	to highlight the entire range (B22..G22)
<Enter>	to confirm the range selection

If you are using 1-2-3 Release 2.2 or higher, as you are issuing the above commands, the information typed will be transferred automatically to the Graph Setting or dialogue screen, which by now should look as shown on the next page.

To view the line graph, select the **View** command from the **/Graph** sub-menu, or if 1-2-3 is in READY mode, press the **F10** function key. At this point, your screen should clear and a line graph, as shown on the next page, should appear on it. Should your computer bleep instead, then you must have made a mistake when defining either the type of graph or the data ranges. If that happens, then press the <Esc> key to return to the **Graph** menu, select **Reset** and start again. If you don't use **Reset** you will find that 1-2-3 remembers the previously defined range settings, which might be rather useful to you if you are defining another graph-type with the same range settings.

The Graph Settings dialogue box and corresponding line graph, are shown below:

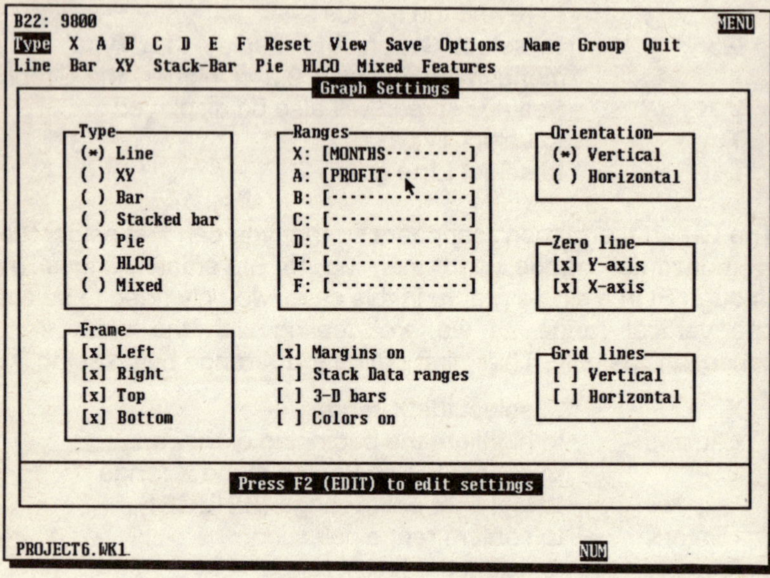

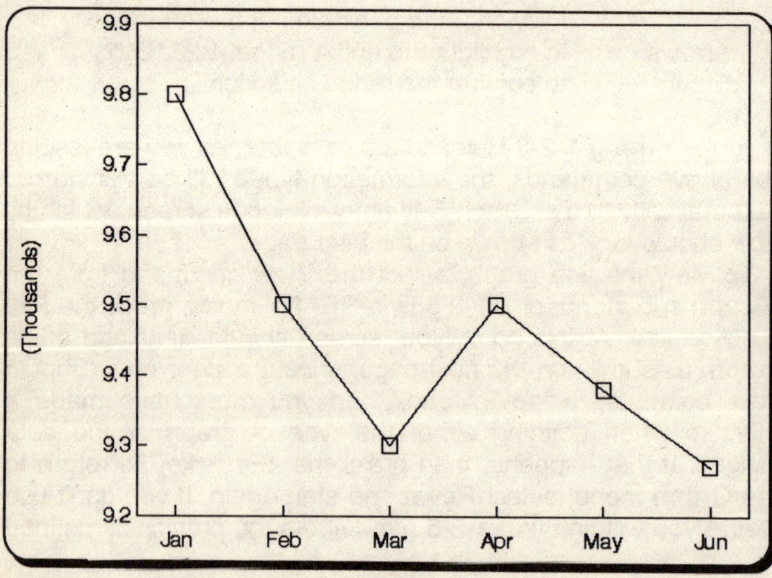

Quick Graphs with SmartIcons

To obtain a 'Quick' graph, highlight the range you want to graph (B21..G22), as shown below:

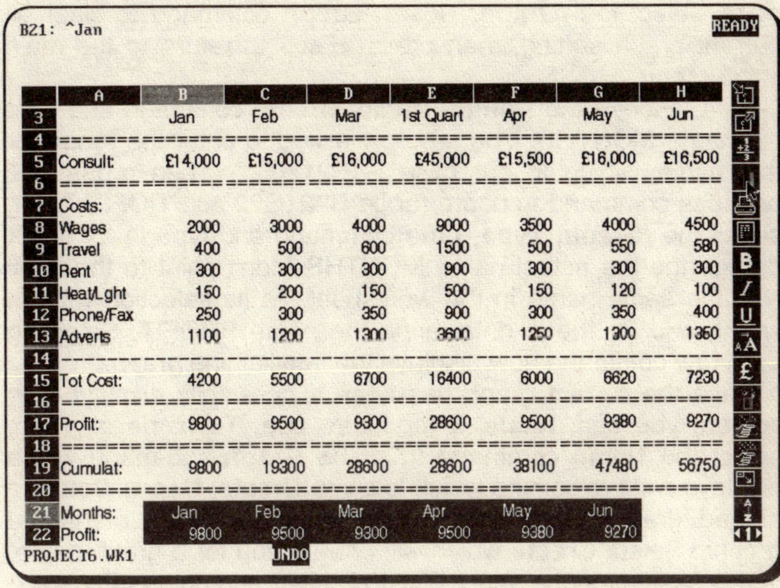

B21: ^Jan READY

	A	B	C	D	E	F	G	H
3		Jan	Feb	Mar	1st Quart	Apr	May	Jun
4	=======	=======	=======	=======	=======	=======	=======	=======
5	Consult:	£14,000	£15,000	£16,000	£45,000	£15,500	£16,000	£16,500
6	=======	=======	=======	=======	=======	=======	=======	=======
7	Costs:							
8	Wages	2000	3000	4000	9000	3500	4000	4500
9	Travel	400	500	600	1500	500	550	580
10	Rent	300	300	300	900	300	300	300
11	Heat/Lght	150	200	150	500	150	120	100
12	Phone/Fax	250	300	350	900	300	350	400
13	Adverts	1100	1200	1300	3600	1250	1300	1350
14	-------	-------	-------	-------	-------	-------	-------	-------
15	Tot Cost:	4200	5500	6700	16400	6000	6620	7230
16	=======	=======	=======	=======	=======	=======	=======	=======
17	Profit:	9800	9500	9300	28600	9500	9380	9270
18	=======	=======	=======	=======	=======	=======	=======	=======
19	Cumulat:	9800	19300	28600	28600	38100	47480	56750
20	=======	=======	=======	=======	=======	=======	=======	=======
21	Months:	Jan	Feb	Mar	Apr	May	Jun	
22	Profit:	9800	9500	9300	9500	9380	9270	

PROJECT6.WK1 UNDO

and press the *Quick Graph* icon (the fourth icon on the first palette - the one with the vertical bars). The following dialogue box is then displayed.

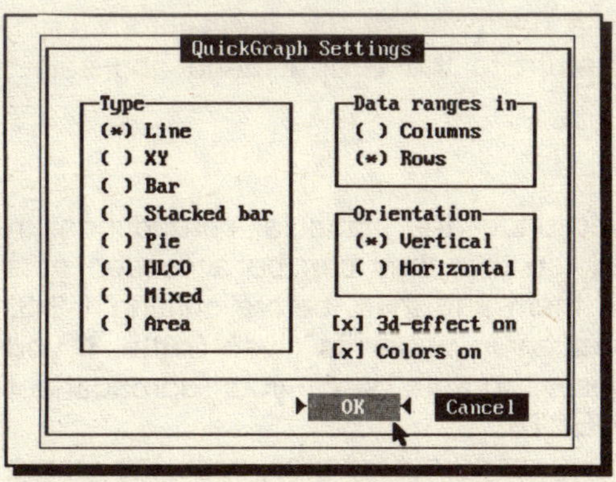

You can now select the 'Type' of graph you want to see, its orientation (vertical or horizontal) and whether in 3D or in colour. On pressing the **OK** button, the graph is drawn for you, automatically.

Naming Ranges and Graphs

It is often more convenient to 'name' a range of data and then use the name rather than the cell addresses in subsequent worksheet operations, including graphing. To illustrate this point, select the **/Graph, Reset, Graph** command to clear all current graph setting, then press <Esc> to return to the main 1-2-3 menu.

Next, choose the **Range, Name, Create** command and type the name MONTHS. You are now asked to enter the range for this name, which in our case is B21..G21. Then repeat the previous command to name range B22..G22 as PROFIT. Next, select the **/Graph, Type, Line** command and type in for the **X** data-range the actual name MONTHS (don't point to the label with the same name in the worksheet, as its selection will not work), and for the **A** data-range the name PROFIT. Selecting the **View** command now displays the familiar line graph.

Once the correct graph has been successfully displayed on screen, you can 'Name' it for future use. To name a graph, select the **Name** command from the **Graph** sub-menu which displays a list of options which lets you **Create, Use** or **Delete** a named graph, **Reset** (delete), or create a **Table** of named graphs. Select **Create** which will prompt you for a graph name. In this case, type the name PROFIT_LINE and press <Enter>.

The settings of the current graph are remembered by 1-2-3, and when you select new settings, the current ones are presented as default so that you can reuse as many of these as you like. This reduces the time required to define new settings for a graph that happens to be rather similar to one you have already defined. To see a bar chart of the same information, simply press <Esc> to return to the **Graph** menu and select **Type, Bar, View.**

Saving Graphs:

Graphs will only be saved under the particular spreadsheet in which they were created (so that they can be accessed at a later stage), if you name them and then, before quitting 1-2-3, you save the spreadsheet again under its given name. If you have named the suggested graph, save your spreadsheet under the filename PROJECT6.

You can save as many separate graphs with the same spreadsheet filename as you like, provided you gave each one a different 'name', using the **/Graph, Name** command. To select any graph and make it current, choose the **/Graph, Use** command (press **F3** to see a list of saved chart names in tabular form, if you have defined lots of them), highlight the required one and press <Enter>.

Note: The **/Graph, Name** command is different from the **/Graph, Save** command. **/Graph, Save** creates a separate file of the current graph on the data disc so that it can be printed with the Lotus 1-2-3 **PrintGraph** program which is one of the options available in the 'Lotus Access System'.

Legends and Titles:

There are several options within the **/Graph, Options** sub-menu which allow you to add information on your graph.

The **/Graph, Options, Legend** selection, allows you to specify the wording of a legend which appears on the x-axis of your graph. In the case of our example, this was not required as the x-axis range itself was descriptive. Legends are not relevant to pie charts.

The **/Graph, Options, Titles** selection allows you to add a two-line title to the whole graph, or add annotation to the x and y axes. To add a title to the previous example, use the **/Graph, Options, Titles, First** option. To annotate the Y axis, choose **/Graph, Options, Titles, Y**, type 'Profit' and press <Enter>.

Drawing a Multiple Bar Chart:

As an exercise, define graph settings for a new bar-type graph which deals with the monthly 'Costs' of Adept Consultants. Start by using the **/Range, Value** command to copy the various costs into a contiguous worksheet range at the bottom of the worksheet, say, starting at cell A23.

As there are six different costs, you must define data-ranges A to F inclusive, so that 6 different bars (corresponding to the six different costs) can be plotted for each month. Use the **/Range, Name, Create** command to name each cost range. Annotate and title your graph, and enter legends to mark the different cross-hatching patterns which represent the various costs. If you are using Release 2.01, the legends describing these costs must be as short as possible (with six costs use only a single letter), if the printout is to be correct.

With 1-2-3 Release 2.2 or higher, use the **/Range, Name, Create** command to name range B24..G30 as COSTS, as shown below. Then, use the **/Graph, Group** command and type the range name COSTS, which causes 1-2-3 to ask whether to use the columns or the rows as data ranges. Select the **Rowwise** option. Next, use the **Options, Legend, Range** command and highlight the labels in range A25..A30.

Only with 1-2-3 Release 2.2 or higher can you select a range of legends. With previous versions you must specify each one separately.

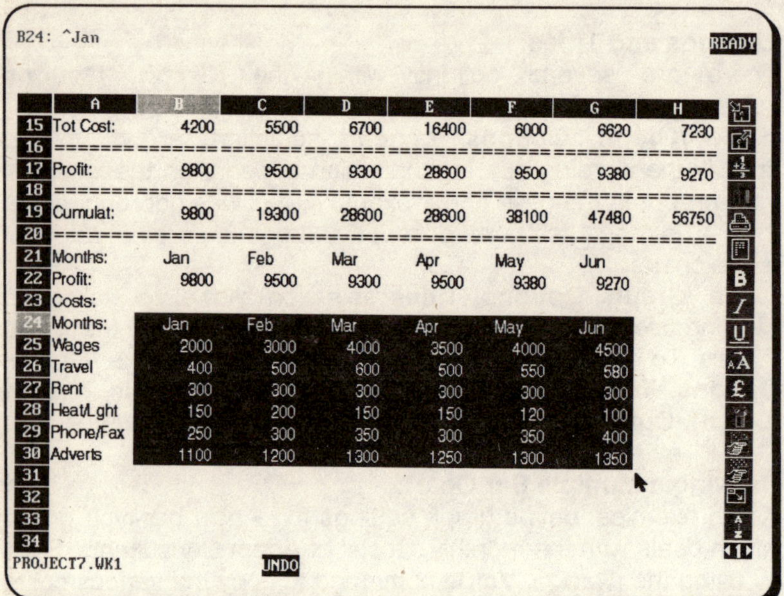

Finally, use the **Title** option to give your bar chart a title and to annotate the two axes, as shown in the Graph Settings screen on the next page.

Don't forget to use the **/Graph, Name, Create** command to give this graph a name - call it COSTS_BAR. The completed graph is also shown on the next page.

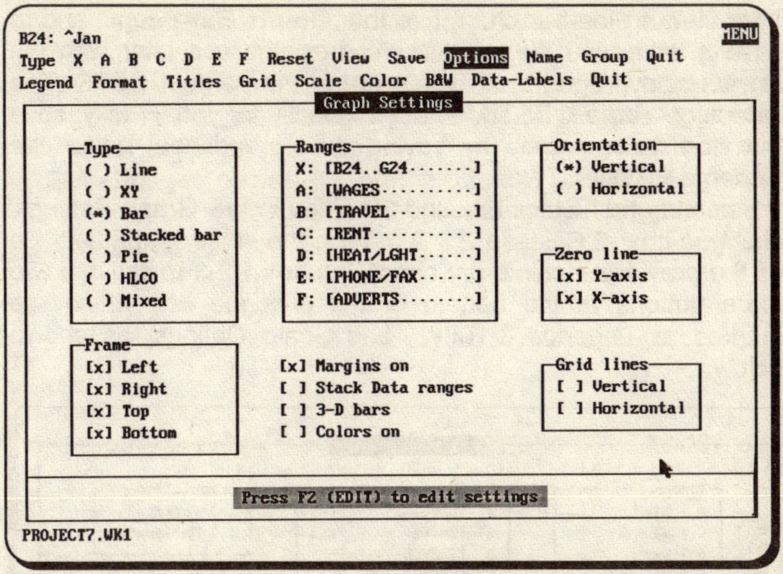
B24: ^Jan
MENU
Type X A B C D E F Reset View Save Options Name Group Quit
Legend Format Titles Grid Scale Color B&W Data-Labels Quit
Graph Settings
Type
( ) Line
( ) XY
(*) Bar
( ) Stacked bar
( ) Pie
( ) HLCO
( ) Mixed
Ranges
X: [B24..G24]
A: [WAGES]
B: [TRAVEL]
C: [RENT]
D: [HEAT/LGHT]
E: [PHONE/FAX]
F: [ADVERTS]
Orientation
(*) Vertical
( ) Horizontal
Zero line
[x] Y-axis
[x] X-axis
Frame
[x] Left
[x] Right
[x] Top
[x] Bottom
[x] Margins on
[ ] Stack Data ranges
[ ] 3-D bars
[ ] Colors on
Grid lines
[ ] Vertical
[ ] Horizontal
Press F2 (EDIT) to edit settings
PROJECT7.WK1

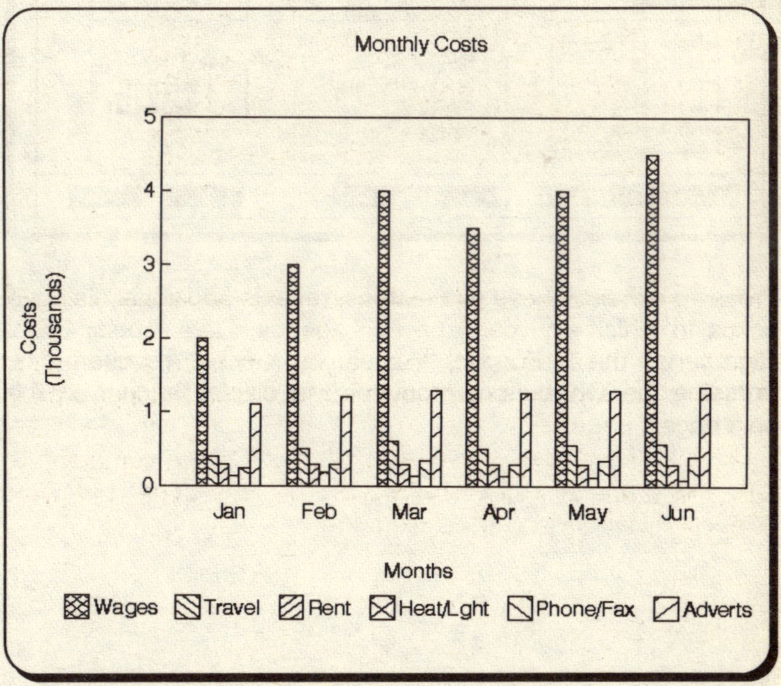
Monthly Costs
Costs
(Thousands)
5
4
3
2
1
0
Jan
Feb
Mar
Apr
May
Jun
Months
Wages
Travel
Rent
Heat/Lght
Phone/Fax
Adverts

After viewing the bar chart, use the **/Graph, Save** command to save it as a .PIC file on disc, for possible use later with the **PrintGraph** program. Give this graph the name COSTS. The extension .PIC will be added automatically for you. Finally, save the worksheet graphs by saving the spreadsheet under the filename PROJECT7.

Selecting the Stack-Bar and 3D-Effec in the 'Graph Settings' dialogue box of Release 2.3 & 2.4 (on the same graph settings as the previous multiple bar chart), causes 1-2-3 to activate two more buttons at the bottom of the dialogue box which are marked as Legends & Titles, and Scale Options, as shown below.

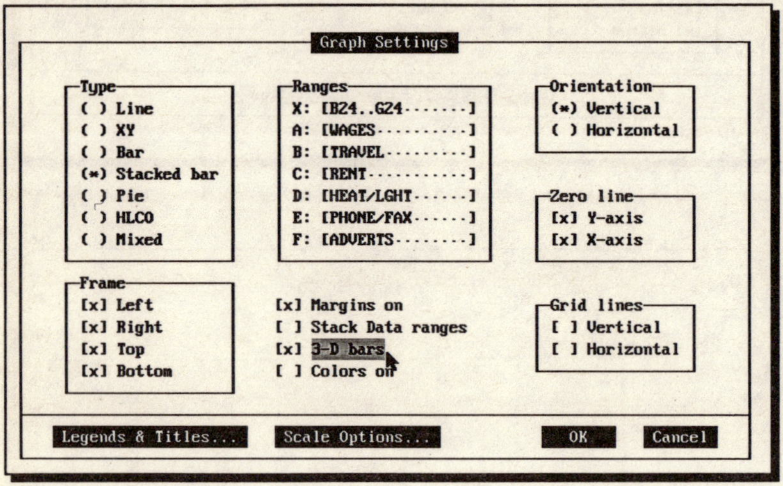

Pressing either of these two buttons, reveals additional dialogue boxes in which you can specify Lagends, Data labels, Label alignment, Titles, Format, Y-scale & X-scale requirements. Pressing the **OK** button, produces the display shown on the next page.

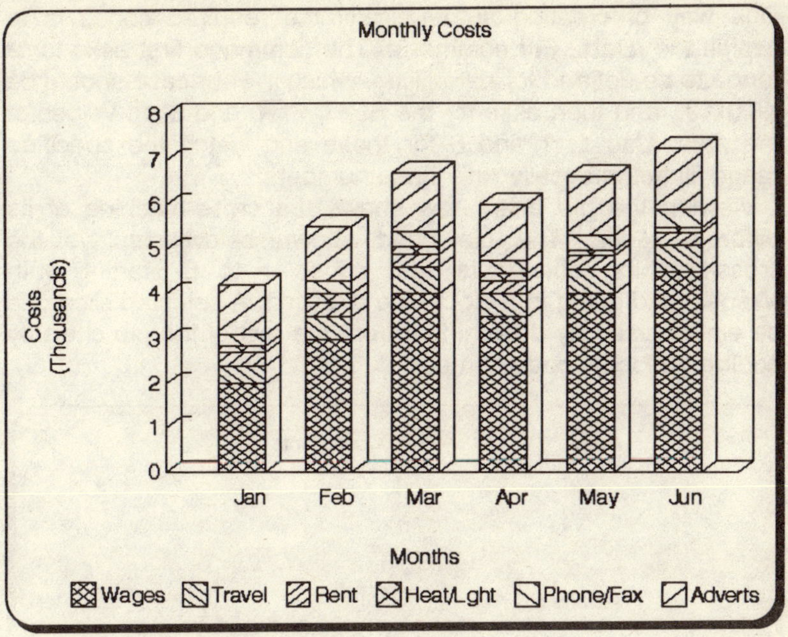

Drawing a Pie Chart:

As a second example, use the 'Average' values of the costs from your worksheet to plot a pie chart. It is advisable to use the **/Graph, Reset, Graph** command to clear all current graph setting, as the new chart you are about to put together is so different from the current one.

Again, define the new graph type as 'Pie' and then set the **X** range to the labels describing the costs (cells A8..A13), then set the **A** (first) range of data to the actual cost values (which are in cells J8..J13) and view the result. You will find that the different parts of the pie chart are all labelled with the words describing the various costs in the worksheet and that percentage values of each cost appear next to them.

Cross-hatching Code Numbers:

We need to provide code numbers for cross-hatching of the pie chart as Lotus 1-2-3 does not automatically shade the slices of a pie chart. The allowable codes are in fact from 0 to 7, each resulting with a different cross-hatching pattern. The codes must be inserted somewhere in the worksheet and the **B** (second) data-range should be set to them.

One way of creating automatically the required codes is to exploit the **/Data, Fill** command. The command first asks for a range to be defined for data filling, which in your case should be K8..K13., and then asks for the **Start**, **Step** and **Stop** values of the data. Use 1, 1 and 6 for these and watch the specified range fill automatically with these numbers.

Viewing the pie chart now shows the cross-hatching of its different slices. The pie chart shown below displays the cross-hatching obtainable with codes 1 to 6 starting with 'Wages' and going in a clockwise direction. A selected slice can be emphasized by detaching it from the rest of the pie chart by adding 100 to its code number.

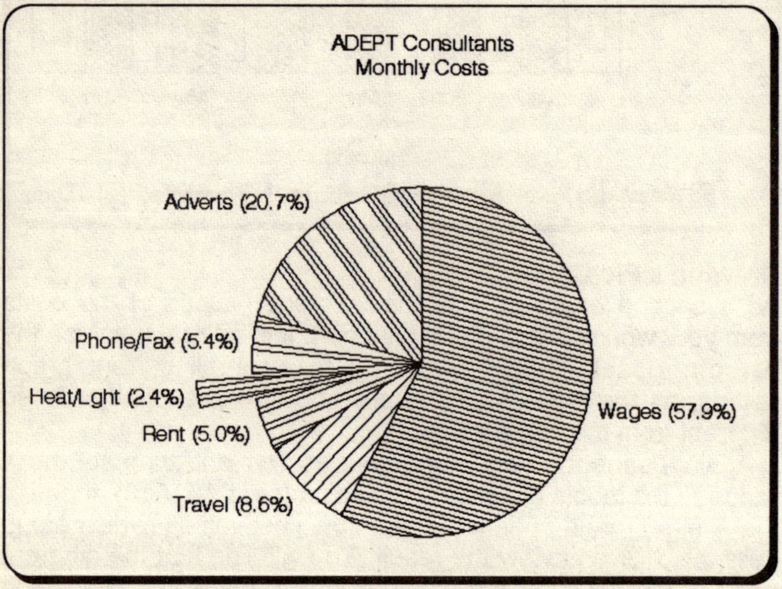

When you are satisfied with your efforts, don't forget to use the **Name, Create** command to give this chart the name COSTS_PIE, then save the worksheet under the filename PROJECT8, so that the graphs are saved with it.

The available cross-hatching patterns against their codes are shown below.

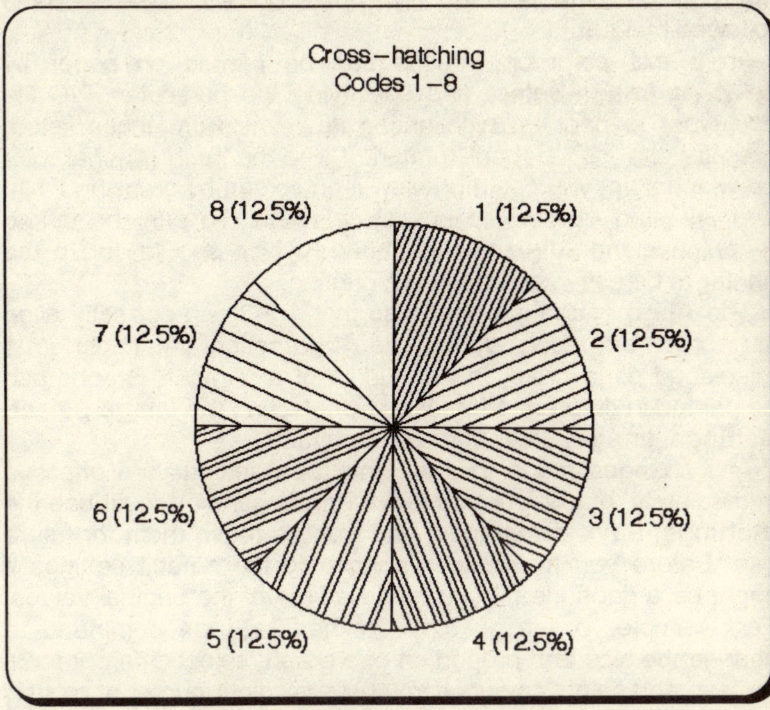

Using the PrintGraph Module

If you are the first person to use the Lotus PrintGraph module you must implement it to accept the 'Saved' graphs which now have the extension .PIC. To do this, quit the worksheet and select **PrintGraph** from the 'Lotus Access System' and select **Settings, Hardware** and **Graphs-Directory** and type

c:\lot123v2\data

followed by <Enter>. This assumes that you have saved the .PIC files in the **data** subdirectory of **\lot123v2** directory on the **c:** drive. Then select **Fonts-Directory** and type

c:\lot123v2

because the 'font' files are kept in the main Lotus 1-2-3 directory.

Now select **Settings**, **Hardware** and then **Printer** to select the combination of printer and density of print required, then **Quit** to return to the Settings menu from where you should select **Save** followed by **Quit**.

From this point on, graphs can be printed on paper by selecting **Image-Select** and specifying the particular .PIC file you want to print by highlighting its name from those listed, pressing the <Spacebar> to mark it with the hash (#) character (at which point you could preview it on screen by pressing **F10**), and pressing <Enter> to accept selection. To print a marked graph, use the **Align, Go** command which should cause the printer to be activated and begin printing.

The **Align** option is needed so that 1-2-3 can correctly align your graph on paper. Without the **Align** option, you might get a misplaced page break in the middle of a printout. Graphs can be printed in different orientation by selecting the **Image-Select, Settings, Image, Size, Manual** command.

Any changes made to the PrintGraph settings are effective immediately, but before you leave PrintGraph you must use the **/Settings, Save** command if you want to retain them for future use. Before you make any changes to the default settings it might be a good idea if you made a note of the original values. For example, you might choose the **/Settings** command to change the size and proportion of a graph, select different fonts for text, and select colours if you have a colour printer or plotter.

However, be careful with such changes (don't save them until you are absolutely satisfied) as printing pie charts some time later might produce an egg shaped graph after 10 minutes of laborious printing if you change the proportion of the graph incorrectly. If you do make any such changes which you save and later discover they are not what you want, choose 'half size' graphs from the **/Settings, Size** menu, and save your choice. If you are not careful, you could end up wasting an awful lot of hours experimenting with PrintGraph. The reason is the slowness with which your printer draws such graphs.

The separateness of the PrintGraph program from the Lotus 1-2-3 program, causes a lot of other problems to users of Release 2.01 and earlier. For example, it is impossible to print a graph and the table of figures from which it was derived on the same sheet of paper. The Always add-in in Release 2.2 and the Wysiwyg add-in in Release 2.3 & 2.4, solves this problem.

5. SPREADSHEET PUBLISHING

The Wysiwyg (what you see is what you get) module that comes with Lotus 1-2-3 Release 2.3 & 2.4, allows you to enhance the appearance of your worksheet both on screen and on paper; you can customise worksheet fonts, add text enhancements (such as bold and underline), shade worksheet ranges, change screen colours, etc. The printed output that you can achieve with Wysiwyg is of high quality, whether you print reports, documents or graphs. Users of earlier versions of 1-2-3 than Release 2.3, can only benefit in a similar way if they have either the Impress (a forerunner of Wysiysg) or the Allways spreadsheet publishing add-ins. However, only the Wysiwyg module is discussed in this book.

Before we look at specific aspects of the Wysiwyg module, we need to prepare a worksheet and discuss some terminology common to both. This is done in the next two sections which you should read first, before you turn to the publishing module itself.

Preparing a Worksheet

To illustrate some of the spreadsheet publishing and graphing capabilities of Wysiwyg, we will now work on the consolidation worksheet (PROJECT5) of the small consulting company we discussed at the end of Chapter 3. However, before we can go on, you will need to complete the entries for the other two quarters of trading of the Adept Consultants' example into the PROJECT4 file and link the quarterly totals to the consolidation file of PROJECT5, which should then be saved as PROJECT9.

Of course, if you don't feel like doing this right now, you can always add manually the quarterly totals in the consolidation worksheet. However, for those who would like to do things properly and/or would like the opportunity to practice what they have learned so far, we list on the next page the data needed in the PROJECT4 file to create the consolidation file. Having made the additions, use the **/Range, Name, Create** command to give the ranges used in the consolidation file relevant names. This is good practice, as discussed in the previous chapter.

	Jul	Aug	Sep	Oct	Nov	Dec
Consult:	17,000	16,000	16,500	18,000	20,000	22,000
Costs:						
Wages	4,000	4,000	4,500	4,000	4,500	5,500
Travel	450	400	550	550	600	650
Rent	300	300	300	300	300	300
Heat/Lght	80	60	90	130	170	240
Phone/Fax	330	170	250	380	400	450
Adverts	1,200	1.000	1,200	1,350	1,400	1,500

Finally, having carried out the suggested changes, don't forget to save worksheet PROJECT4 under its original name.

Next, retrieve the consolidation worksheet PROJECT5 and edit existing linking formulae by replacing references to actual cell ranges in the source file by named ranges, then add the additional linking formulae needed to fill the worksheet. Completing this work is quicker than imagined, provided you adopt a liberal use of the EDIT **(F2)** key and /**Copy** command. The final contents of the PROJECT9 file, should look as follows:

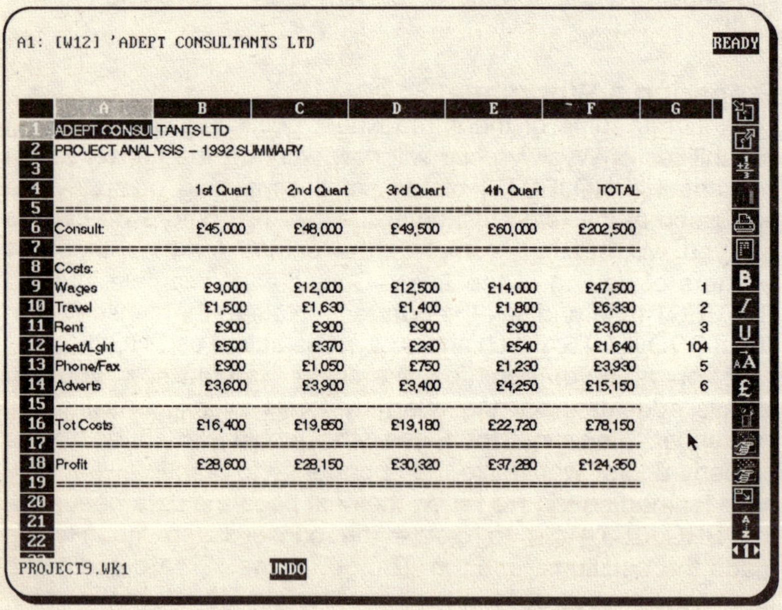

A1: [W12] 'ADEPT CONSULTANTS LTD READY

	A	B	C	D	E	F	G
1	ADEPT CONSULTANTS LTD						
2	PROJECT ANALYSIS – 1992 SUMMARY						
3							
4		1st Quart	2nd Quart	3rd Quart	4th Quart	TOTAL	
5	==========	==========	==========	==========	==========	==========	
6	Consult:	£45,000	£48,000	£49,500	£60,000	£202,500	
7	==========	==========	==========	==========	==========	==========	
8	Costs:						
9	Wages	£9,000	£12,000	£12,500	£14,000	£47,500	1
10	Travel	£1,500	£1,630	£1,400	£1,800	£6,330	2
11	Rent	£900	£900	£900	£900	£3,600	3
12	Heat/Lght	£500	£370	£230	£540	£1,640	104
13	Phone/Fax	£900	£1,050	£750	£1,230	£3,930	5
14	Adverts	£3,600	£3,900	£3,400	£4,250	£15,150	6
15	----------	----------	----------	----------	----------	----------	
16	Tot Costs	£16,400	£19,850	£19,180	£22,720	£78,150	
17	==========	==========	==========	==========	==========	==========	
18	Profit	£28,600	£28,150	£30,320	£37,280	£124,350	
19	==========	==========	==========	==========	==========	==========	
20							
21							
22							

PROJECT9.WK1 UNDO

Next, define a pie chart of the yearly costs and then save it as a .PIC file giving it the name YEARCOST. Later on, we will use this file when we discuss the individual publishing modules.

Font Styles

When you first use the Wysiwyg module, you will find that there are eight character fonts resident which you can use to enhance the looks of your worksheet. These fonts, called the font set, can be replaced with other typefaces of varied size from a list supplied with the module, or a library of soft fonts, if you happen to have purchased them from a third party.

There are two ways of specifying the size of a character font; a 'point' is approximately 1/72 of an inch, and determines the height of a character, while a 'pitch' is the number of characters that can fit horizontally in one inch. The spacing of a font is either 'fixed' (monospaced) or 'proportional'. With fixed spacing, each character takes up exactly the same space, while proportionally spaced characters take up different spacing (an 'i' or a 't' take up less space than a 'u' or a 'w'). Thus, the length of proportionally spaced text can vary depending on which letters it contains. However, numerals take up the same amount of space whether they have been specified as fixed or proportional.

Which fonts you choose is largely dependent on your printer. Here you can experiment to your heart's delight, but it will take time. One thing you must bear in mind is that 1-2-3 uses screen fonts to display characters on screen and printer fonts to print characters with a printer. If you choose printer fonts for which there are no screen fonts, 1-2-3 will use the nearest screen font to display your work on screen, which might not be exactly what you will see when you print your work.

The Wysiwyg Module - Release 2.3 & 2.4

The Wysiwyg module loads automatically with 1-2-3 Release 2.4. With Release 2.3, you will have to load it yourself by first loading 1-2-3 and, when the program displays a blank worksheet and is in the READY mode, then

1. Press ADDIN (Alt+**F10**)
2. Select **Attach**
3. Choose WYSIWYG.ADN
4. Select **No-Key**
5. Select **Invoke**
6. Choose WYSIWYG
7. Select **Quit**.

This way of loading Wysiwyg into memory, as opposed to assigning it to one of the APP1 to APP3 (Alt+**F7** to Alt+**F9**) keys, allows you to use the colon (:) method for accessing the Wysiwyg menu. If you want Wysiwyg to load automatically whenever you load 1-2-3, then

1. Select **/Worksheet, Global, Default**

which causes the 'Default Settings' dialogue box to be displayed,

2. Press **F2** (EDIT) function key, or click the Auto-attach add-ins field of the dialogue box, and press <Enter>
3. Type in the entry box 1:[........] WYSIWYG as the add-in you want to attach and press <Enter>
4. Press the **Update** button.

Next time you load 1-2-3, Wysiwyg will be loaded automatically into memory, and invoked.

Selecting Wysiwyg Commands:

When Wysiwyg is active, the main Lotus 1-2-3 menu can be activated by pressing the slash (/) key (and thereafter by moving the mouse pointer into the menu area). You can invoke the Wysiwyg menu by pressing the colon (:) key on the keyboard (and thereafter by moving the mouse pointer into the menu area). Wysiwyg menu commands can be selected by either typing their first letter or by pointing with the mouse and clicking the left mouse button. When a command has been chosen, pressing the right mouse button has the same effect as pressing <Esc> on the keyboard.

Once you have activated either the main 1-2-3 menu or the Wysiwyg menu, moving the mouse pointer in the menu area displays the currently active menu. You can toggle between the two menus by pressing the right mouse button.

If you are a left-handed person and wish to switch the mouse buttons around so that the left button is used for the right (and vice versa), then use the Install program and select the Wysiwyg options. Other options can be used to generate fonts for printing and screen display, or add soft fonts from a disc to use with Wysiwyg.

The screen dump below, shows the top-half of the screen when the Wysiwyg menu, in Release 2.4, is displayed.

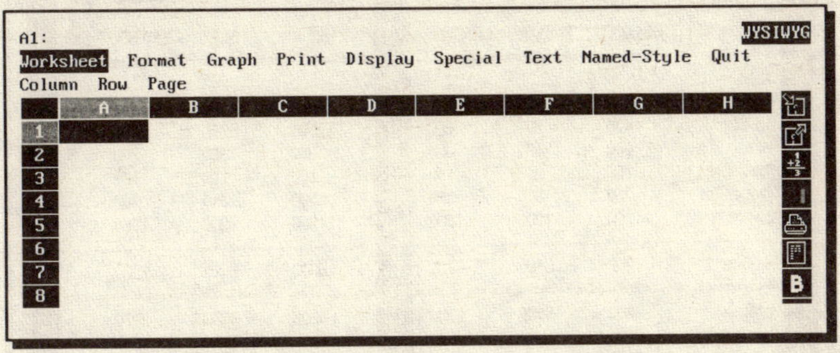

Mouse Shortcuts in Wysiwyg:

You can use the mouse to specify worksheet ranges when asked by the program. You can even specify a range before selecting a command which can prove useful when trying to apply a variety of formats to a range without having to specify the range for each command. These can be achieved as follows:

- Point to one corner of the range, click the left mouse button and drag the mouse to the opposite corner of the cell range, then release the mouse button.
- Highlighting a range and then selecting a command, causes 1-2-3 to carry out the command without asking for the range. The specified range remains highlighted (unless you move the cell pointer, press <Esc>, or click either mouse button) ready for selecting the next command. When you have finished with all the commands you intend to apply to the highlighted range, click the left mouse button.

Further, you can use the mouse to create vertical or horizontal windows by pointing to the box located above row1 and to the left of column A, pressing the left mouse button and dragging the mouse to the right or down, respectively, until the desired window size is reached, then releasing the mouse button. Retrieve PROJECT6 and then split the screen vertically to obtain the following display:

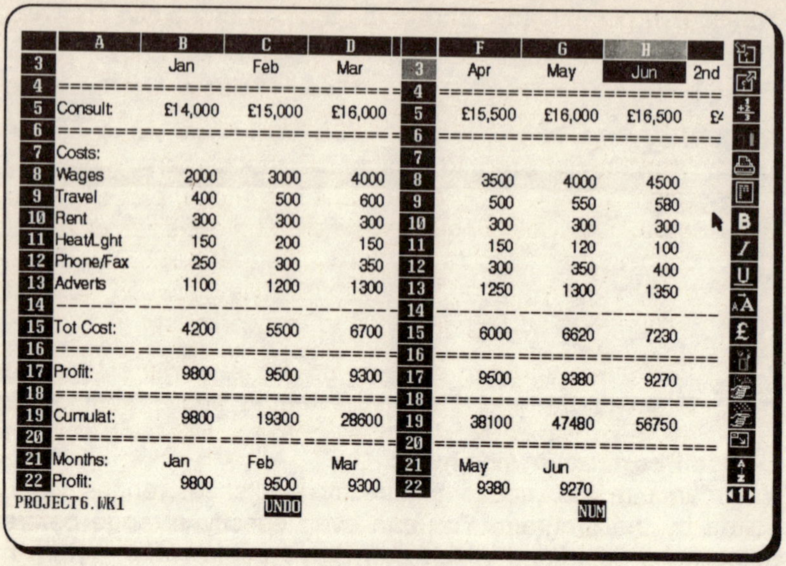

	A	B	C	D		F	G	H	
3		Jan	Feb	Mar	3	Apr	May	Jun	2nd
4	======	======	======	======	4	======	======	======	===
5	Consult:	£14,000	£15,000	£16,000	5	£15,500	£16,000	£16,500	£4
6	======	======	======	======	6	======	======	======	===
7	Costs:				7				
8	Wages	2000	3000	4000	8	3500	4000	4500	
9	Travel	400	500	600	9	500	550	580	
10	Rent	300	300	300	10	300	300	300	
11	Heat/Lght	150	200	150	11	150	120	100	
12	Phone/Fax	250	300	350	12	300	350	400	
13	Adverts	1100	1200	1300	13	1250	1300	1350	
14	------	------	------	------	14	------	------	------	---
15	Tot Cost:	4200	5500	6700	15	6000	6620	7230	
16	======	======	======	======	16	======	======	======	===
17	Profit:	9800	9500	9300	17	9500	9380	9270	
18	======	======	======	======	18	======	======	======	===
19	Cumulat:	9800	19300	28600	19	38100	47480	56750	
20	======	======	======	======	20	======	======	======	===
21	Months:	Jan	Feb	Mar	21	May	Jun		
22	Profit:	9800	9500	9300	22	9380	9270		

To clear such windows, move the mouse pointer to the box above row1 of the added window and drag the mouse left or up to move the box to its original position.

The Wysiwyg Commands:
There are eight commands in the main Wysiwyg menu which can be used to enhance what Lotus 1-2-3 displays, or prints. What these commands can achieve, is listed below.

> **:Worksheet** is used to control the width of a column or a range of columns, the height of a row or a range of rows, and to insert or remove a page break.

> **:Format** is used to format worksheet data in any of eight fonts, add text enhancements such as bold, italics, or underline, select a different colour for a range, add a variety of horizontal and vertical lines to a range, including drop shadows, and shade a range.

> **:Graph** is used to place 1-2-3 graphs anywhere in a worksheet, and then enhance them with colours, text, arrows, and geometric shapes. You can even view and add external graph files saved under the .PIC and .CGM formats, or create free-hand drawings and annotations.

:Print is used to specify the printer, interface and font cartridges, orientation and resolution of the output, paper type and size, margins, titles, headers, footers and preview a printed range on screen.

:Display is used to customise the screen display by selecting between graphics and text mode, black & white and colour, selecting between six different sizes of zoom, choosing the colours for the worksheet background and data, specifying the cell pointer style between solid or outline, and adding grid lines to the worksheet.

:Special is used to copy or move the format of a range to another range, import the format and/or settings of another worksheet to the current file, and export formatting information to disc in a .FM3, .FMT, or .ALL file format.

:Text is used to enter information in a worksheet as if you were using a word processor. Data can be entered directly in a range (instead of in the control panel) with word wrap, font and formatting control. Text alignment is within the specified range (instead of within cells).

:Named-Style is used to assign names to groups of formats by defining up to eight such groups, so that you can later format easily and consistently other worksheet ranges with the same group of formats.

Adding a Graph to a Worksheet Using Wysiwyg:
To add a graph to your current worksheet (you should have PROJECT9 on your screen), invoke Wysiwyg, move to cell location A22 and use the **:Graph, Add** command and specify the YEARCOST file as the .PIC file to be added to your worksheet within the range A22..F41. The result should be similar to the screen dump shown on the next page.

This worksheet will be used to illustrate some of the capabilities of Wysiwyg. First, we will print the worksheet range A1..F41, in a report form as it stands. Then, we will format and enhance the actual worksheet data layout, step by step, each time printing a more enhanced report, in order to cover as many Wysiwyg enhancing commands as possible.

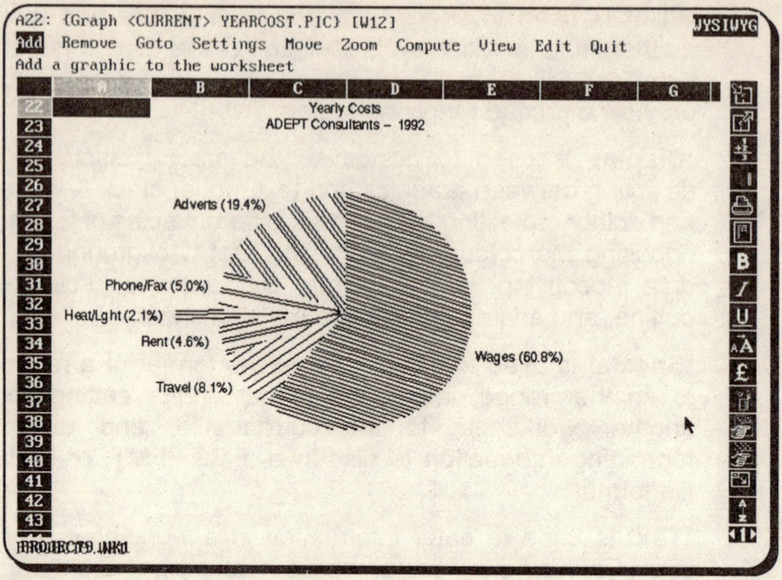

Now use the **:Print, Range, Set** command and specify cell range A1..F44, followed by the **2:A4** option in the **Layout, Page-Size** command. Then, in the **Titles, Header** option, type the words 'Income & Expenditure Report' in the **Footer** option, type 'December 1992||Page#'. The resultant Print Settings screen is shown below.

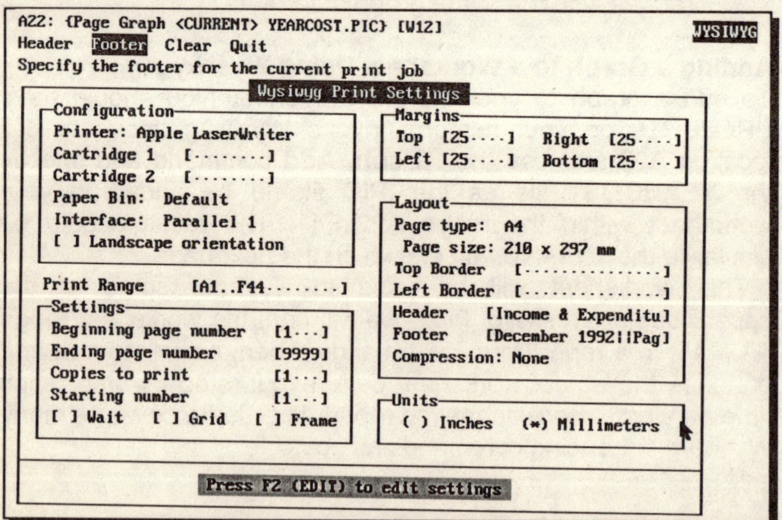

There are four special characters that can be used to format printed information. The vertical bar (|) is used to separate left-aligned, centred, and right-aligned portions of a header or footer, the hash sign (#) indicates a page number, the 'at' sign (@) indicates the current date, and the backslash (\) followed by a cell address can be used to copy cell contents to the header or footer.

You can preview the layout of your work so far, on a full page display, by selecting the **:Print, Preview** command, and/or you can print it on paper by selecting the **:Print, Go** command. However, before attempting to print on paper, make sure that you have used the **:Print, Config** command in order to select the appropriate printer driver. Also make sure that the whole of the selected range of the current worksheet fits on a single report page. If not, use the **/Worksheet, Column, Column-Range, Set-Width** command to set range A1..F1 to a width of 9 characters. The printout is shown on the next page.

Obviously, before this report becomes acceptable we need to use quite a bit of cosmetic surgery, particularly on the layout of the worksheet data. Another area that needs attention is the default type styles available with Wysiwyg which might not be available to your printer. However, before we start doing so, save the current worksheet under the filename REPORT1W.

Income & Expenditure Report

ADEPT CONSULTANTS LTD
PROJECT ANALYSIS - 1992 SUMMARY

	1st Quart	2nd Quart	3rd Quart	4th Quart	TOTAL
Consult:	£45,000	£48,000	£49,500	£60,000	£202,500
Costs:					
Wages	£9,000	£12,000	£12,500	£14,000	£47,500
Travel	£1,500	£1,630	£1,400	£1,800	£6,330
Rent	£900	£900	£900	£900	£3,600
Heat/Lght	£500	£370	£230	£540	£1,640
Phone/Fax	£900	£1,050	£750	£1,230	£3,930
Adverts	£3,600	£3,900	£3,400	£4,250	£15,150
Tot Costs	£16,400	£19,850	£19,180	£22,720	£78,150
Profit	£28,600	£28,150	£30,320	£37,280	£124,350

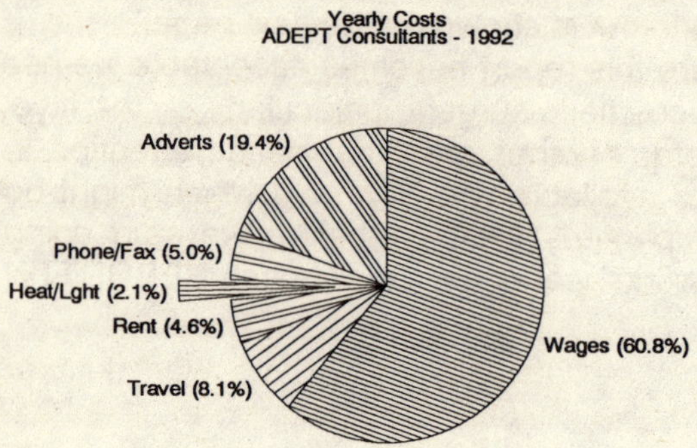

December 1992 Page1

The Wysiwyg Type Styles:
You can access the Wysiwyg font set with the **:Format, Font** command. In Release 2.3 & 2.4, the eight fonts include Swiss typeface in 12, 14, and 24 point size (selected with font options 1 to 3), and Dutch typeface in 6, 8, 10, and 12 point size (selected with font options 4 to 7, and Xsymbol typeface in 12 point size (selected with font option 8).

These fonts can be replaced by using the **:Format, Font, Replace** command, which allows you to replace any of the default fonts (1-8) with a typeface of your choice from **Swiss, Dutch, Courier, Xsymbol,** and **Other** (with the latter including a list of 18, mainly fonts used with a PostScript printer), with point sizes ranging from 3 to 72. However, you should only select those fonts which are supported by your printer.

With some printers, even if you choose the correct character fonts for that printer, 1-2-3 will use the printer's graphics capability to print your work when you select the **:Print, Go** command, and in some cases the output produced might be of inferior quality. If, that is the case with your printer, you could try selecting the **/Print, Printer, Go** command (you will have to specify the **Range** again), which might improve the printout, but since the printer will be operating in text mode, the graph in the included range will not be printed.

Best output results can only be obtained when using a laser printer with PostScript capability. So, if you want to produce high-quality reports, and you have access to a PostScript printer, then use the Install program to install it as a second printer, then select the **:Print, Config, Printer** command to make it the current printer.

From then on, use the **:Print, File** command which sends print output to an encoded file on disc. Such a file can be printed on a laser printer by using the DOS command

COPY *Filename*.ENC/B LPT1

on the computer connected to it, without needing the 1-2-3 program. Clearly, *Filename* refers to the name of the file on disc to which you sent your output. The extension .ENC is added to your chosen name by 1-2-3.

Wysiwyg Formatting:

We shall now use various Wysiwyg formatting commands to improve the looks of the 1992 report on Adept Consultants Ltd. We carry out the following improvements:

1. Delete row 1 of the worksheet by using the **/Worksheet, Delete** command.
2. Add the text '||ADEPT Consultants Ltd' to the report header, using the **:Print, Layout, Titles, Header** command so that the additions appear on the extreme right-hand side of the printed page.
3. Replace the equals and minus signs now appearing in rows 4, 6, 14, 16, and 18, by first erasing the contents of each of the specified rows using the **/Range, Erase** command, then use the **:Worksheet, Row, Set-Height** command to set the height of each of the specified rows to 5 points. Next, use the **:Format, Lines, Double, Top** command to draw double horizontal lines at the top edge of each cell in the range for all the specified rows, except row 14. For row 14 use a single horizontal line at the top edge of each cell in the required range.
4. Centre the report title (in A1) by using the **:Text, Align, Center** command and specifying A1..F1 as the range within which it is to be aligned. Next, use the **:Text, Set** command to set the range to be used with the **:Text, Edit** option, press <Enter> to accept the displayed edit range and press NAME (**F3**) to reveal a sub-menu from which choose **Italics,** followed by **F3**, **Outline**, and pressing <Esc> to finish.

Save the result as REPORT2W. The top-half of your worksheet should now look as shown on the next page.

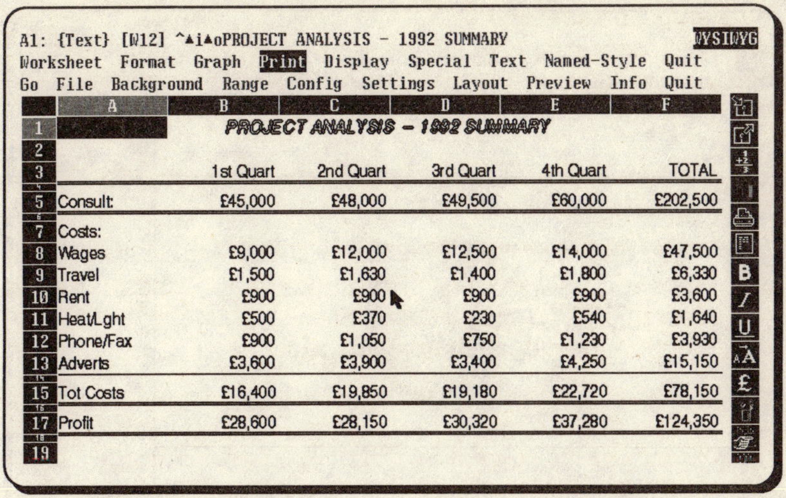

A1: {Text} [W12] ^▲i▲oPROJECT ANALYSIS - 1992 SUMMARY WYSIWYG
Worksheet Format Graph Print Display Special Text Named-Style Quit
Go File Background Range Config Settings Layout Preview Info Quit

	A	B	C	D	E	F
1		PROJECT ANALYSIS - 1992 SUMMARY				
2						
3		1st Quart	2nd Quart	3rd Quart	4th Quart	TOTAL
4						
5	Consult:	£45,000	£48,000	£49,500	£60,000	£202,500
6						
7	Costs:					
8	Wages	£9,000	£12,000	£12,500	£14,000	£47,500
9	Travel	£1,500	£1,630	£1,400	£1,800	£6,330
10	Rent	£900	£900	£900	£900	£3,600
11	Heat/Lght	£500	£370	£230	£540	£1,640
12	Phone/Fax	£900	£1,050	£750	£1,230	£3,930
13	Adverts	£3,600	£3,900	£3,400	£4,250	£15,150
14						
15	Tot Costs	£16,400	£19,850	£19,180	£22,720	£78,150
16						
17	Profit	£28,600	£28,150	£30,320	£37,280	£124,350
18						
19						

5. Remove the graph from the display by using the **:Graph, Remove** command, then remove the second line of the graph title by using the **/Graph, Options, Titles, Second** command, backspacing to delete the displayed text and pressing <Enter>, then use **/Graph, Options, Titles, First** command and change the chart title from 'Yearly Costs' to 'COSTS PROJECTIONS. Next, use the **:Graph, Add, Current** command to re-insert the edited pie chart in range A21..F40.

6. Add text to the graph portion of the display by first using the **:Graph, Goto** command and select <CURRENT>, which moves the cell pointer to the beginning of the graph area (in this case A21). Next, select the **:Graph, Edit** command, specifying the graphic to edit as A21 by pressing <Enter>, choosing the **Add, Text** option and typing the text 'For the Year 1990'. Use the arrow keys to place the text in the graph, centrally positioned, under its main caption, then use the options **Add, Line** and **Add, Arrow** to add a horizontal line and an inclined arrow.

Save the result as REPORT3W. The bottom-half of your worksheet should now look as follows:

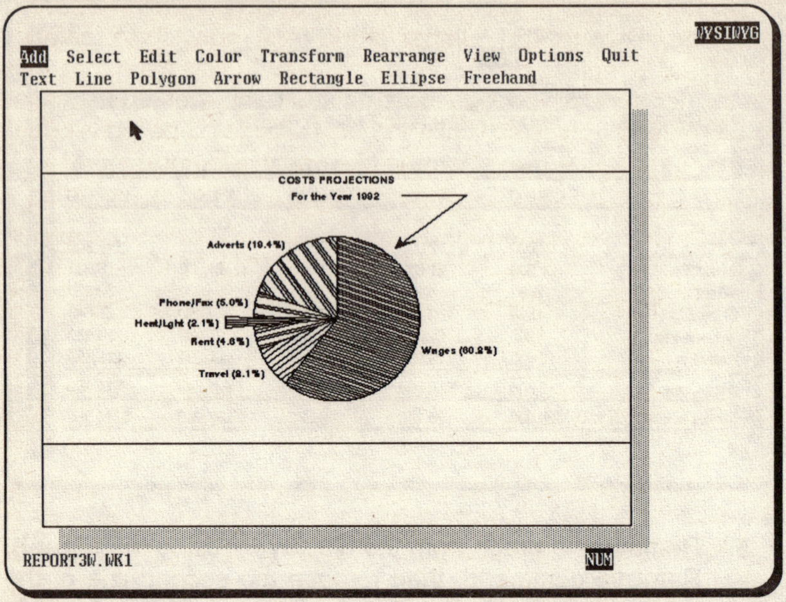

Note: Objects within a graphic window (which can be a line of text, a geometric shape, or a free-hand drawing) that you have added with the **:Graph, Edit** commands, can be edited, moved or removed. However, before you can carry out any of these commands, you must 'select', or identify such objects using the **:Graph, Edit, Select** command (or when using the mouse, by pointing to the required object and double clicking the left mouse button). When an object has been selected, small filled squares appear on its outer edges. You can move such objects by pointing to one of the small filled squares and dragging them to a new position.

Replacing the Wysiywg Font Set:

The next lot of improvements to the looks of the worksheet requires the substitution of part of the default font set for another set of fonts, the choice of which depends entirely on your printer. Do note, however, that you might be limited in the number of fonts you can use in a single worksheet by the actual size of memory in your printer.

In what follows, the Swiss printer font has been chosen, as an example of how to replace fonts; you might have to make a different choice.

Thus, to replace a font, use the **:Format, Font, Replace** command, highlight the number of the font you wish to replace and select a replacement from the displayed list. Note that the first printer font is the one used to print the worksheet as a whole, unless you specifically format a range to be printed by another font. Below, we show the choices made here.

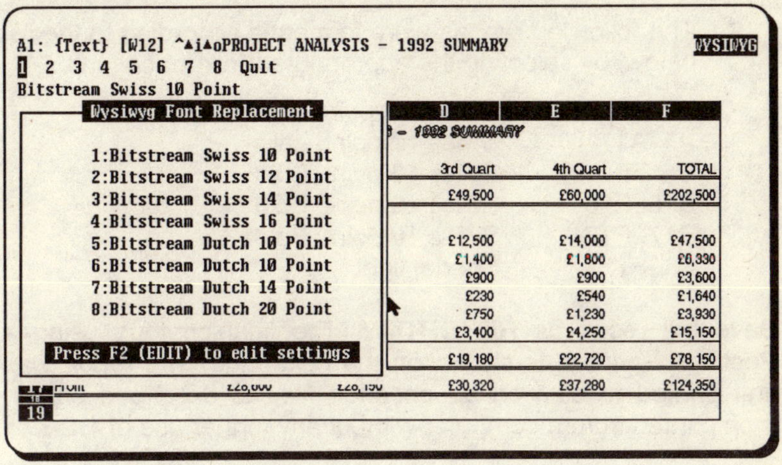

7. In order to be able to format the title of the report 'PROJECT ANALYSIS - 1990 SUMMARY' with a 16 point Swiss font, thus making it appear larger, you will have to shorten it somewhat, otherwise you might find that one or two of its end letters will not be printed out, even though they appear on the screen. Therefore, use the 1-2-3 EDIT (**F2**) key to shorten the title to 'PROJECT ANALYSIS SUMMARY, then use the **:Format, Font** command, select the required font by highlighting it and pressing <Enter>. Next, enter the range you want to format with this font and press <Enter>.

Note: A range can be highlighted before selecting a command which might prove useful when more than one enhancement is to be applied to the same range, without having to specify the range each time. For example, in order to change the font of a range, then follow it by shading the same range, first highlight the range by dragging the mouse. Do <u>not</u> press <Enter> at this point, but select the required command.

On selecting a command, Wysiwyg will not prompt you for a range, but will carry out the command on the predefined range which remains highlighted until you either move the cell pointer or press <Esc>. Thus, in this way you can choose a number of commands, one after the other, applying enhancement to a range successively.

8. The following ranges were formatted according to the list below, by selecting the appropriate **:Format** options:

A1..A1	Swiss, 16 point
A5..A17	Swiss 12 point, Italic
B5..F5	Swiss 10 point, Bold
B15..F15	Swiss 10 point, Bold
B17..F17	Swiss 10 point, Bold
F3..F17	Shade, light

Save the result as REPORT4W. The final printout, using a PostScript printer, is shown on the next page. The report was first printed to disc on an encoded file, as described earlier, then printed from a computer without any further use of 1-2-3.

Removing Wysiwyg from Memory:
Wysiwyg can be removed from memory by pressing ADDIN (Alt+**F10**) and choosing the **Detach** option. However, before removing Wysiwyg from memory, make sure you have saved your work with the **/File, Save** command, otherwise all formatting information will be lost.

Output on a PostScript Printer

Income & Expenditure Report ADEPT Consultants Ltd

PROJECT ANALYSIS SUMMARY

	1st Quart	2nd Quart	3rd Quart	4th Quart	TOTAL
Consult:	**£45,000**	**£48,000**	**£49,500**	**£60,000**	**£202,500**
Costs:					
Wages	£9,000	£12,000	£12,500	£14,000	£47,500
Travel	£1,500	£1,630	£1,400	£1,800	£6,330
Rent	£900	£900	£900	£900	£3,600
Heat/Lght	£500	£370	£230	£540	£1,640
Phone/Fax	£900	£1,050	£750	£1,230	£3,930
Adverts	£3,600	£3,900	£3,400	£4,250	£15,150
Tot Costs	**£16,400**	**£19,850**	**£19,180**	**£22,720**	**£78,150**
Profit	**£28,600**	**£28,150**	**£30,320**	**£37,280**	**£124,350**

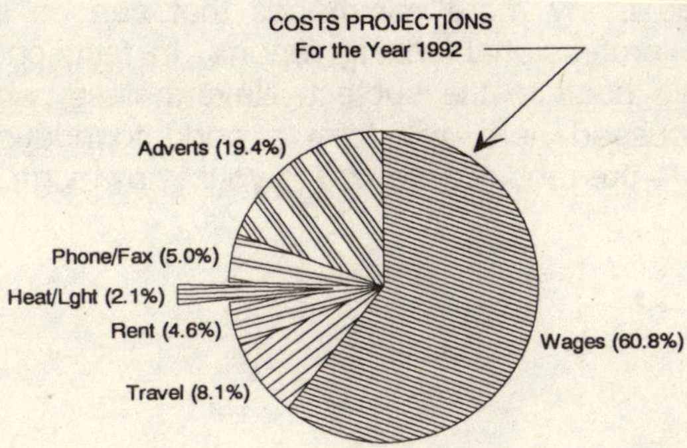

December 1992 Page1

* * *

Wysiwyg has many more commands that can be used to produce more professional-looking reports. In fact, one could devote a whole book to the subject. Nevertheless, what little has been discussed here, will form a good foundation from which to explore the module and add to your knowledge.

* * *

6. DATABASE MANAGEMENT

A 1-2-3 database is a worksheet range which contains related information, such as 'Customer's Names', 'Consultancy Details', 'Invoice No.', etc. A phone book is a simple database table, stored on paper. In Lotus 1-2-3 each record is entered as a worksheet row, with the fields of each record occupying corresponding columns.

A worksheet can contain many databases, each organised around a specific theme or requirement, and used for storing information so that it is quickly accessible. To make accessing the data easier, each row, or **record,** of data within a database is structured in the same fashion, i.e. each record will have the same number of columns or **fields**.

We define a database and its various elements as follows:

Database	A collection of related data organised in rows and columns in a worksheet file. A worksheet file can contain many different databases
Record	A row of information relating to a single entry and comprising one or more fields
Field	A single column of information of the same type, such as name of customers.

Setting-up a Database

In order to investigate the various database functions, such as sorting, searching, date calculations, etc., we first need to set-up a worksheet in the form shown overleaf.

Note that in creating a database, the following rules must be observed:

1. The top row of the database must contain the field labels, one per column, which identify the fields in the database. The second and subsequent rows of such a database must contain records; no blank rows should be inserted between the field labels and the actual records.

2. Field labels must be unique within a given database.

3. Entries under each field must be of the same type.

4. A database can contain a maximum of 256 fields and 8,191 records.

We assume that the 'Invoice Analysis' of Adept Consultants is designed and set out as shown below with the listed field titles and field widths. Formatting information is given below.

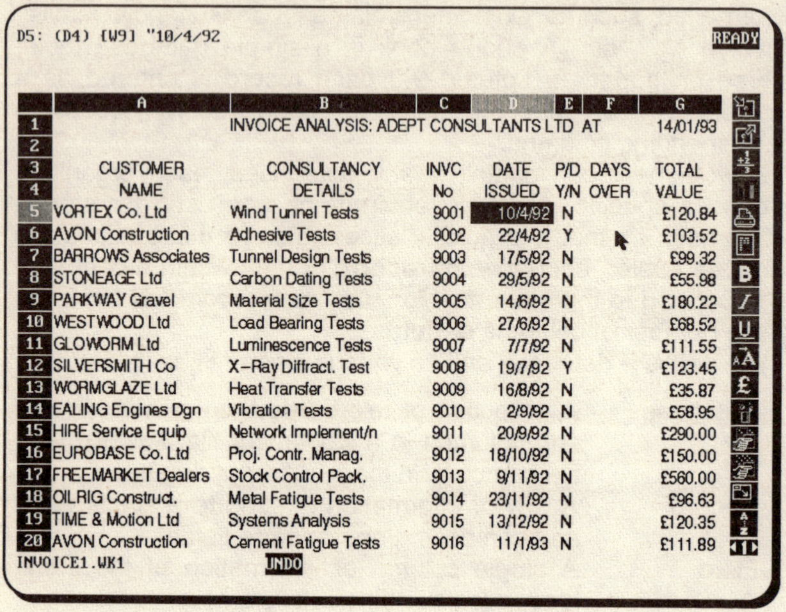

D5: (D4) [W9] "10/4/92 READY

	A	B	C	D	E	F	G
1		INVOICE ANALYSIS: ADEPT CONSULTANTS LTD AT					14/01/93
2							
3	CUSTOMER	CONSULTANCY	INVC	DATE	P/D	DAYS	TOTAL
4	NAME	DETAILS	No	ISSUED	Y/N	OVER	VALUE
5	VORTEX Co. Ltd	Wind Tunnel Tests	9001	10/4/92	N		£120.84
6	AVON Construction	Adhesive Tests	9002	22/4/92	Y		£103.52
7	BARROWS Associates	Tunnel Design Tests	9003	17/5/92	N		£99.32
8	STONEAGE Ltd	Carbon Dating Tests	9004	29/5/92	N		£55.98
9	PARKWAY Gravel	Material Size Tests	9005	14/6/92	N		£180.22
10	WESTWOOD Ltd	Load Bearing Tests	9006	27/6/92	N		£68.52
11	GLOWORM Ltd	Luminescence Tests	9007	7/7/92	N		£111.55
12	SILVERSMITH Co	X–Ray Diffract. Test	9008	19/7/92	Y		£123.45
13	WORMGLAZE Ltd	Heat Transfer Tests	9009	16/8/92	N		£35.87
14	EALING Engines Dgn	Vibration Tests	9010	2/9/92	N		£58.95
15	HIRE Service Equip	Network Implement/n	9011	20/9/92	N		£290.00
16	EUROBASE Co. Ltd	Proj. Contr. Manag.	9012	18/10/92	N		£150.00
17	FREEMARKET Dealers	Stock Control Pack.	9013	9/11/92	N		£560.00
18	OILRIG Construct.	Metal Fatigue Tests	9014	23/11/92	N		£96.63
19	TIME & Motion Ltd	Systems Analysis	9015	13/12/92	N		£120.35
20	AVON Construction	Cement Fatigue Tests	9016	11/1/93	N		£111.89

INVOICE1.WK1 UNDO

Use the **/Worksheet, Column, Set-Width** command to change the width of the various columns to those given below, and then enter the abbreviated titles, centrally positioned, in two rows as shown in the worksheet above. These widths were chosen so that the whole of the worksheet could be seen on the screen at once.

Column	*Title*	*Width*	*Type*
A	CUSTOMER NAME	19	Default
B	CONSULT DETAILS	20	Default
C	INVOICE No	6	Fixed, 0 decimal
D	DATE ISSUED	9	Date, type 4
E	PAID? (Y/N)	3	Default
F	DAYS OVER	6	Fixed, 0 decimal
G	TOTAL VALUE	9	Currency, 2 decimal

Use the **/Range, Format, Fixed** command to format column C and F to 0 (zero) decimal places, and then the **/Range, Format,**

Currency command to format column G to 2 decimal places, before entering information. The dates in Column D were entered with the quotes (") prefix. Column F will be calculated later using a formula which relies on information held in columns D and E. However, for the time being, leave this column empty and, when you complete the other entries, save the resultant worksheet under the filename INVOICE1.

Sorting a Database

The records within the above database are in the order in which they were entered, with the 'Invoice No' shown in ascending order. However, once records have been entered, we might find it easier to browse through the information if it was sorted in alphabetical order of, say, 'Customer Name'. Lotus 1-2-3 has an easy to use sort function. To use it, place the cell pointer at the beginning of the sort range (in this case A5), and use the **/Data, Sort, Data-Range** command, then press

<.>	to anchor beginning of sort range
<Arrows>	to highlight the sort range (A5..G20)
<Enter>	to confirm range selection
P	to select **Primary-Key**
<Enter>	to confirm primary range selection (A5)
A	to select Ascending sort order
<Enter>	to confirm selection
G	to select **Go**.

Issuing these commands, produces a sorted database under the 'Customer Name', but information under a given customer might not be in invoice order and, therefore, chronologically in the wrong order (note, for example, the invoice order of AVON Construction on your screen).

To remedy this, select the **Secondary-Key** sort field (you don't even have to confirm the sort block range or the primary sort fields, as 1-2-3 remembers these), and specify the 'Invoice No' column. If you want to reset any of these 'remembered' ranges, then choose the appropriate sort function and press <Esc> to allow re-definition of the specific choice.

With Release 2.3 & 2.4, as you enter information on the range to be sorted, the primary and secondary keys, and their order of sorting, the program copies and displays the information on a

'Sort Settings' dialogue box, as shown below.

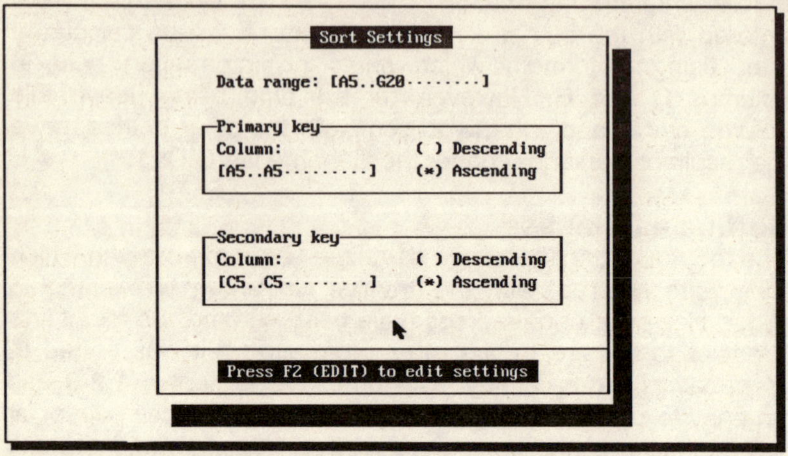

Having defined C5 as the **Secondary-Key** sort field, selecting **Go** displays the following screen:

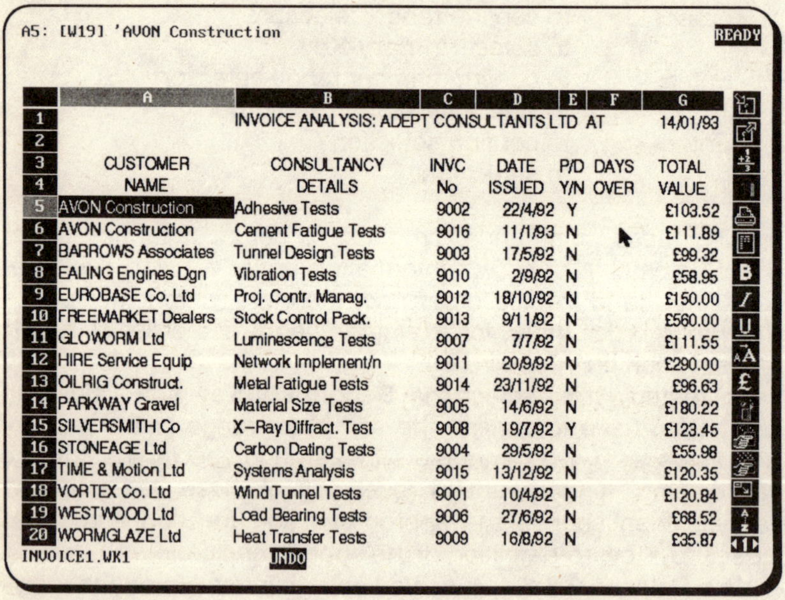

	A	B	C	D	E	F	G
1		INVOICE ANALYSIS: ADEPT CONSULTANTS LTD AT					14/01/93
2							
3	CUSTOMER	CONSULTANCY	INVC	DATE	P/D	DAYS	TOTAL
4	NAME	DETAILS	No	ISSUED	Y/N	OVER	VALUE
5	AVON Construction	Adhesive Tests	9002	22/4/92	Y		£103.52
6	AVON Construction	Cement Fatigue Tests	9016	11/1/93	N		£111.89
7	BARROWS Associates	Tunnel Design Tests	9003	17/5/92	N		£99.32
8	EALING Engines Dgn	Vibration Tests	9010	2/9/92	N		£58.95
9	EUROBASE Co. Ltd	Proj. Contr. Manag.	9012	18/10/92	N		£150.00
10	FREEMARKET Dealers	Stock Control Pack.	9013	9/11/92	N		£560.00
11	GLOWORM Ltd	Luminescence Tests	9007	7/7/92	N		£111.55
12	HIRE Service Equip	Network Implement/n	9011	20/9/92	N		£290.00
13	OILRIG Construct.	Metal Fatigue Tests	9014	23/11/92	N		£96.63
14	PARKWAY Gravel	Material Size Tests	9005	14/6/92	N		£180.22
15	SILVERSMITH Co	X-Ray Diffract. Test	9008	19/7/92	Y		£123.45
16	STONEAGE Ltd	Carbon Dating Tests	9004	29/5/92	N		£55.98
17	TIME & Motion Ltd	Systems Analysis	9015	13/12/92	N		£120.35
18	VORTEX Co. Ltd	Wind Tunnel Tests	9001	10/4/92	N		£120.84
19	WESTWOOD Ltd	Load Bearing Tests	9006	27/6/92	N		£68.52
20	WORMGLAZE Ltd	Heat Transfer Tests	9009	16/8/92	N		£35.87

Now re-sort the database in ascending order of 'Invoice No' so that you obtain the original data entry screen display.

Using Functions in a Database

Functions can be used in a database to assist with data manipulation, for example, calculating the number of days an invoice is overdue. In addition, you can use special database functions to perform statistical calculations on information held in a database. These are listed in Appendix B.

Date Arithmetic:

There are several date functions which can be used in 1-2-3 to carry out date calculations. For example, typing the function @DATE(93,1,14) - 14/1/93 backwards, works out the number of days since 31 December 1899, while typing @NOW (as in cell G1 of the worksheet), gives the number of days (in decimal) since the beginning of the century, but using the internal clock. The decimal part has to do with time. These date numbers can only be seen if you have not used the **/Worksheet, Global, Format, Date** command. If you use this command and select option **4 (Long Intn'l)**, then the cell displays the actual date in the usual form (14/1/93).

Another function, the @DATEVALUE, allows a date entered in the declared format of the spreadsheet (such as that in cell D5 - 10/4/92) to be used in calculations. Thus, typing

```
@NOW-@DATEVALUE("10/4/92") or
@NOW-@DATEVALUE(D5)
```

gives the difference in days, if the appropriate worksheet cell is formatted for integer (Fixed, 0 decimals) numbers, between now and the mentioned date.

We will use these two functions to work out the number of overdue days of the unpaid invoices in our example, by typing in cell F5 the following formula:

```
@NOW-@DATEVALUE(D5)
```

If the record in row 5 of the worksheet refers to the data of VORTEX Co. Ltd., then the result should be 280 days, provided you are actually performing this calculation on 14/1/93, otherwise your result will differ substantially from the one discussed above. The reason for this is, of course, that the @NOW function returns different numerical values when used at different dates.

To get the same results as those shown in what follows, change the contents of cell G1 to "14/01/93, then edit or re-type the formula in cell F5 to replace the @NOW function with @DATEVALUE($G$1) where $G$1 causes an 'absolute' reference to be made to the contents of cell G1. The complete formula in cell F5 should now be

@DATEVALUE($G$1)-@DATEVALUE(D5)

However, before you proceed to copy the above formula to the rest of the F column of the database data block, you should take into consideration the fact that, normally, such information is not necessary if an invoice has been paid. Therefore, you need to edit the above formula in such a way as to make the result conditional to non-payment of the issued invoice.

The @IF Function:
The @IF function allows comparison between two values with the use of a special 'logical' operators (for other operators see list under section 'Order of Priority in Formulae' in Chapter 2). The logical operators we can use are listed below.

Logical operators

=	Equal to
<	Less-than
>	Greater-than
<=	Less-than or Equal to
>=	Greater-than or Equal to
<>	Not-Equal to

The general format of the @IF function is as follows:

@IF(Comparison, Outcome-if-true, Outcome-if-false)

which contains three arguments separated by commas. The first argument is the logical comparison, the second is what should happen if the outcome of the logical comparison is 'true', while the third is what should happen if the outcome of the logical comparison is false.

Thus, we can incorporate the @IF function in the formula of cell F6 to calculate the days overdue only if the invoice has not been paid, otherwise the string 'N/A' should be written into the appropriate cell should the contents of the corresponding E column of a record be anything else but N. To edit the formula in cell F5, highlight the cell and use the EDIT (**F2**) key. Then press the <Home> cursor key to place the cursor at the beginning of the existing formula in the control area at the top of the worksheet and insert

@IF(E5="N",

then press the <End> cursor key to move the cursor to the end of the existing entry and add

," N/A")

The edited formula in cell F6 should now correspond to what is shown as the contents of that cell below. Now copy this formula to the rest of the appropriate range (F6..F20) and compare your results with those shown below.

```
F5: (F0) [W6] @IF(E5="N",@NOW-@DATEVALUE(D5),"   N/A")                READY
```

	A	B	C	D	E	F	G
1		INVOICE ANALYSIS: ADEPT CONSULTANTS LTD AT					14/01/93
2							
3	CUSTOMER	CONSULTANCY	INVC	DATE	P/D	DAYS	TOTAL
4	NAME	DETAILS	No	ISSUED	Y/N	OVER	VALUE
5	VORTEX Co. Ltd	Wind Tunnel Tests	9001	10/4/92	N	280	£120.84
6	AVON Construction	Adhesive Tests	9002	22/4/92	Y	N/A	£103.52
7	BARROWS Associates	Tunnel Design Tests	9003	17/5/92	N	243	£99.32
8	STONEAGE Ltd	Carbon Dating Tests	9004	29/5/92	N	231	£55.98
9	PARKWAY Gravel	Material Size Tests	9005	14/6/92	N	215	£180.22
10	WESTWOOD Ltd	Load Bearing Tests	9006	27/6/92	N	202	£68.52
11	GLOWORM Ltd	Luminescence Tests	9007	7/7/92	N	192	£111.55
12	SILVERSMITH Co	X-Ray Diffract. Test	9008	19/7/92	Y	N/A	£123.45
13	WORMGLAZE Ltd	Heat Transfer Tests	9009	16/8/92	N	152	£35.87
14	EALING Engines Dgn	Vibration Tests	9010	2/9/92	N	135	£58.95
15	HIRE Service Equip	Network Implement/n	9011	20/9/92	N	117	£290.00
16	EUROBASE Co. Ltd	Proj. Contr. Manag.	9012	18/10/92	N	89	£150.00
17	FREEMARKET Dealers	Stock Control Pack.	9013	9/11/92	N	67	£560.00
18	OILRIG Construct.	Metal Fatigue Tests	9014	23/11/92	N	53	£96.63
19	TIME & Motion Ltd	Systems Analysis	9015	13/12/92	N	33	£120.35
20	AVON Construction	Cement Fatigue Tests	9016	11/1/93	N	4	£111.89

INVOICE1.WK1 UNDO

WARNING: It is important that you enter the date, in cells which will be used later for calculations, in the format that you have specified as your replacement to the default 'Date' format of your worksheet. It should be obvious that unless the @NOW function, which uses the specified internal format for date, is of the same type as the entered dates in other cells, to which you intend to apply 'date' arithmetic, then the result of such calculations will be incorrect.

If you have to change the default 'date' format, then use the **/Worksheet, Global, Default, Other, International, Date** command and choose the type preferred (option **B** in the previous example). However, make quite sure that you use the **Update** command (one level back - pressing Q once - after selecting the date type) to make such a choice permanent. If you don't use the **Update** command, even if everything appears as it should be this time, when you reload your worksheet later, the fields containing the results of 'date' calculations will be filled with ERR, because the worksheet would have reverted back to its default 'date' format. If you get such errors, follow the suggestions above and don't forget to use CALC (**F9**) to recalculate the worksheet.

After making the above suggested changes to your worksheet, save the result under the filename INVOICE2.

Frequency Distribution:

A frequency distribution of data allows us to find how many values in a specified range fall within specified numeric intervals (otherwise known as the bin range).

Thus, if we want to find out how many unpaid invoices exist in our database within 0-30, 31-60, 61-90, etc., days, then we need to specify the bin range in a column of the database and allocate another column to receive the frequency values. We choose to insert two columns between the existing F and G columns of the database by highlighting column G and using the **/Worksheet, Insert, Column** command, moving the cell pointer to the right once so as to highlight the range G5..H5 and pressing <Enter>. Then, move the cell pointer to A1 and use the **/Worksheet, Titles, Vertical** command to freeze the titles of column A so they remain visible while working with columns H and I. Next, use the **/Range, Format, Fixed** command to format the ranges in the two new columns to the following:

Range	*Title*	*Width*	*Type*
G5..G20	BIN RANGE	6	Fixed, 0 decimals
H5..H20	FREQ DIST	5	Fixed, 0 decimals

Now enter the values you want to use as intervals for the calculation of the frequency distribution into the bin range column, in this case G5..G20, as shown in the worksheet output display below. You could use the **/Data, Fill** command to do this the easy way.

To calculate the frequency distribution, highlight cell H5 and use the **/Data, Distribution** command, then press

<←>	to highlight beginning of data range (F5)
<.>	to anchor beginning of range
<↓>	to highlight range (F5..F20)
<Enter>	to confirm highlighted area
<←>	to highlight beginning of bin range (G5)
<.>	to anchor beginning of range
<↓>	to highlight range (G5..G20)
<Enter>	to confirm highlighted area

The result of the frequency distribution is shown below.

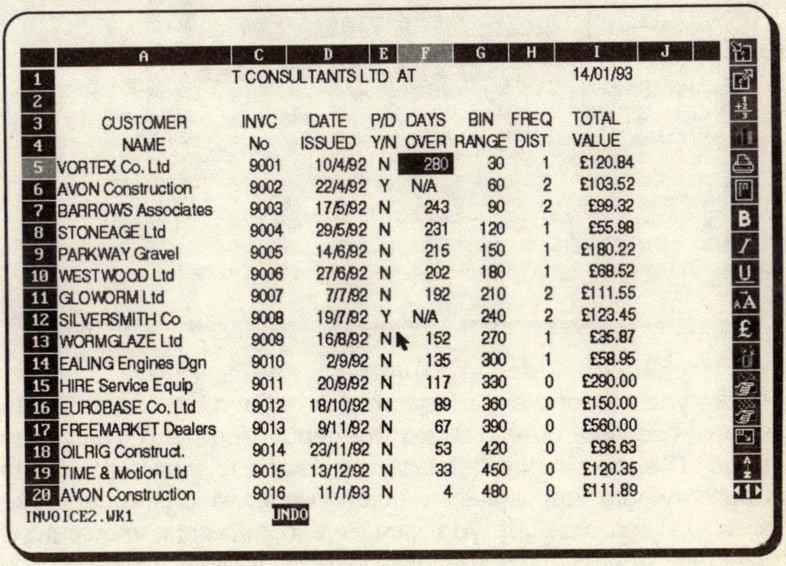

	A	C	D	E	F	G	H	I	J
1		T CONSULTANTS LTD AT						14/01/93	
2									
3	CUSTOMER	INVC	DATE	P/D	DAYS	BIN	FREQ	TOTAL	
4	NAME	No	ISSUED	Y/N	OVER	RANGE	DIST	VALUE	
5	VORTEX Co. Ltd	9001	10/4/92	N	280	30	1	£120.84	
6	AVON Construction	9002	22/4/92	Y	N/A	60	2	£103.52	
7	BARROWS Associates	9003	17/5/92	N	243	90	2	£99.32	
8	STONEAGE Ltd	9004	29/5/92	N	231	120	1	£55.98	
9	PARKWAY Gravel	9005	14/6/92	N	215	150	1	£180.22	
10	WESTWOOD Ltd	9006	27/6/92	N	202	180	1	£68.52	
11	GLOWORM Ltd	9007	7/7/92	N	192	210	2	£111.55	
12	SILVERSMITH Co	9008	19/7/92	Y	N/A	240	2	£123.45	
13	WORMGLAZE Ltd	9009	16/8/92	N	152	270	1	£35.87	
14	EALING Engines Dgn	9010	2/9/92	N	135	300	1	£58.95	
15	HIRE Service Equip	9011	20/9/92	N	117	330	0	£290.00	
16	EUROBASE Co. Ltd	9012	18/10/92	N	89	360	0	£150.00	
17	FREEMARKET Dealers	9013	9/11/92	N	67	390	0	£560.00	
18	OILRIG Construct.	9014	23/11/92	N	53	420	0	£96.63	
19	TIME & Motion Ltd	9015	13/12/92	N	33	450	0	£120.35	
20	AVON Construction	9016	11/1/93	N	4	480	0	£111.89	

INVOICE2.WK1 UNDO

From the frequency distribution display it can be seen that there is 1 invoice within the period 0-30 days, 2 invoices within the period 31-60 days, 2 between 61-90, 1 between 91-120, etc. Save this worksheet under the filename INVOICE3.

Searching a Database

A database can be searched for specific records that meet the criteria established by the use of the **/Data, Query** command. We will use the database of worksheet INVOICE3 to illustrate the method by searching the database with the criterion relating to the frequency distribution of invoices.

Assuming that the database is on your screen, select the **/Data, Query** command, which causes the following 'Query Settings' screen to be displayed:

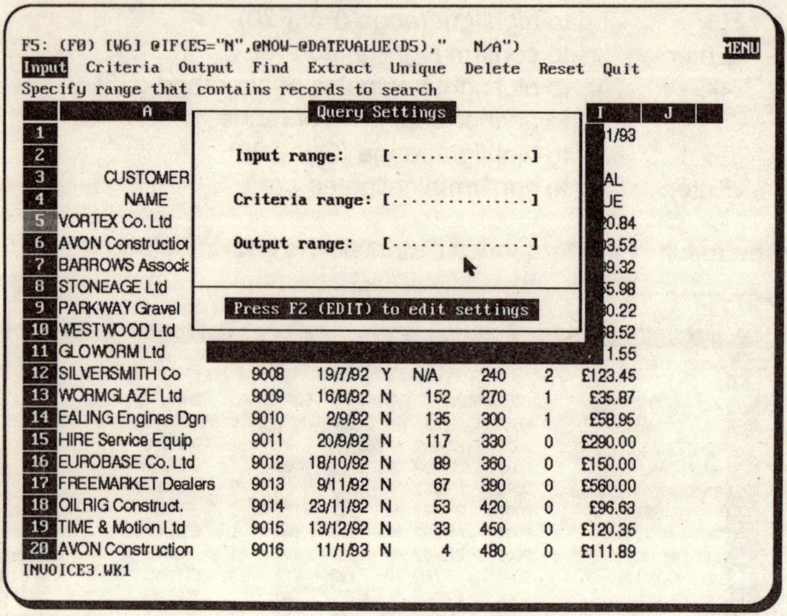

Before you can use any of the search options, you must create at least two data query ranges; the input range and the criteria range. The input range defines your database, while the criteria range is where you define the criteria under which the database is to be searched. If you use any commands which copy selected records from the database to another range in the worksheet, then you must also define an output range.

The various query options and their description are listed on the next page in order of appearance.

Option	*Description*
Input	Specifies the range of the records you want to manipulate
Criteria	Specifies the range that contains selected criteria for searching or manipulating a database input range
Output	Specifies the range where you want the results of a query by the Extract or Unique option to be placed
Find	Locates and highlights the records in the input range that match the criteria in the criteria range
Extract	Copies to the output range those records from the input range that match the criteria specified in the criteria range
Unique	Copies to the output range those unique records (omits duplicate records) from the input range that match the criteria specified in the criteria range
Delete	Deletes the records in the input range that match the criteria in the criteria range
Reset	Clears the settings for the input, criteria, and output ranges.

To illustrate how some of these options work, first use the **/Worksheet, Titles, Clear** command to unfreeze any columns or rows so that you can use the cursor keys to point to the entire database range, then specify the input range of the data, using the **/Data, Query, Input** command, which must include the field names (in our example this range is A4..I20).

Next, set-up two more ranges in the worksheet, one for specifying the criteria for the search, and the other for copying records extracted from the database (the latter is only needed if the **Extract** or **Unique** options are used). To do this, first copy some or all of the field names of the database (we will choose to copy all of them) to an empty area of the worksheet, say, K4..S4 which will form the first line of the 'criteria range' and label this area CRITERIA RANGE in cell K2. Then, copy again the same field names to K12..S12 and label that area OUTPUT RANGE in cell K10.

Finally, set the width of the cells and format them according to the table below which correspond to those of the database.

Column	*Field*	*Width*	*Type*
K	NAME	W19	Default
L	DETAILS	W20	Default
M	No	W6	F0
N	ISSUED	W9	D4
O	Y/N	W3	Default
P	OVER	W6	F0
Q	RANGE	W6	Default
R	DIST	W5	Default
S	VALUE	W9	C2

Save the resultant worksheet under the filename INVOICE4. The criteria and output ranges are shown below:

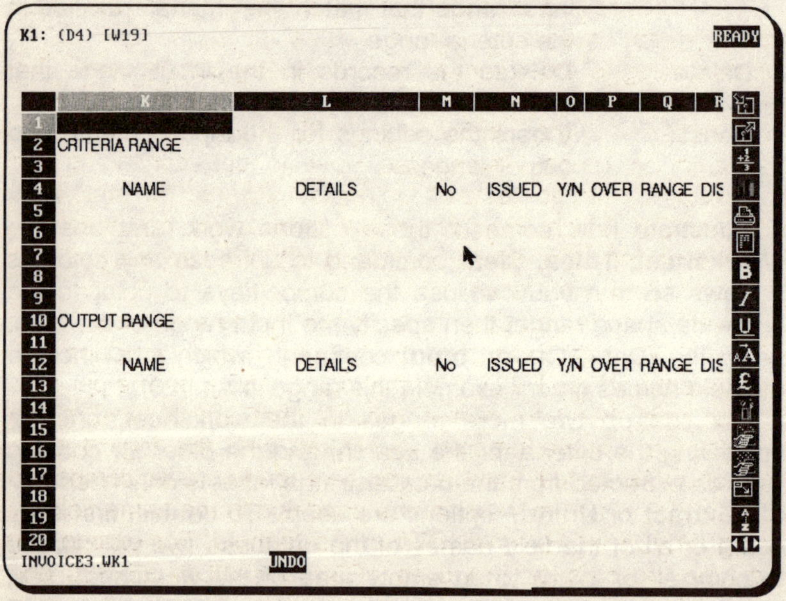

Finding and Deleting Records:

To search the database for all the details of our customers whose invoices fall within a Bin Range of 80 or more days, but whose frequency distribution is greater than 0, we need to type in cell Q5 the criterion +G5>=80 and in cell R5 the criterion +H5>0, where G5 and H5 are the appropriate fields of the first record of the database data.

In general, criteria must be entered in the second and subsequent rows of the criterion range, with each criterion entered below the copy of the appropriate field name. A label or a value may be entered exactly as it appears in the database or the two special characters ? and * can be used to match any single character of a label or all characters to the end of the label. Preceding a label with a tilde (~), causes the search of all labels except for that one. Thus, ~Y* searches the database for all records with an entry in that field which does not begin with Y.

Thus, to search a database for values, either enter the value as the exact criterion or use a formula, such as +G5>=80 in which the logical operators (<, <=, >, >=, <>) can be used. The logical formula generates a value of 1 if the condition is TRUE or a value of 0 if the condition is FALSE. This value appears in the criterion range, unless the specific cell containing the formula is formatted as 'text', using the **/Range, Format, Text** command in which case the actual formula (or part thereof - depending on the width of the cell) will appear in the corresponding criterion cell.

Several criteria can be entered, either in the same row, if you want 1-2-3 to search for records that match every criterion (i.e. criteria entered are linked with the logical AND), or one per row, if you want 1-2-3 to search records that satisfy any of the criteria (i.e. criteria entered are linked with the logical OR). Compounded logical formulas can be used to create compound criteria that match more than one condition in the same field by using #AND#, #OR# or #NOT# in the formula. For example, if we type the criterion in Q5 as +G5>=80#AND#+G5<330 and erased that in R3 (unwanted criteria must be erased rather than over-typed with a space), we would retrieve the same records that will be retrieved by the use of the two separate criteria, discussed previously.

Finally, before we can search a database, we need to specify the criterion range, which must include the field names and at least one following row in which the criteria for the search appear (in our example K4..S5), via the **/Data, Query, Criterion** command. Criteria may be included that refer to one field or to several (up to 32) fields of the database. Do not specify an empty line as part of the criterion range, as this has the effect of searching the database for <u>all</u> records.

To search the database for the criteria discussed above, use the **/Data, Query, Find** command which causes 1-2-3 to highlight the first record that matches the criteria which in this case is that of BARROWS Associates. Pressing the down arrow key finds the next record that matches the chosen criteria. If there are no more records (there should be 8 consecutive records in all), 1-2-3 bleeps. You can peruse through the chosen records backwards by pressing the up arrow key. Again, if there are no more records that match the chosen criteria, 1-2-3 bleeps when the up arrow key is pressed.

Extracting Records:

The **/Data, Query, Extract** command copies records that match the chosen criteria from the database to the output range of the worksheet, while the **/Data, Query, Unique** command does the same thing, but does not copy repeated records. However, before selecting either of these commands, you must use the **/Data, Query, Output** command to specify the output range into which data is to be copied.

It is imperative that the area below the output range is sufficiently long to accommodate all the extracted records. In our example, as we have chosen the output area to be in a part of the worksheet which has nothing below it, we can specify the output range as K12..S12. Specifying the output range by only the row of field names causes the entire area under these field names to be cleared before the extracted records are copied into the output range. So, beware! If an output range of more than one row is specified, 1-2-3 does not erase the contents of the worksheet below the output range, but if such a multiple-row output range is not large enough to contain all the records that meet the criteria, an error message will be displayed.

The criteria we used previously with the **/Data, Query, Find** command were such that 8 records were found, one of which referred to a customer who had already paid the relevant invoice. To eliminate this customer, add into the criteria selection the entry ~Y in cell O5 and use the **/Data, Query, Extract** command to extract the following records.

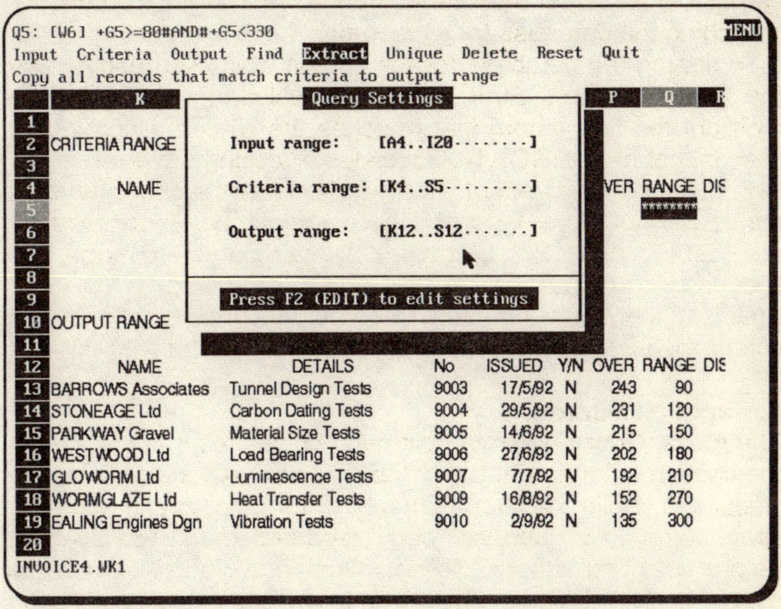

When the **/Data, Query, Extract** command is being executed, the mode indicator changes to MENU, and with Release 2.2 and higher, the 'Query Settings' screen or dialogue box is also displayed. After the records have been copied into the output range, selecting **Quit** causes 1-2-3 to return to the READ mode.

7. USING MACROS

A macro is a set of instructions made up of a sequence of key-strokes and commands that you would normally have typed onto the keyboard, but which you type instead into your worksheet as cell entries. After entering and naming a macro it can be invoked by simply typing its name. Thus, a macro is a list of commands which is used to perform a complete task and is used whenever we wish to save time in performing repetitive commands or make a worksheet easier to use.

Creating a Simple Macro

We will now use the worksheet saved under PROJECT3 (see the beginning of Chapter 3) to show how we can add macros to it, to perform 'what-if' type of projections by, say, increasing the 'Wages' bill by 15%. If you haven't saved PROJECT3 on disc, it will be necessary for you to enter the information shown below into 1-2-3 so that you can benefit from what is to be introduced at this point. Having done this, save it under PROJECT3.

If you have saved PROJECT3, then enter 1-2-3 and when the mode indicator reads READY, use the **/File, Retrieve** command to load the file. What should appear on screen is shown below.

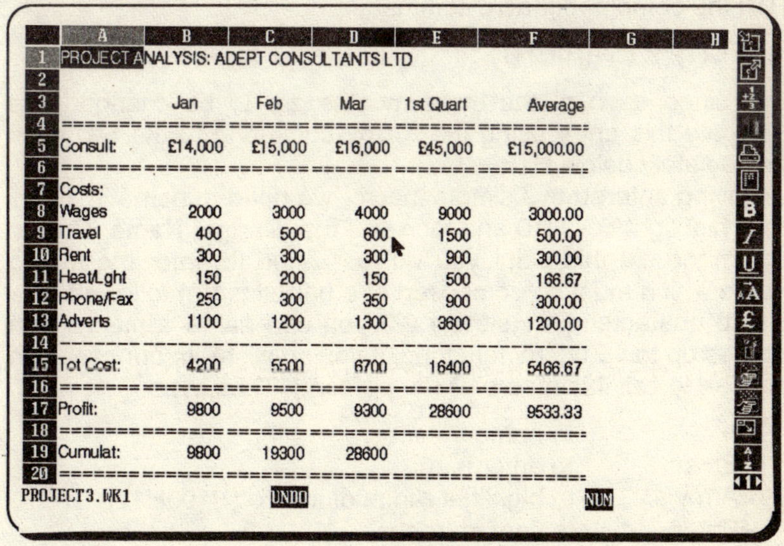

	A	B	C	D	E	F	G	H
1	PROJECT ANALYSIS: ADEPT CONSULTANTS LTD							
2								
3		Jan	Feb	Mar	1st Quart	Average		
4	======	======	======	======	======	=========		
5	Consult	£14,000	£15,000	£16,000	£45,000	£15,000.00		
6	======	======	======	======	======	=========		
7	Costs:							
8	Wages	2000	3000	4000	9000	3000.00		
9	Travel	400	500	600	1500	500.00		
10	Rent	300	300	300	900	300.00		
11	Heat/Lght	150	200	150	500	166.67		
12	Phone/Fax	250	300	350	900	300.00		
13	Adverts	1100	1200	1300	3600	1200.00		
14	------	------	------	------	------	---------		
15	Tot Cost:	4200	5500	6700	16400	5466.67		
16	======	======	======	======	======	=========		
17	Profit:	9800	9500	9300	28600	9533.33		
18	======	======	======	======	======	=========		
19	Cumulat:	9800	19300	28600				
20	======	======	======	======	======	=========		

PROJECT3.WK1 UNDO NUM

What we would like to do now is to edit the entries under 'Wages' so that this part of the costs can be increased by 15%. One way of doing this would be to multiply the contents of each cell containing the wages value by 1.15. To do this, we would start by highlighting cell B8 then pressing EDIT (**F2**) to allow us to edit the value in it by adding to the entry '*1.15' which has the effect of multiplying the contents of the cell by 1.15 which would increase its contents by 15%. We would then press <Enter>, press the <Right> arrow key to move to cell C8 and repeat the whole procedure. The exact steps, after highlighting cell B8, are:

Manual Procedure	*Equivalent Macro Steps*
Press F2 to edit cell	EDIT}
Type	'*1.15'*1.15
Press <Enter>	~
Press <Right> arrow	{RIGHT}

Macros must be entered in an empty part of the worksheet in columnar fashion. Each command could be entered in a different row cell of that column, but since a number of commands can be combined - provided the entry is less than 240 characters long - we choose to do just that by typing in cell H10 the combined macro commands

{EDIT}*1.15~{RIGHT}

and since each of the three months are to be changed, we replicate this entry using the **/Copy** command to the two rows immediately below H10.

Having entered this simple macro, we need to name it. To do this, highlight cell H10 and then use the **/Range, Name, Create** command. At this point you will be asked to enter the macro name which must be composed of a backslash (\) followed by a single character (in Release 2.2 you can name a macro with names up to 15 characters long, if you so wish). In our case, we choose to call this macro **\P** (for percent). Thus, type

\P	to name the macro
<Enter>	to enter name
<Arrows>	to highlight range of macro (H10..H12)
<Enter>	to confirm range

It is also a good idea to name your macro on the worksheet itself so that you can remember its name later. To do this, move the highlighted bar to the cell immediately to the left of the first macro entry and type **'\P**.

Before executing any macro, save your worksheet, in this case under the filename MACRO1. This is a simple precaution, because should things go wrong and your macro does unpredictable things to your worksheet, it will be easier to reload the worksheet and edit the incorrect macro than it would be to also have to correct the original worksheet!

To allow viewing of as much of the macro as possible, we have reduced the width of column G to 5 characters. Your screen should now display the following information:

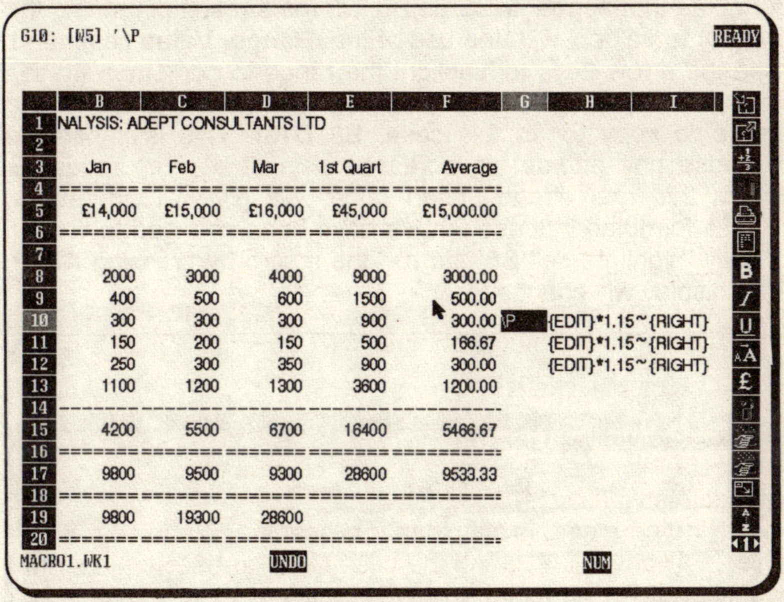

To use this macro, highlight the first cell to be updated (in this case B8), press Alt+**P** - in Releases 2.2 & higher, you can also press RUN (Alt+**F3**) and select the name of the macro you want to run from the menu of named ranges. Watch the changes that take place in cell range B8..D8 as a result of the three line macro (an empty row signifies the end of a macro), and beyond to F8, since the contents of cells E8 and F8 depend on the contents of cells B8..D8.

We could use the same macro to increase the other costs by a different percentage, by editing it, but this would be rather an inefficient way of doing it. A better method is to allocate a cell for the % increase, say cell H7, and edit the macro so that reference to that cell is made in absolute terms. For example, in cell G7, type

Incr=

and in cell H7 type the actual % increase (in the previous case this would have been 1.15). Then, edit the macro to:

{EDIT}*$H$7~{RIGHT}

copy it to the next two consecutive rows, and change the formulae that appear in range B8..D8 (as a result of running the macro) to values, with the use of the **/Range, Value** command. Use the arrow keys to highlight the range to copy from (in this case, B8..D13). On pressing <Enter> you will be asked for the range to copy to (in this case, B8..D13). This is imperative because any attempt to increase costs of a given range for which this has already been done, will give wrong results, unless formulae in these ranges have been changed to values. Finally, highlight cell B8 and run the macro by pressing **Alt+P**. The display will change to:

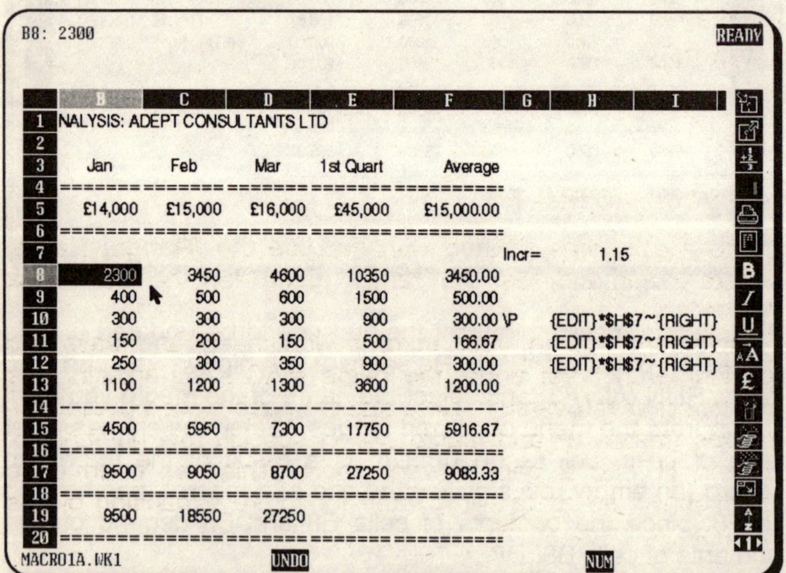

	B	C	D	E	F	G	H	I
1	NALYSIS: ADEPT CONSULTANTS LTD							
2								
3	Jan	Feb	Mar	1st Quart	Average			
4	======	======	======	======	==========			
5	£14,000	£15,000	£16,000	£45,000	£15,000.00			
6	======	======	======	======	==========			
7						Incr=	1.15	
8	2300	3450	4600	10350	3450.00			
9	400	500	600	1500	500.00			
10	300	300	300	900	300.00	\P	{EDIT}*$H$7~{RIGHT}	
11	150	200	150	500	166.67		{EDIT}*$H$7~{RIGHT}	
12	250	300	350	900	300.00		{EDIT}*$H$7~{RIGHT}	
13	1100	1200	1300	3600	1200.00			
14	------	------	------	------	----------			
15	4500	5950	7300	17750	5916.67			
16	======	======	======	======	==========			
17	9500	9050	8700	27250	9083.33			
18	======	======	======	======	==========			
19	9500	18550	27250					
20	======	======	======	======	==========			

Now change the value in cell H7 to 1.20, to attempt to increase the recently increased values in B8..D8 by an additional 20%. You will notice in fact, that as soon as you change the contents of H7, the actual values in cells B8..D8 also change to reflect this new change. This, of course, will inevitably lead to errors, unless you incorporate the command **/Range, Value** within an additional macro which should be executed prior to any attempt to change the contents of H7. Such a macro could incorporate the following commands:

'/RVB8..D13~B8..D13~

Implement this macro in cell H8 of your current worksheet, name it **\V** and save the resulting worksheet under the name MACRO2. This macro should be run prior to attempting to change the contents of cell H7. Try it.

Range Names in Macros:
When writing macros it is a good idea to use range names throughout. This allows you to change the location of certain portions of the macro without having to keep track and having to change references to cell addresses; reference to such cells is made by range name rather than discrete cell addressing. For example, the **\V** macro discussed earlier which had the commands

'/RVB8..D13~B8..D13~

could be rewritten to incorporate the range name 'Costs' as follows:

'/RVCosts~Costs~

where 'Costs' was defined with the use the **/Range, Name, Create** command, as the range name for the cell block B8..D13.

Implement this in your current worksheet, and save the resulting worksheet under the name MACRO2, replacing the previously saved version. Note that we have placed both these macros (macro **\P** and macro **\V**) on specific row numbers of column H with a gap between them. This has been done intentionally, so as to allow room for future expansion of this example.

What you should have on your screen, is the following display:

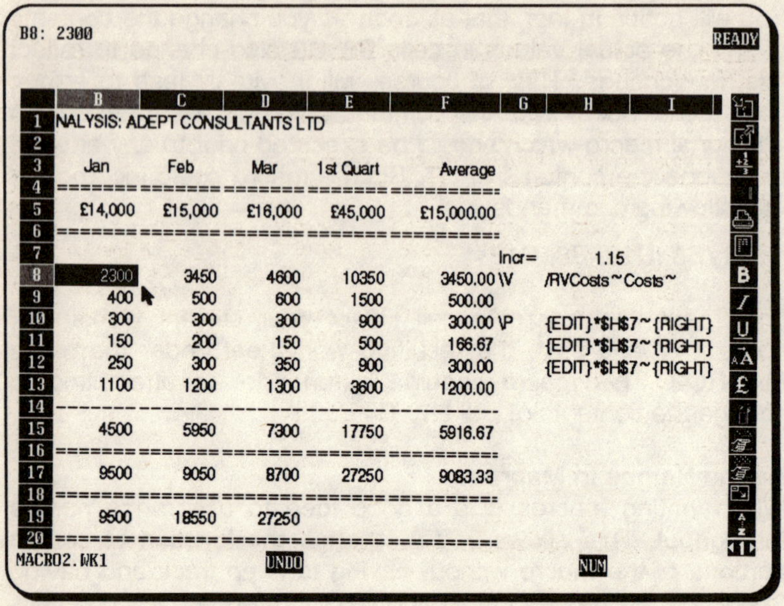
B8: 2300 READY

	B	C	D	E	F	G	H	I
1	NALYSIS: ADEPT CONSULTANTS LTD							
2								
3	Jan	Feb	Mar	1st Quart	Average			
4	======	======	======	======	==========			
5	£14,000	£15,000	£16,000	£45,000	£15,000.00			
6	======	======	======	======	==========			
7						Incr=	1.15	
8	2300	3450	4600	10350	3450.00	\V	/RVCosts~Costs~	
9	400	500	600	1500	500.00			
10	300	300	300	900	300.00	\P	{EDIT}*$H$7~{RIGHT}	
11	150	200	150	500	166.67		{EDIT}*$H$7~{RIGHT}	
12	250	300	350	900	300.00		{EDIT}*$H$7~{RIGHT}	
13	1100	1200	1300	3600	1200.00			
14	------	------	------	------	----------			
15	4500	5950	7300	17750	5916.67			
16	======	======	======	======	==========			
17	9500	9050	8700	27250	9083.33			
18	======	======	======	======	==========			
19	9500	18550	27250					
20	======	======	======	======	==========			

MACRO2.WK1 UNDO NUM

A final addition to the above macros could be made to allow for user entry of the 'increment' value from the keyboard, rather than having to edit cell H7. This can be achieved by the use of the GETNUMBER macro command, which allows the user to enter a number which is then inserted into the specified cell in the worksheet. The general format of this macro command is:

{GETNUMBER prompt-string,location}

Other available macro commands are listed in Appendix D.

In our particular case, the GETNUMBER command takes the following form:

{GETNUMBER "Enter increment ",H7}~

which is typed into cell H9. Don't forget to use the **/Range, Name, Create** command to re-define macro **\V** to its new range, which now should be H8..H12.

Save the resulting worksheet under the filename MACRO3, before using it. Your screen should now display what is shown on the next page.

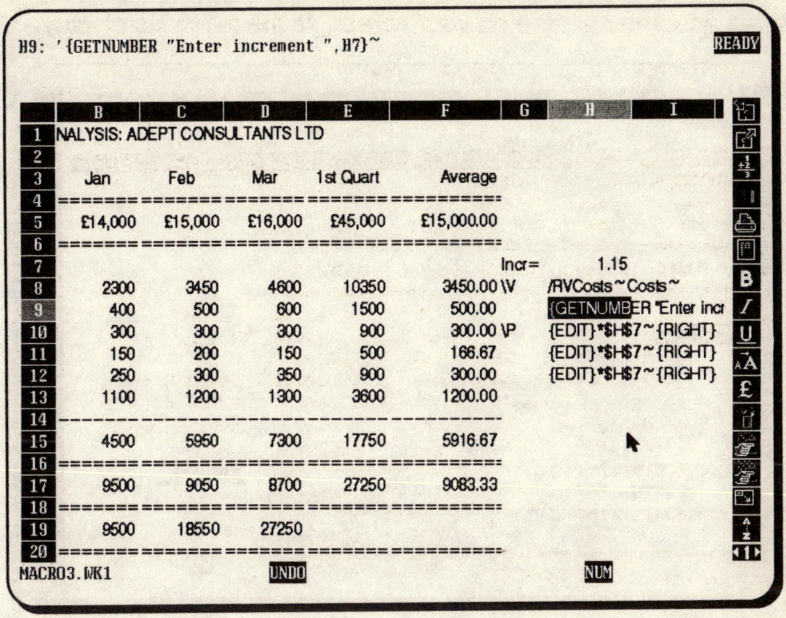

As a second example, use the **/Range, Name, Create** command to name the cell block A1..F20 as 'Analysis', then write a macro that will print to the printer the specified range name. Remember that to print the named range manually you would require to issue the **/Print, Printer, Range** command, then type the range to be printed and press <Enter> to confirm the range selection and then select the commands **Align, Go, Quit**.

Error Checking in Macros:

A macro should be written in such a way as to anticipate any mistakes that might be made by the user. This requires error checking to be incorporated into it so that it provides for possible re-entry of data, rather than cause abrupt exit from the particular application.

With this in mind, the macro displayed on the next page, has been added to the file MACRO3, incorporating range names and an error routine, as shown overleaf.

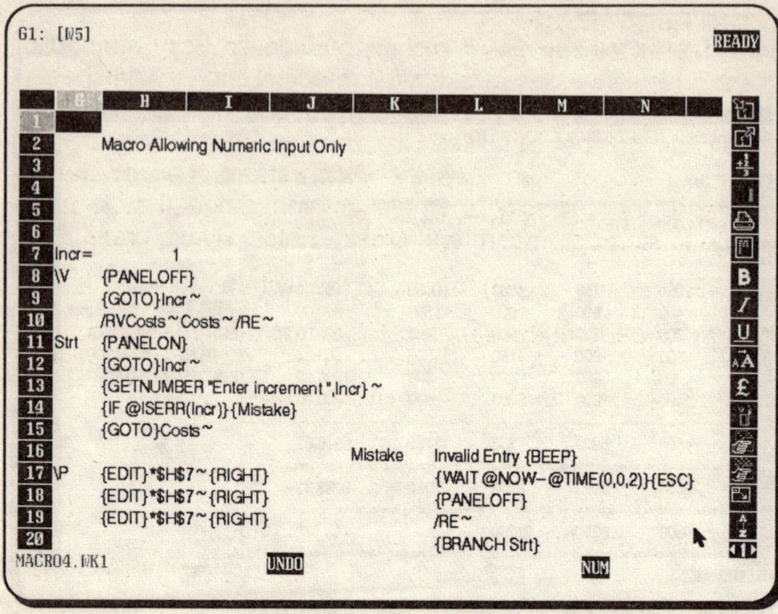

Make sure that you use the **/Range, Name, Create** command to name the appropriate ranges as follows:

Name	*Range*
Incr	H7
\V	H8..H15
Strt	H11
Mistake	L16
\P	H17..H19
Costs	B8..D13

The macro checks to see if an error results from a non-numeric entry, and if so, it causes the internal speaker to bleep, and asks for data re-entry. If all is well, the macro causes the cursor to be placed at the beginning of the 'Costs' range so that you can choose which of the various cost categories you would like to update by activating macro **\P**. Before you run the amended macro, save it under the filename MACRO4.

Macro Learn Mode

Lotus 1-2-3 Release 2.2 & higher, provide an easy method of entering repetitive key-stroke type macros into a worksheet - the LEARN mode. Before this feature can be used, a learn range has to be specified in an unused section of the worksheet. To do this, use the **/Worksheet, Learn, Range** command, then specify a single column range that is large enough to store the macro and press <Enter>. Next, press

LEARN (Alt+**F5**) to turn on the learn feature

and start to perform the series of tasks you want to record.

While this feature is activated, the LEARN indicator is displayed at the bottom of your worksheet. After you have finished, press

LEARN (Alt+**F5**) to toggle off the learn feature

If you look at the learn range now, you will see all the instructions for a macro already typed out. Now name and then run your macro in the usual way. If you want to include another macro in the one you are recording, then enter its range name in braces { }.

As an exercise, use the LEARN mode to create another macro in the MACRO4 file, which can save your worksheet. Compare the result with your manually generated one.

Macro Keys

Most key-strokes can be entered in a macro by typing the appropriate key. All the special macro keys must be typed as shown in the list below. In addition all special keys (with the exception of the <Enter> key symbol) must be enclosed in braces. You can use upper- or lower-case letters when entering the special key names.

Macro Key	*Description*
~	Enter key
{~}	Tilde appears as ~
{{ } and { }}	Braces appear as { and }
{ABS}	ABS (F4); cycles a cell address through relative, absolute, and mixed in POINT and EDIT modes

{APP1}	APP1 (Alt+F7) key
{APP2}	APP2 (Alt+F8) key
{APP3}	APP3 (Alt+F9) key
{APP4}	APP4 (Alt+F10) key
{BIGLEFT}	Move left one screen
{BIGRIGHT}	Move right one screen
{BS}	BkSp; backspace key, erases character to the left of the cursor. If a range is selected, it erases the current range
{CALC}	CALC (F9); recalculate formulae in READY mode or converts a formula into its current value in VALUE and EDIT modes
{DEL}	Del; delete key, used in EDIT mode only
{DOWN}	Down arrow key
{EDIT}	EDIT (F2); places highlighted entry on the control panel for editing
{END}	End key
{ESC}	Esc key
{GOTO}	GOTO (F5); moves cell pointer to specified cell
{GRAPH}	GRAPH (F10); view graph most currently specified
{HELP}	This is new to Release 2.2 & higher. It produces the same effect as pressing HELP (F1) so that by capturing the keystroke in a {GET} command, the user is allowed to access the Help screens written for the particular macro.
{HOME}	Home key
{INS}	Ins (insert) key
{LEFT}	Left arrow key
{MENU}	Brings up the 1-2-3 main command menu; the same effect as using the slash (/) or less-than (<) key
{NAME}	NAME (F3); produces a menu of the current range names in POINT mode
{PGDN}	PgDn key
{PGUP}	PgUp key
{QUERY}	QUERY (F7); repeats the last **/Data Query** command

{RIGHT}	Right arrow key
{TABLE}	TABLE (F8); repeats the last **/Data Table** command
{UP}	Up arrow key
{WINDOW}	WINDOW (F6); switches pointer between the two windows when there is a split screen. In Releases 2.2 & higher it can be used to turn on and off the display of settings sheets.

To specify two or more consecutive uses of the same key, use a repetition factor within the braces. For example,

{RIGHT 2} causes the cell pointer to move right twice.

Debugging a Macro

Writing macros can lead to mistakes which you must find and correct. To help you with this task, 1-2-3 provides the STEP mode which allows you to check the execution of your macro step by step. Using this technique, you can see exactly what the macro is doing and where it is going wrong.

To invoke the STEP mode, press the STEP (Alt+**F2**) key. The status indicator at the lower right corner of the worksheet will display the word STEP, and invoking a macro after that, causes its execution to be paused after processing each of its key-strokes.

In Release 2.2 & higher, the STEP mode has been enhanced to make it easier to locate errors in a macro. Each time you press a key to execute another macro instruction, 1-2-3 replaces the STEP indicator with the cell address of the cell that contains the macro instruction being executed and the contents of that cell. The current macro instruction (the one to be executed next) is highlighted.

Finally, when all the macro commands have been executed, 1-2-3 displays the STEP indicator to remind you that you are still in single step mode. If you press the STEP (Alt+**F2**) key again, the status indicator disappears and any macros you may invoke after that will execute normally.

* * *

Lotus 1-2-3 has many more commands and functions which can be used to build and run your applications in special ways. What this book has tried to do is to introduce you to the overall subject and give the beginner a solid foundation on which to build future knowledge.

* * *

APPENDIX A - INDICATORS

Indicators are highlighted words that appear either in the top right-hand corner of 1-2-3's control panel, or at the bottom of the screen, There are two types of indicators: Mode and Status. The Wysiwyg module indicators are mostly the same as those used in 1-2-3.

Mode Indicators:
Mode indicators appear during every operation of 1-2-3 at the top right-hand corner of the screen. They inform the user of the current state or condition of 1-2-3's operation. The table below lists all the mode indicators with their associated description. The macro command {INDICATE} creates special indicators which are displayed in the same way.

Indicator	*Description*
EDIT	The current entry is being edited or needs to be edited
ERROR	An error has occurred. Press HELP (**F1**) to display a help screen, or <Esc> to clear it
FILES	A list of files is being displayed
FIND	A **/Data, Query, Find** operation is in progress
FRMT	A format line is being edited during a **/Data, Parse** operation
HELP	The help facility has been invoked
LABEL	A label is being entered
MENU	A command menu is being displayed
NAMES	A menu of existing range, graph, print setting, or @function names is being displayed
POINT	The cell pointer is pointing to a cell or a range of cells
READY	1-2-3 is ready to receive data or a command
STAT	A status screen is being displayed
VALUE	A number or formula is being entered
WAIT	A command or process is being executed
WYSIWYG	The Wysiwyg menu has been activated.

Status Indicators:
Status indicators appear on the bottom status line of the screen and inform the user of the status of the program or of a key. For example, CALC indicates that the worksheet's formulae need to be recalculated, while CAPS indicates that the <Caps Lock> key is on. The table below lists all the status indicators and gives their description.

Indicator	*Description*
CALC	The worksheet's formulae need to be recalculated; press the CALC key (**F9**).
CAPS	The <Caps Lock> key is on
CIRC	The worksheet contains a formula that refers to itself (occurs only when the recalculation order is 'Natural', which is the default state). To locate the formula use the **/Worksheet, Status** command
CMD	Program is pausing during a macro execution
END	The <End> key has been pressed
MEM	Less than 4KB of memory is available
LEARN	The LEARN (Alt+**F5**) key has been pressed to turn on the learn feature and 1-2-3 is recording your key-strokes
NUM	The <Num Lock> key is on
OVR	The overstrike mode is on; press the <Ins> key to return to INSERT mode
RO	The status of the current file is read-only
SCROLL	The <Scroll Lock> key is on
SST	A macro currently being run in single-step mode is waiting for user input
STEP	The single-step mode has been activated by pressing the STEP (Alt+**F2**) key
UNDO	The UNDO (Alt+**F4**) key has been pressed to cancel any changes made since 1-2-3 was last in READY mode.

APPENDIX B - @FUNCTIONS

Lotus 1-2-3's @functions are built-in formulae that perform specialised calculations. Their general format is:

@name(arg1,arg2,...)

where 'name' is the function name, and 'arg1', 'arg2', etc., are the arguments required for the evaluation of the function. Arguments must appear in a parenthesized list as shown above and their exact number depends on the function being used. However, there are seven functions that do not require arguments and are used without parentheses. These are: @ERR, @FALSE, @NA, @NOW, @PI, @RAND, and @TRUE.

There are four types of arguments used with @functions: numeric values, range values, string values and conditions, the type used being dependent on the type of function. Numeric value arguments can be entered either directly as numbers, as a cell address, a cell range name or as a formula. Range value arguments can be entered either as a range address or a range name, while string value arguments can be entered as an actual value (a string in double quotes), as a cell address, as a cell name or a formula. Condition arguments would normally use logical operators or refer to an address containing a logic formula.

Types of Functions

There are several types of functions, such as mathematical, logical, financial, statistical, string, date and time, special, and database. Each type requires its own number and type of arguments. These are listed below under the various function categories.

Mathematical Functions:

Mathematical functions evaluate a result using numeric arguments. The various functions and their meanings are as follows:

Function	*Description*
@ABS(X)	Returns the absolute value of X
@ACOS(X)	Returns the angle in radians, whose cosine is X (arc cosine of X)

@ASIN(X)	Returns the angle in radians, whose sine is X (arc sine of X)
@ATAN(X)	Returns the angle in radians, between $\pi/2$ and $-\pi/2$, whose tangent is X (arc tangent of X - 2 quadrant)
@ATAN2(X,Y)	Returns the angle in radians, between π and $-\pi$, whose tangent is Y/X (arc tan of Y/X - 4 quadrant)
@COS(X)	Returns the cosine of angle X (X must be in radians)
@EXP(X)	Raises e to the power of X
@INT(X)	Returns the integer part of X
@LN(X)	Returns the natural logarithm (base e) of X
@LOG(X)	Returns logarithm (base 10) of X
@MOD(X,Y)	Returns the remainder of X/Y
@PI	Returns the value of π (3.1415926)
@RAND	Returns a random number between 0 and 1
@ROUND(X,N)	Returns the value of X rounded to N places
@SIN(x)	Returns the sine of angle X (X must be in radians)
@SQRT(X)	Returns the square root of X
@TAN(X)	Returns the tangent of angle X (X must be in radians).

Logical Functions:

Logical functions produce a value based on the result of a conditional statement, using numeric arguments. The various functions and their meanings are as follows:

Function	*Description*
@FALSE	Returns the logical value 0
@IF(Cr,X,Y)	Returns the value X if Cr is TRUE and Y if Cr is FALSE
@ISAAF(Name)	Returns 1 (TRUE) if Name is a defined add-in @function, else returns 0 (FALSE)

@ISAPP(Name)	Returns 1 (TRUE) if Name is a currently attached add-in, else returns 0 (FALSE)
@ISERR(X)	Returns 1 (TRUE) if X contains ERR, else returns 0 (FALSE)
@ISNA(X)	Returns 1 (TRUE) if X contains NA, else returns 0 (FALSE)
@ISNUMBER(X)	Returns 1 (TRUE) if X contains a numeric value, else returns 0 (FALSE)
@ISSTRING(X)	Returns 1 (TRUE) if X contains a string value, else returns 0 (FALSE)
@TRUE	Returns the logical value 1.

Financial Functions:

Financial functions evaluate loans, annuities, depreciation and cash flows over a period of time, using numeric arguments. The various functions and their meanings are as follows:

Function	*Description*
@CTERM(Rt,Fv,Pv)	Returns the number of compounding periods for an investment of present value Pv, to grow to a future value Fv, at an interest rate Rt
@DDB(Ct,Sg,Lf,Pd)	Returns the double-declining depreciation allowance of an asset, with original cost Ct, salvage value Sg, life Lf, and period Pd
@FV(Pt,Rt,Tm)	Returns the future value of a series of equal payments, each of equal amount Pt, earning a periodic interest rate Rt, over a number of payment periods in term Tm
@IRR(Gs,Rg)	Returns the internal rate of return of the series of cash flows in a range Rg, based on the approximate percentage guess Gs
@NPV(Rt,Rg)	Returns the net present value of the series of future cash flows in range Rg, discounted at a periodic interest rate Rt

@PMT(Pl,Rt,Tm)	Returns the amount of the periodic payment needed to pay off the principal Pl, at a periodic interest rate Rt, over the number of payment periods in term Tm
@PV(Pt,Rt,Tm)	Returns the present value of a series of payments, each of equal amount Pt, discounted at a periodic interest rate Rt, over a number of payment periods in term Tm
@RATE(Fv,Pv,Tm)	Returns the periodic interest rate necessary for a present value Pv to grow to a future value Fv, over the number of compounding periods in term Tm
@SLN(Ct,Sg,Lf)	Returns the straight line depreciation allowance of an asset for one period, given the original cost Ct, predicted salvage value Sg, and the life Lf of the asset
@SYD(Ct,Sg,Lf,Pd)	Returns the sum-of-the-years' digits depreciation allowance of an asset, given the original cost Ct, predicted salvage value Sg, life Lf, and period Pd
@TERM(Pt,Rt,Fv)	Returns the number of payment periods of an investment, with amount of each payment Pt, the periodic interest rate Rt, and the future value of the investment Fv

Statistical Functions:

Statistical functions evaluate lists of values using numeric arguments or cell ranges. The various functions and their meanings are as follows:

Function	*Description*
@AVG(Rg)	Returns the average of values in range Rg
@COUNT(Rg)	Returns the number of non-blank entries in range Rg

@MAX(Rg)	Returns the maximum value in range Rg
@MIN(Rg)	Returns the minimum value in range Rg
@STD(Rg)	Returns the population standard deviation of values in range Rg
@SUM(Rg)	Returns the sum of values in range Rg
@VAR(Rg)	Returns the population variance of values in range Rg

String Functions:
String functions operate on strings and produce numeric or string values dependent on the function.

Function	*Description*
@CHAR(X)	Returns the LICS (Lotus International Character Set) character that corresponds to the code number X
@CLEAN(Sg)	Removes control characters from a string
@CODE(Sg)	Returns the LICS code number for the first character in string Sg
@EXACT(Sg1,Sg2)	Returns 1 (TRUE) if strings Sg1 and Sg2 are exactly alike, otherwise 0 (FALSE)
@FIND(Ss,Sg,Sn)	Returns position at which the first occurrence of search string Ss begins in string Sg, starting the search from search number Sn
@LEFT(Sg,N)	Returns the first (leftmost) N characters in string Sg
@LENGTH(Sg)	Returns the number of characters in string Sg
@LOWER(Sg)	Converts all the letters in string Sg to lower-case
@MID(Sg,Sn,N)	Returns N characters from string Sg beginning with the character at Sn
@N(Rg)	Returns the numeric value in the upper left corner cell in range Rg

@PROPER(Sg)	Converts all words in string Sg to first letter in uppercase and the rest in lower-case
@REPEAT(Sg,N)	Returns string Sg N times. Unlike the repeating character (\), the output is not limited by the column width
@REPLACE(O,S,N,Ns)	Removes N characters from original string O, starting at character S and then inserts new string Ns in the vacated place
@RIGHT(Sg,N)	Returns the last (rightmost) N characters in string Sg
@S(Rg)	Returns the string value in the upper left corner cell in range Rg
@STING(X,N)	Returns the numeric value X as a string, with N decimal places
@TRIM(Sg)	Returns string Sg with no leading, trailing or consecutive spaces
@UPPER(Sg)	Converts all letters in string Sg to uppercase
@VALUE(Sg)	Returns the numeric value of string Sg.

Date and Time Functions:

Date and time functions generate and use serial numbers to represent dates and times. Each date between 1 January, 1900 and 31 December 2099 has an integer serial number starting with 1 and ending with 73050. Each moment during a day has a decimal serial number starting with 0.000 at midnight and ending with 0.99999 just before the following midnight. Thus the value 0.5 indicates midday. The various functions and their meanings are as follows:

Function	*Description*
@DATE(Yr,Mh,Dy)	Returns the date number of Yr,Mh,Dy
@DATEVALUE(Ds)	Returns the date number of date string Ds
@DAY(Dn)	Returns the day of the month number (1-31) of date number Dn

@HOUR(Tn)	Returns the hour number (0-23) of time number Tn
@MINUTE(Tn)	Returns the minute number (0-59) of time number Tn
@MONTH(Dn)	Returns the month number (1-12) of date number Dn
@NOW	Returns the serial number for the current date and time
@SECOND(Tn)	Returns the second number (0-59) of time number Tn
@TIME(Hr,Ms,Ss)	Returns the time number of Hr,Ms,Ss
@TIMEVALUE(Ts)	Returns the time number of time string Ts
@YEAR(Dn)	Returns the year number (0-199) of date number Dn.

Special Functions:
Special functions perform a variety of advanced tasks, such as looking up values in a table. The various functions and their meanings are as follows:

Function	*Description*
@(Ca)	Returns the contents of the cell referenced by cell address Ca
@CELL(At,Rg)	Returns the code representing the attribute At of range Rg
@CELLPOINTER(At)	Returns the code representing the attribute At of the highlighted cell
@CHOOSE(X,V0,..,Vn)	Returns the Xth value in the list V0,..,Vn
@COLS(Rg)	Returns the number of columns in the range Rg
@ERR	Returns the value ERR
@HLOOKUP(X,Rg,Rn)	Performs a horizontal table look-up by comparing the value X to each cell in the top index row, in range Rg, then moves down the column in which a match is found by the specified row number Rn

@INDEX(Rg,Cn,Rw,[W])	Returns the value of the cell in range Rg at the intersection of column-offset Cn, row-offset Rw and worksheet-offset W; used to refer to a look-up table with relative positions rather than the specified values required by @HLOOKUP and @VLOOKUP
@NA	Returns NA (not available)
@ROWS(Rg)	Counts the rows in range Rg
@VLOOKUP(X,Rg,Cn)	Performs a vertical table look-up by comparing the value X to each cell in the first index column, in range Rg, then moves across the row in which a match is found by the specified column number Cn.

Database Functions:

Database functions perform calculations on a database. The database, called the input range, consists of records, which include fields and field names. A criterion range must be set up to select the records from the database that each function uses. The various functions and their meanings are as follows:

Function	*Description*
@DAVG(Ip,Os,Cr)	Returns the average of the values in the offset column Os, of the input range Ip that meet the criteria in the criterion range Cr
@DCOUNT(Ip,Os,Cr)	Returns the number of non-blank cells in the offset column Os, of the input range Ip that meet the criteria in the criterion range Cr
@DMAX(Ip,Os,Cr)	Returns the maximum value in the offset column Os, of the input range Ip that meet the criteria in the criterion range Cr
@DMIN(Ip,Os,Cr)	Returns the minimum value in the offset column Os, of the input range Ip that meet the criteria in the criterion range Cr

@DSTD(Ip,Os,Cr)	Returns the population standard deviation of the values in the offset column Os, of the input range Ip that meet the criteria in the criterion range Cr
@DSUM(Ip,Os,Cr)	Returns the sum of the values in the offset column Os, of the input range Ip that meet the criteria in the criterion range Cr
@DVAR(Ip,Os,Cr)	Returns the population variance of the values in the offset column Os, of the input range Ip that meet the criteria in the criterion range Cr.

APPENDIX C - MACRO COMMANDS

There are a large number of advanced macro commands available in 1-2-3 each one of which has a specified syntax. This takes one of the following two forms:

{Keyword}
{Keyword arg1,arg2,...,argn}

and must be typed into a macro with the prescribed number of arguments. Uppercase and lower-case letters are equivalent in macro keywords and are, therefore, interchangeable. However, it is a good idea to always use a different case for macro commands from that of range names. In the examples given in this book, all macro commands are entered in uppercase, while range names are entered in lower-case. This makes it easier to distinguish between the two.

Note that incorrect macro commands result in an error when the macro is invoked, and not when the macro command is entered. Also, note that there is an important difference between macros and @functions. If you place your macros in any place other than their own worksheet or file, commands that disrupt the sheet layout, such as **/Move, /Worksheet, Insert**, or **/Worksheet, Delete** commands with macros, 1-2-3 does not adjust specified cell address, therefore the macro will not work correctly.

Some macro commands, such as GETNUMBER, change the contents of cells in the worksheet. However, 1-2-3 may not always update or recalculate the worksheet after each macro command is executed. Normally, the inclusion of a tilde (~), which executes an <Enter> at the end of a command accomplishes this, while others require the inclusion of either the CALC (**F9**) instruction, or the {RECALC} macro command, as the next macro instruction. In the following list, a superscript R (^{R}) against a command indicates that a {RECALC} command must be used, while a superscript tilde ($^{\sim}$), indicates that a ~ must be used before the worksheet is updated.

Optional arguments are placed in square brackets ([..]), and advanced macros which are new to Release 2.2 & higher, or have been greatly enhanced, are shown with a superscript N (^{N}) against their name.

?	{?} stops macro execution temporarily for keyboard input or to allow you to move the cell pointer
BEEP	{BEEP [Num]} causes the speaker to beep. Num is an optional number from 1 to 4 used for different tones (the default value is 1)
BLANK[~]	{BLANK Loc} erases the contents of a specified cell location given by Loc or a range of cells such as A1..A9
BORDERSOFF[N]	{BORDERSOFF} turns off the worksheet frame; similar to {FRAMEOFF}
BORDERSON[N]	{BORDERSON} turns worksheet frame back on; similar to {FRAMEON}
BRANCH	{BRANCH Loc} causes macro execution to branch to a different location
BREAK[N]	{BREAK} clears the control panel contents and returns 1-2-3 to READY mode
BREAKOFF	{BREAKOFF} disables the <Ctrl+Break> key during macro execution
BREAKON	{BREAKON} enables the <Ctrl+Break> key function
CLOSE	{CLOSE} closes a file that has been opened with the OPEN command
CONTENTS[R]	{CONTENTS Dest,Sour,[Wdth],[Frmt]} places the contents of Source cell, if a 'string', into Destination cell as a label. If the contents of the Source cell are numeric and the *optional* arguments of Width and Format are different from those of the Source cell, then 1-2-3 takes the number in Source together with specified Width and Format and stores it as a left-aligned label in Destination cell
DEFINE[R]	{DEFINE Loc1:Type1,Loc2:Type2,.Locn.} specifies Location cells and declares Types of arguments to be passed to a subroutine
DISPATCH	{DISPATCH Loc} branches indirectly to the specified destination, given by Loc

FILESIZE[R] {FILESIZE Loc} determines the number of bytes in a currently opened file and places it in a specified Location

FOR[R] {FOR Count,Start,Stop,Step,Startloc} executes repeatedly the macro subroutine that begins at the Start location. Count is a cell in which 1-2-3 holds the current number of repetitions, while Startloc is the first cell, or range name, of the subroutine to be executed

FORBREAK {FORBREAK} cancels execution of current FOR loop

FRAMEOFF[N] {FRAMEOFF} turns off the display of the worksheet frame

FRAMEON[N] {FRAMEON} turns on the display of the worksheet frame

GET[R] {GET Loc} stops macro execution temporarily and stores a single character you type in a specified cell given by Loc

GETLABEL[~] {GETLABEL Prompt,Loc} stops macro execution temporarily, prompts you with Prompt string and stores the characters you type as a label in a specified cell given by Loc

GETNUMBER[~] {GETNUMBER Prompt,Loc} stops macro execution temporarily, prompts you with Prompt string and stores the characters you type as a number in a specified cell given by Loc

GETPOS[R] {GETPOS Loc} determines the current position of the file pointer in an open file and displays it in Loc

GRAPHOFF[N] {GRAPHOFF} removes a graph displayed by {GRAPHON} and re-displays the worksheet

GRAPHON[N] {GRAPHON [Na],[Nodis]} displays: with no arguments the current graph, the graph named Na, or no graph display but makes Na current

IF	{IF Cond} executes the command that follows, in the same cell, if Cond is true, else moves control to next line down
INDICATE[N]	{INDICATE [String]} shows String as the mode indicator
LET[R]	{LET Loc,String} stores an entered label or {LET Loc,Num} stores an entered number, in a specified cell given by Loc
LOOK[R]	{LOOK Loc} scans the keyboard for input during macro execution and stores that character in Loc
MENUBRANCH	{MENUBRANCH Loc} stops macro execution to allow selection from a customised menu with user-defined choices. The upper left-corner of the menu is given by Loc
MENUCALL	{MENUCALL Loc} stops macro execution to allow menu selection and executes the corresponding macro as a subroutine. The upper left-corner of the menu is given by Loc
ONERROR[R]	{ONERROR Loc,[Msg]} branches to Loc if an error occurs during macro execution. The error message can be optionally recorded at location Msg
OPEN	{OPEN Filename,Mode} opens the specified file in the current directory for reading or writing. Mode is a single character (R for Read, W for Write, M for Modify, or A for Append) which describes the type of file access
PANELOFF[N]	{PANELOFF [Clear]} freezes the control panel during macro operation. If optional Clear is set, the panel is also cleared
PANELON	{PANELON} enables control panel redrawing
PUT[R]	{PUT Loc,Col,Row,String} puts a string or {PUT Loc,Col,Row,Num} puts a number, in the specified Location within a specified range

QUIT	{QUIT} terminates macro execution and returns control to the keyboard
READ[R]	{READ Bytes,Loc} reads a number of bytes (characters) from a file into a cell specified by Loc
READLN[R]	{READLN Loc} copies a line of characters from the currently open file into the specified location
RECALC	{RECALC Loc,[Condit],[Iternum]} recalculates the formulae in a specified range, row by row. Condit and Iternum are optional arguments; Condit is evaluated after the range Location is calculated and if Condit is FALSE, it calculates the range again; Iternum specifies the number of times the range is calculated
RECALCCOL	{RECALCCOL Loc,[Condit],[Iternum]} Recalculates the formulae in a specified range, column by column under the same conditions as RECALC
RESTART	{RESTART} cancels the subroutine and clears the subroutine stack
RETURN	{RETURN} returns from a subroutine
SETPOS	{SETPOS Pointer} sets the file Pointer in the currently opened file into a new position
subroutine_name	{subroutine_name} calls a subroutine
SYSTEM[N]	{SYSTEM Cmd} halts 1-2-3 session to execute DOS command Cmd, then macro continues
WAIT	{WAIT Timenum} suspends macro execution for a specified time
WINDOWSOFF[N]	{WINDOWSOFF} disables redrawing the display screen during macro execution
WINDOWSON[N]	{WINDOWSON} enables normal screen redrawing
WRITE	{WRITE String} copies String into the open text file
WRITELN	{WRITELN String} adds String, plus a carriage return and line-feed sequence, to the open text file.

INDEX

NOTES

NOTES

COMPANION DISC TO THIS BOOK

This book contains many pages of file/program listings. There is no reason why you should spend many hours typing them into your computer, unless you wish to do so or need the practice.

The COMPANION DISC for this book comes with all the listings, organised into a separate subdirectory for each chapter. It is available in both 3.5-inch and 5.25-inch formats.

COMPANION DISCS for all books written by the same author(s) and published by BERNARD BABANI (publishing) LTD, are also available and are listed at the front of this book. Make sure you specify the BP book number and the book title in your order.

ORDERING INSTRUCTIONS

To obtain your copy of the disc companion, fill-in the order form below, enclose a cheque (payable to **P.R.M. Oliver)** or a postal order, and send it to the address given below.

Book No.	Book Name	Unit Price	Total Price
BP ___		£2.50	
BP ___		£2.50	
BP ___		£2.50	
Name		Sub-total	£............
Address			
....		P & P	£.... 0.45
....			
		Total Due	£............
Disc Format 3.5-inch....... 5.25-inch.......			
Send to: P.R.M. Oliver, CSM, Pool, Redruth, Cornwall, TR15 3SE			

PLEASE NOTE

The author(s) are fully responsible for providing this Companion Disc service. The publishers of this book accept no responsibility for the supply, quality, or magnetic contents of the disc, or in respect of any damage, or injury that might be suffered or caused by its use.

Past Poets - Future Voices

2010 Poetry Competition for 11-18 year-olds

Scotland & The North Of England

Edited by Allison Jones

First published in Great Britain in 2010 by

YoungWriters

Remus House
Coltsfoot Drive
Peterborough
PE2 9JX
Telephone: 01733 890066
Website: www.youngwriters.co.uk

Book Design by Ali Smith & Tim Christian

SB ISBN 978-0-85739-170-4

Foreword

Young Writers was established in order to promote creativity and a love of reading and writing in children and young adults. We believe that by offering them a chance to see their own work in print, their confidence will grow and they will be encouraged to become the poets of tomorrow.

Our latest competition 'Past Poets - Future Voices' was specifically designed as a showcase for secondary school pupils, giving them a platform with which to express their ideas, aspirations and passions. In order to expand their skills, entrants were encouraged to use different forms, styles and techniques.

Selecting the poems for publication was a difficult yet rewarding task and we are proud to present the resulting anthology. We hope you agree that this collection is an excellent insight into the voices of the future.

Contents

Hurworth School, Hurworth

Kelso High School, Kelso

Pensby High School for Girls, Heswall

The Poems

Immaterial Innocence

The hammer fell sharply,
I saw the look on his face,
It seemed made of metal
Just the end of a routine case.

It's a moment of shock and horror
To see your life ended by people you don't know
And to have people watching in the same room
Like some kind of sick show.

I could almost taste my own blood
As my demise was laid out in front of me,
My innocence is immaterial,
They decided I would never be free.

So now as I walk slowly
Towards that sinister-looking chair,
I can't help but bow my head
And run my fingers through my hair.

As I sit down slowly,
My heart quickens to the point of break.
'Please, you have to believe me,
I'm innocent for Heaven's sake.'

They are covering my face now
With that God-forsaken sack,
I have to say I'm going now,
I'm never coming back.

John Weatherston (16)
Abronhill High School, Abronhill

War?

Regiment 114, paratrooper, Private Sheperd . . .
One more person lost to this colossus. War? Yeah, that's it
'Go fight for your country and die a hero?'
Not one lie in that sentence.

'You become the hero of the neighbourhood,
But they don't know that you've left for good -
You're in the army now.
There, missiles flying over your head -
How to survive? Get out of bed!'

I once heard that in a song,
Not too far away from the truth in honesty . . .
But it's what we signed up for.
'The army - guns and glory'!

Ha, ha, recruits come in so naïve,
I was one of them at one point,
But now I know! Now I understand . . .
'The army - dirt and death'!

Ahh, that's more like it - death.
The plague sweeps through here every day -
Women, children, innocents for Christ's sake,
And for what?
Oil?

Another thing spoon-fed to the public,
We're here to fight for the war against terrorism!
But where are the terrorists?
Us?
Them?

We stand proud, wearing the badge of honour,
This mark of power.
The only thing we wear is a uniform that hides our cruelty,
The barbaric causes of the army - oil.

Young men die every day,
To fuel the money-making colossus of America.
We're not even from America,
And yet we starve and slaughter so the disgrace will prosper!

No longer for this soldier, oh no, Sheperd?
One more casualty for the fire of power and money.

Scott Walker (16)
Abronhill High School, Abronhill

Good Vs Evil

Good vs evil
Right vs wrong
Freedom vs greed
Sins vs virtues
To which do you belong?

Good vs evil
Courage vs fear
Love vs lust
Light vs dark
The cowardice so sheer.

Good vs evil
Creativity vs excess
The originality and imagination vs
The greed, glut and obsess.

The seven deadly sins
Can kill a person's soul,
But the seven heavenly virtues
Can create a common goal.
The war between good and evil
Never rests.

Marc Hamilton (12)
Abronhill High School, Abronhill

Day Vs Night

As the day draws to a close,
The faint blackness creeps across the sky,
The sun pops his head over the horizon,
And battles on.
The stars shake off their shyness,
One by one they emerge from the dark lilac sky,
The sun's beams are still jagging out,
As he battles on through the light grey clouds,
Soon after the moon's wise face can be seen,
But she doesn't push her light as much as the sun,
The sun is getting restless, competitive,
As he fights a losing battle,
The moon laughs quietly to herself,
Knowing all too well that the sun will have to give up soon,
The darkness and the outgoing stars dance on the sky,
Not looking for any competition at all,
The stars giggle at the sun's attempts to keep them away,
Knowing it is impossible,
Then the sun finally lets go,
Letting the moon win the battle
She knew she'd win all along.

Emma Hamilton (13)
Abronhill High School, Abronhill

This Is Just To Say . . .

(Inspired by 'This Is Just To Say . . . ' by William Carlos Williams)

This is just to say
I've had a brilliant day
Eating all your food
I'm in a good mood
Forgive me, it was delicious
Sis, stop getting suspicious
I'll buy you a lolly
And get you a dolly
I'm really, really sorry.

Danny Fraser (12)
Abronhill High School, Abronhill

Flower Vs Weed

Weed - I will strangle you with my long, thin hands
If you don't get out of my way.
Flower - Was that a threat because I would rather stay
If you want my spot you will have to pay.
Weed - Well then let's fight, but for you my friend
It won't be a pretty sight.
Flower - I would win with my giant muscles, you are as thin as a twig,
you really should eat more Brussels.
Weed - No way! I'm so much stronger,
Plus my body's so much longer.
Flower - And we all know who wins when it comes to the boys.
Weed - Me, of course.
Flower - Don't be so silly, I'm pretty and frilly,
My nails are so long and fine and my eyes sparkle and shine.
Weed - But my lips are so plump,
You look worse than a tree stump.
Flower - I have the power, I'm sweet, you're sour.

Then the weed ran away
And didn't dare come back any other day.

Rachael MacBride (12)
Abronhill High School, Abronhill

The Chain

A chain
A chain, all gold and shiny.
A chain, that is all I have left.
That chain is broken now, much like us.
Our family is apart but only for a while.
The pain of the break is over for you,
No pain and suffering,
You shall hurt no more.
The chain will be fixed soon.
As our family go one by one,
Until we're up there with you.

Ross McGill (16)
Abronhill High School, Abronhill

Sun Vs Moon

She lifts her face and opens her eyes
And lets her light flood the sky,
She is always cheery and will always smile
She'll not go away as she stays for a while,
Her fingers are long and almost touch the ground,
It is always bright when she is around.

She disappears as her enemy comes,
But now it is her enemy's turn.

He comes after the sun goes to bed.
His job starts as she rests her head,
Watching over us in the night,
Making sure that the children are alright,
Although he dances around the midnight sky,
He still looks after us, because he's a caring kind of guy.

Niamh Allison (12)
Abronhill High School, Abronhill

Fire Vs Water

The fire wrapped his arms and legs around the building,
But as he took hold, the water sprang out the hose.
The fire tried all he could to destroy the building,
But the water's cool tongue licked at the flames.

The fire started to get upset as he started to disappear
And the water felt good as she started to take over.
The fire felt weak and started to lose his breath,
But the water was full of stamina.

Losing consciousness, the fire took his last dying breaths,
The water was overjoyed at winning this battle.
The fire was gone, disappeared, leaving huge, black scars,
Once again the water had defeated its enemy,

Fire!

Chanice Young (12)
Abronhill High School, Abronhill

Wind And Trees

The force of the wind,
And the strength of the trees,
It's a full day battle.

The wind ferociously pushes the trees,
It bashes them hard
But the trees are not to be moved.

The trees stand tall and fierce,
But the furious wind smashes into them
Like a raging bull.

The trees' leaves are knocked off balance,
And the trees still haven't budged.
Tomorrow is the start of another battle.

Colin Wilson (13)
Abronhill High School, Abronhill

Sun Vs Rain

The sun smiles down on us,
And it gives us warmth,
But the rain showers us,
And makes us wet.
The sun reaches out
And makes us warm.
But the rain cries down
And keeps us cool.
The sun gives us light,
With all its might,
But the rain clouds make it dark,
So the stars can twinkle,
Like a spark.

Megan Nicoll (12)
Abronhill High School, Abronhill

Crime And Justice

There is no good without evil
No light without dark
As for crime and justice
Each edging ahead like racing horses

Crime strikes like a knife slice
Justice keeps the street clean at night
Crime tries to stand and fight
Justice responds with force and might

Crime is like a virus
Justice is the thing that makes us better
However, the fight between them
Will go on forever, and ever and ever and ever and ever.

Ross Kernan (12)
Abronhill High School, Abronhill

Day Vs Night

Every morning, a battle begins,
And day is always the winner,
It pushes night, right out of sight,
And leaves it there to simmer.

The sun will shine from dawn till dusk,
She'll sit there in her space,
Then night will come and push her down,
And take over his rightful place.

Night will lie in his glory,
Then the sun will do what she thinks is right,
Can you see the pattern here?
This is day and night.

Robyn McQuade (13)
Abronhill High School, Abronhill

Summer And Winter

His breath whooshes down the chimney, swirling the ashes.
Icy fingers of unexpectedly chilly draughts.
They creep beneath the floorboards, under the doors
And up my leg, tormenting me.
Old man Winter skulks around my house,
Waiting to come inside.

Six months later we see Lady Summer, dancing around the daisies.
Her hands warmer than fire.
When she touches me, she burns me.
To me she is special.
She smiles at me, then leaves.
Winter is just around the corner . . . again.

Laura Burns (12)
Abronhill High School, Abronhill

Shoes Vs Handbags

One can have shoes; one can have handbags.
Shoes are shiny, colourful and comfy.
Handbags hold all of your essentials,
Like lipgloss, phone and purse.
But how can you compare?

Shoes have different types,
Like pumps, heels and boots.
Handbags make shoulder, clutch and purses.

A girl cannot live without both,
You may say compromise, and yes you could,
But maybe shoes and handbags are what a girl needs.

Ivory Bennett (12)
Abronhill High School, Abronhill

The Hammer And The Nail

The hammer swung vigorously towards the nail,
But the nail jumped away just in time.
The hammer screamed as his face hit the wall,
The nail shouted, 'Ha, ha, you missed me that time!'

The hammer immediately picked himself up,
And so the nail quickly started to run.
The hammer then tripped up the nail,
And the nail fell on its bum.

'Ha ha!' the hammer shouted.
'Now you know who is number one!'

Holly Graham (12)
Abronhill High School, Abronhill

This Is Just To Say . . .

(Inspired by 'This Is Just To Say . . . ' by William Carlos Williams)

I borrowed that fiver on the table
Please, don't get mad
It was just for sweets
Please, don't get mad
I'll give you it back at the end of the week
Please, don't get mad
I'll treat you like royalty every day
Please, don't get mad
You are the best mum in the entire world
Please, don't get mad.

Calum Dempsey (12)
Abronhill High School, Abronhill

A Question

If you could be with your special someone,
If you could keep them by your side forever,
Who would you choose?
A question.
A question that was grabbed by my heart, before I could.
A question that I had been wanting to ask before I lost the words.
A question asked by a very special and very beautiful friend of mine.
But a pointless question
She knew the answer
And so did I.

Calum Rooney (16)
Abronhill High School, Abronhill

Sea And Wind

The sea's waves roared at the land,
The wind whispered through the trees.
The sea smashed the rocks
And the wind whistled through the long, green grass.
The sea jumped over the pier,
The wind angrily blew towards the sea.
But the sea backed away,
And so did the wind.
The sea got on with its business,
And so did the wind.

Mason Black (13)
Abronhill High School, Abronhill

Hurricane Vs Seaside

A raging and very strong oblivion,
Wiping out everything in its path,
Go too near and feel its wrath,
Always angry, never nice,
Get caught in it, pay the price.

Happy, jolly and really cheerful,
Nobody there is at all fearful,
The waves walk gently on the shore,
People are happy more and more.

Jordan Fallenstein (13)
Abronhill High School, Abronhill

Water Vs Fire

The water roared at the fire,
As it started to tire,
The fire was winning the fight,
As it started to become night,
The fire was pushing against the water,
Then the clouds came over faster and faster,
Then the rain stamped out the fire,
The water won the fight even though
It started to tire.

Dean Murdoch (13)
Abronhill High School, Abronhill

This Is Just To Say . . .

(Inspired by 'This Is Just To Say ... ' by William Carlos Williams)

I have taken all my things
And packed them away
I may not be an angel
But now I'm away
I am sorry
Forgive me
'Cause I've taken all the money
And run away.

Robyn Seath (12)
Abronhill High School, Abronhill

Death Date

The path is gone,
And I'm alone.
The coldness grips me,
As my eyesight becomes uncontrollably blurry.
The trees grab at my tattered clothes,
Piercing my cold skin like jagged arrows.
My body starts hurting like no pain before,
Soon to be accompanied by the icy downpour.

I see the light, it's as white as snow,
It has that amazing, shimmering glow.
I feel it taking over,
It is absolute torture.
The pain punctures my heart,
Like a dartboard targeted by a dart.

I'm dying alone,
My last word, a mere groan.
Goodbye cruel world,
My body is now curled.
Awaiting my fate,
Record this day as my death date.

Jack Bowey (14)
Academy 360, Sunderland

He Was Always There

She had grown up thinking she was never good enough,
How all her siblings would shine above her.
She felt invisible, unknown at the least,
But yet, there was something different about her,
Something special.

Her mother always made her do everything,
Every little speck of perfection was through her.
Her father, well, he was a great man,
Told her he loved her day in, day out.
Yet the mother was different, a horrible kind of different.
She hurt the little girl, inside and out.

The little girl had always been capable of doing one thing,
That one thing was singing.
She'd hum little songs to herself now and again.
Her dad always smiled, knowing it made her happy,
But the mother had no happiness for her,
None at all, not even an ounce.

It was a warm day, the little girl loved it,
She ran into the warm sun, beating down on her dry skin.
She lay under a tree, singing to herself, smiling.
There began loud shouting -
Her mother.
She ran from her mother, behind the tree,
Making sure she was safe.

Her mother began to speak.
She had never spoken to the girl like this before.
She was not shouting, not cursing,
But apologising.
The girl whimpered from behind the tree.
She didn't care what her mother had to say,
She couldn't care less anymore.
After all the pain she had been put through over the past thirteen years,
The girl didn't want anything to do with her, nothing at all.
Her dad came behind her, cuddling her from behind.

She looked up, smiling with happiness.
'Daddy, can I come home?'
He smiled, bright white teeth gleaming,
'Of course you can, you're my girl.'

Despite everything she'd been put through,
She loved her dad, he was there for her when no one else was.
He was her happiness all along,
He made her complete.

Amy Mitchell-Hall (14)
Academy 360, Sunderland

String Quartet

The flat, empty serenade of a cold, wet violin,
Drips away in the rain.
Yet what happens to the violinist?
Temper sweet, his mind embodies with his medicine
Of the bitter ale that is alcohol.

A displeased centrality of that of the viola
Covers itself with plea and sickness
Over an un-heartfulness of use.
In this dampness of a box,
Yet now an empty, hollow violin player
Cowers away in such rapid shivers
Of bills and bailiffs.

Heat of exhausted flames bite away
Like a virus on an old, burnt cello.
Its disuse of once high timbre
Qualities put to shame by a snapped bow,
The cellist cast his shaded black eyes
Onto a screen of silver to direct his
Large self to inject his body with that
Of food and supplements.

Louis Robson (13)
Academy 360, Sunderland

The Ending

The end will come in life,
It always does.
In some way or another,
It comes.

You never know when it's coming,
Tomorrow or today.
It could be far, it could be near,
Maybe a month, maybe a year.
Maybe two, maybe more,
You know it's coming, that's for sure.
Autumn, winter, summer or spring,
Would it bother you which season it was in?

Would you mind if it was slow?
Or would you rather a single blow?
Quick or slow, you might not know,
You know it's coming before you go.

In the dark or in the light?
At midday, or at midnight?
You'll close your eyes and then you'll fall,
Then you know it's the end after all.

There are shells, there are knives,
And they both can end a life,
There are so many ways to die,
So many ways for you and I.
Don't be scared, don't you cry,
You'll know it's coming, you'll do your best,
You'll lay your hands upon your chest.

The end will come in life,
It always does.
In some way or another,
It comes.

Kitty Rayner (14)
Academy 360, Sunderland

Summer Love Dies

As the bright orange sun
Sets one last time
I close my eyes tight
And whisper goodbye,
I've lived my life
And now it's done,
I'm leaving now,
But it's been fun.

I've had good times and bad,
Stayed happy and true,
For all of the memories,
I thank you.

You had my heart from
The very first day,
From the moment we met,
That one summer day.

I saw you and
You saw me,
I felt happy,
Finally free.
You healed my heart
And held me close,
When you were there,
Time just froze.

You have my heart,
You own my soul.
You are the one
Who makes me whole.

Aylise Bailey (14)
Academy 360, Sunderland

War Bound

Lost in the smoke, caught in the cloud
Just can't be heard, just can't be loud
Stuck in the battle, found on the ground
Lots of dead bodies, piled in a mound
One is all it takes, two is just too much
Lost all of their feelings, lost even their touch.

One minute you're safe, the next you are sorry
Close to your death, but no need to worry
You still have your team, back to back together
When you start doing your job, the bodies drop like a feather
Even when you're inside, you still think out there
Figuring out your next plan, as dangerous as a bear.

First you're in your base, next you're on your way
Fighting for your country, living another day
No need to speak a word, your actions say it all
A war, man versus man, no one left feeling small
Death, death, death, we do all we can
But when you're out in battle, no one gives a damn.

Going into this forest, making our way through
Ensuring that our life is yet so true
Not making a mistake, going through flawless
Until one moment, when you end up lifeless
Just by one bullet, you end up staring down a bright light
And end up knowing, you've just fought your final fight.

Ryan Dodd (14)
Academy 360, Sunderland

Untitled

They look at me, smile then cry,
But in their hearts I'll never die.
Forever in their heads I'll be,
I know they will remember me.

My brothers always envied me,
I was just something they could never be.
For many years to come,
I'll always be their favourite son.

I love them all so dearly,
But I've never shown it clearly.
Some things happen for a reason,
But that reason is hardly clear.

Just love, wish and hope,
To keep your family near.
They'll visit me, I know they will,
Just like they visited me when I was ill.
Everything was easy back then,
It's quite hard trying to remember when.

But my life is over now.

Sarah Markham (14)
Academy 360, Sunderland

Untitled

Shopping, shopping,
I love shopping,
Shopping is good,
Shopping is my
Livelihood.

I search for bargains galore,
Ready to hit the dance floor.

France, France, oh France,
The country of passion and dance.

Danica Green (14)
Academy 360, Sunderland

So What?

So what if I arrive at school after the bell?
Doesn't mean you have to tell.
So what if I sit by myself in class?
You don't have to mutter when you all pass.
So what if I'm pale? It's my skin.
It's just because I'm not fake from a tin.
So what if my shoes talk to me?
Isn't poverty plain to see?
So what if I'm dark and black inside?
For when you attack I have to hide.
So what if I cut myself?
It's you that mess up my mental health.
So what if I like the band Slipknot?
It is your loss to not!
So what if I've never met a boy?
Just because you get played like a toy.

So what, I'm me,
Why can't you just see?
Leave me, please leave me!

Chelsea Benson (14)
Academy 360, Sunderland

The War And After

The Nazis had us surrounded
Every one of the Nazis took aim
Landing near us was a friendly ship
Landmines were scattered everywhere
Many years later
Everyone survived
To this day
Obelisk stones are scattered all over the war zone
Wait if you have the chance
ID is needed to see this wonderful sight
Not unless you were in the war.

Kyle Crampton (14)
Academy 360, Sunderland

The Battle

Lost in the wilderness of the battlefield
Holding my weapons, I am expected to yield
A burden of disaster, destruction and death,
I am a soldier, bringing other men to their terminal breath.

Cruel and merciless, but never fearless
Leaving the enemy lying motionless.
As troops hit the ground, their bodies will be found,
Lying, releasing no signs of sound.

Their faces swell with anguish,
Agonising screams of a distant language
No attempt at translation,
Just sheer, stomach-churning intimidation.

The horrors of war, as men hit the floor
If only this city was like it was before.
I am a soldier and expected to kill
Leaving every enemy, permanently still.

Ryan Walker (14)
Academy 360, Sunderland

Happy Dancer

Happy dancer, a shopper I am,
As I dance from shop to shop,
Cheerful I am.
I leap, jump and hop,
In and out of shops,
Around and around I go.

I hear a beat everywhere I go,
There's a burst of energy in me,
Then my feet start tapping,
Then punching out dance moves.

And there I go!
I dance around, opening my mind.

Abbigail Coyne (14)
Academy 360, Sunderland

I Am Proud

Can you be as proud as me?
My brothers are in the army.
New adventures,
New stories.
One went to Afghanistan,
How scary that was.
Three months he was away,
'Long time no see,' I would say.

The other one has just started,
I'm still a bit scared.
He is down at Harrogate,
Then home, bashing COD and then the real thing.

My lovely brothers if you knew
How proud I am,
I love you both,
My best brothers, Chris and Dan.

Katie Robertson (13)
Academy 360, Sunderland

I Am What I Am

Do you know what you're doing?
Do you think you will learn?
I hope you get what you've done to me in return.
Look in the mirror,
What do you see?
Take a look at you, take a look at me.
So what if I'm stupid?
So what if I'm fat?
I'm always me
And you can't beat that.
So what if I'm not famous?
So what if I'm not cool?
I'm not afraid of what I am
You stupid little fool!

Arran Conlin (14)
Academy 360, Sunderland

Lost For Words

Lost for words I sit in silence,
As I listen to the rhythmic tweeting in the bushes,
The jogger goes by without even stopping,
With the singing of the iPod just gradually stopping,
The pot of water starts to whistle
As I drag my feet along the bristle.
The whistling stops as I lift the pot,
The boiling hot water starts to blot.
The window slams shut,
I see that mutt
Walking past the gate.

I hurdle the fence like an athlete runner,
As I chase off that very stupid bragger.
He brags all day like a repetitive dagger,
Even though I'm lost for words, I sit in silence.

Joshua Tumilty (13)
Academy 360, Sunderland

I Follow The Beat!

A single dancer
Spinning, twirling and floating on one spot
As I point my toe
I bend down below
Under a spotlight

Slowly but active
A couple danced
As they glanced as they pranced
All night long to their special song

As I pop and hop and jam and break
I'm dancing hard as my legs ache
But as I flip and slide all day
I just love dancing
In any way!

Shantelle Polley (13)
Academy 360, Sunderland

Loneliness

A young girl shaking in silence
Covered in bruises by horrific violence.

A young girl unhappy and helpless
Also lonely and quite defenceless.

A young girl's mother who couldn't care less
But somehow caring for all the rest.

A young girl beaten day by day
As if she was a punch bag which could fray.

A young girl with not a lot of friends
Apart from one whose friendship will never end.

A young girl lonely no longer
Day by day growing stronger.

Jake Clark (14)
Academy 360, Sunderland

Every Day

As I wake up each day to get dressed
I always seem to feel depressed
I hear them talking and calling my name
I put my head down and walk with shame
The school bell rings as first lesson starts
The dread creates fear in our hearts
I sit there and do my work
As all the bullies call me a jerk
Lesson finishes, I start to walk out
Then the big, bad bullies fling my books about
Everywhere I go I just seem to see
All the bullies picking on me
I try to ignore it but it's still in my head
I can't wait to go home, just to go to bed.

Brogan Burrell (13)
Academy 360, Sunderland

Splash, Splash, Splash

Splash, splash
I see you in a flash.
I have to dash
Otherwise I will get soaked,
As your tail goes
Crash!

Swish, swish
As you eat a fish.
You get distracted by a bee
Which flies into a nearby tree.

I love you
And I hope you love me too!

Megan McMurrough (13)
Academy 360, Sunderland

Mr Footballer

Mr Footballer, oh footballer
Why do you not run?

Your legs are so strong
Now run to the sun

The goal is your sun
Its light shining bright

The defence is in fright
Of your strength and your might

Now you are set
Send the ball to the back of the net.

Aaron Smith (14)
Academy 360, Sunderland

Untitled

Alone in the room
Stood a young girl
Ready to face her doom.
Creeping footsteps down the stairs
She will enter if she dares.
She stood there, looking around
She turned to listen for some sound.
She opened the cupboard with fear
But as she looked in, it was all clear.

Gabby Bridge (14)
Academy 360, Sunderland

View Of The Past

I loved the days when we had to earn for what wanted.
I loved the days when no one cared about what we looked like.
I loved the days when drugs weren't even thought about.
But that was the past and this is now!
I loved the days when we used to have fun and laughter.
I loved the days when I had a life.
But all of that passed away the day I ruined my life
And I loved the days when a diet was a four-letter word
And no one cared!

Sarah Copeland (14)
Academy 360, Sunderland

Untitled

Hitting bags and loads of noise
People cheering for their kids
Kids working really hard
People punching really fast
Kids training really good
Getting faster every day.

Jordan Dinsdale (13)
Academy 360, Sunderland

Confused

He drives me crazy, he drives me mad,
He makes me happy, he makes me sad.
He'll always be crazy, this I know,
He'll always put on a show
To Mam and Nan, they don't even know
How evil he really is, he smirks and grins
When he gets his own way.
I sometimes hate him, but really I love him so,
But it's all good because he's my brother you know.

Sophie Smart (13)
Academy 360, Sunderland

Morals

What's become of our morals today?
They seem to have got up and gone away
While there are children in Africa without a house
We moan about the temperature like a big girl's blouse
There are children who go to bed starving
While we observe a turkey before we start the carving
So don't question me about my morals, I know where they've gone
They've been in my heart, where they should have been all along.

Jordan Smith (13)
Academy 360, Sunderland

Regret

Dad is sitting talking to himself;
I am waiting over him.

He is a ball of fury.
'What did I do wrong? I tried to stop it.
He killed her, she's dead.
I'm just in a wheelchair because I could have done more,
I could have walked her, protected her
With all my power.
Now I can't, I'm useless and no one needs me.'

Now his heart is a thumping stone.

'People hate to see me,
They can't know what I see.
I might as well, I might as well . . .'

I have no tears for him, no voice to
Cry through, no hand to hold out.
My ghost with frozen eyes.

Andrea Elder (12)
Auchmuty High School, Glenrothes

Bonfire

Bright red, orange flames licking round the black, charred wood,
Specks of ash scintillating, like bubbles in lemonade, rising
Ticker tape in the midnight sky, a New York parade.

Crackling, hissing, popping, the damp wood dries and burns.
Thickly smelling smoke is autumn toadstools swamped in the forest;
Potatoes in the glowing cinders wait to be eaten, by adults, by children

Enchanted in a circle, their faces in the darkness
Of the hill and the beacon, drawing its flock to worship.

Aldra Corbett (14)
Auchmuty High School, Glenrothes

Powder Blue

Your pale, white skin so
Beautiful, so cold your voice.
There's comfort in your eyes so
Blue in that dark dress, by the fountain's
Side, your hand running through the water
Making ripples.

When rain falls in your hair, I wonder.
I thank the angels' sky for letting you
Lay by the fountain's eye.

Shaunie Donaldson (15)
Auchmuty High School, Glenrothes

Alphabet Of Assumptions

Alcohol, abortions, abuse
Beatings, bullying, bereavement
Crying, cocaine, casualty
Death, dilemmas, disappointment
Exams, effort, exhaustion
Family, friend, failure?
Gaming, girls, grades
Help!
Intelligence, inspiration, imagination
Jokes, joy, jammin'
Kaleidoscope, knowledge, karma
Laughter, love, loyalty
Music, money, melodrama
Noise, naughtiness, never-ending
Optimism, opportunities, Oxford?
Passion, palaver, parties
Quiet!
Riots, romance, reality
Stereotypes!

Emily Anderson (14)
Balfron High School, Balfron

This Is Me

I don't know how I'm supposed to act
I'm not an emo and that's a fact
I might dress differently from you
And dye my hair pink purple and blue
Sure, I'm depressed sometimes
It doesn't mean I cut myself a million times
Okay, so I have a scar on my wrist . . .
I was drunk, okay? I was p*****!
And when I got home my cat was on my bed
So I moved it and left a gleaming thread
Blood. It shone. It shone red.
So I picked the scab, I picked it till it stayed
And I'd play around with a knife blade.

But everything's changing
My life's rearranging
I'm growing into a young adult
But my classmates, they still insult
Like a broken record they must throw
The nasty words that hurt me so
I've changed school thrice
But everyone knows now. I've paid the price
I've learned from my mistakes
Though my life I tried to take
I've learned the value of my life
And I dropped that nasty knife
That convinced me my life was awful.

Well, I say, I'm glad.

Keira Curtis (14)
Balfron High School, Balfron

Why?

Why do you hate me?
I never asked to be a gypsy.
We are all the same inside.
You and your stupid stereotypes.
You drink, you do drugs.
I don't, but you still call me a dirty gypsy.
You steal booze,
But you call me a thief.
I just want to be accepted,
So do you.
Sometimes,
I think the world should be
Reversed.
So then you'll know what it's like
And then maybe there'll be peace
And no stereotypes.

Leannah Gardner (12)
Balfron High School, Balfron

Life's Jigsaw

Just as some people die alone
So too some people live alone
Just as some people live alone
So too some people live together
Just as some people live together
So too some people start together
Just as some people start together
So too some people are born together
Just as some people are born together
So too some people grow old together
Just as some people grow old together
So too some people die together
Just as sadness tears us apart
Happiness brings us back together.

Amy Graydon (16)
Balfron High School, Balfron

Wondering

If you are sad and you feel bad,
Or if you cry and let out a sigh,
Or if your smile has disappeared,
And people say you're really weird,
Your heart is turning into stone,
And people argue in your home,
Your friends are all turning on you
And you haven't got a clue,
Whatever is happening to you?

You're a teenager and sometimes
That is the way you will feel.

Amy Steedman (12)
Balfron High School, Balfron

We Can See You!

When you see a field of dancing flowers
Or a forest of pines and oaks
Filled with leafy glades
Be very careful what you say and do
For we can see you!

When you wander alone
Through forests green
We follow you unseen
For we are the elven folk
And we guard nature's world!

When you fall, slip and stumble
Through a forest green
And feel yourself being lifted up
By hands unseen and guided back to the path
We are there!

When the air grows cold
And you think you hear
The twang of elven bows
And the clash of mighty swords
We are at war with nature's foes!

So when you see a field of dancing flowers
Or a forest of pines and oaks
Filled with leafy glades
Be very careful what you say and do
For we can see you!

Remember that!

Ailsa Duncan (11)
Casterton School, Carnforth

The Cruel Criminal Accusation Of Cassie Chrissie Cornenear

Cassie Chrissie Cornenear
Is waiting in the hall.
Waiting for the trollish teacher
And her screeching trumpet call.

Waiting to be called back
Through the slick, brown classroom door
And see what hellish torture
The teacher has in store.

Cassie had not meant it,
She did not mean to be rude,
She really did not mean to start
This teacher-student feud.

But everyone knew potato
Was not spelt with an 'E',
And that desert had one 'S'
Was plain for all to see.

When she pointed out to teacher
That three plus three was six,
She was not, as teacher shouted,
'Up to your tricksy tricks.'

She just wanted everyone to know
That was good and kind,
Besides, teacher made lots of mistakes
Which really were easy to find.

So when the classroom door flings out
And teacher stomps into view,
Poor Cassie Chrissie Cornenear
Does not know what to do.

Then teacher opens wide her mouth
Revealing ragged teeth
And screams at her, 'Your bright blue eyes
Can't hide the dark beneath.

You would be hung, drawn and quartered
If only I had my way,
Now, Cassie Chrissie Cornenear,
What do you have to say?'

Standing in perfect silence,
Cassie thinks hard and long
Of teacher's many follies
And of what she had done wrong.

Then she raises her pointed chin
And says with all her might,
'If correcting spelling mistakes is wrong,
Then I don't want to be right.'

Corin Rowell (15)
Cults Academy, Aberdeen

Truffle McKenzie (An Excerpt)

Truffle McKenzie and the Planet of the Ants:

Truffle woke up, covered in sweat,
He'd had a strange dream he would rather forget.
A sewer king and a pelican, rude,
He'd eaten a cake, it had tasted quite good.
He pulled his furry body out of bed,
He yawned and scratched his head,
He went downstairs, turned on the TV,
Made himself a cup of tea.
Then suddenly upon the door a loud knock,
Truffle gasped a gasp of shock.
He got to his feet and picked up a spear,
He opened the door and giggled in fear,
For there on the doorstep it was as he'd thought,
It was the bacon police - he had been caught.
He knew that escape he must
And at the police the spear he thrust,
But it bounced off their salted hide,
The police laughed and kicked the spear aside.
They gargled with guffaws, dripping with fat,
'We'll baconise you, you despicable cat.'
'I'm not a cat, I'm a racoon!'
The police apologised and left the room.
'Sorry for the misunderstanding.'

Euan Ferguson (17)
Cults Academy, Aberdeen

Crowds - Haiku

On the thronging street
People are crushed cheek by jowl
Watching the parade.

Scott Anderson (13)
Fraserburgh Academy, Fraserburgh

Happiness - Haiku

The sun on my face
As I sip fresh lemonade -
No clouds in the sky.

Sarah Alexander (13)
Fraserburgh Academy, Fraserburgh

Happiness - Haiku

Friends watching chick flicks
With lots of cakes and cookies
I can't help but smile.

Julie Stephen (13)
Fraserburgh Academy, Fraserburgh

City Nights - Haiku

On the city streets
All the lights and dark, dark nights
Being rushed and crushed.

Jordan Rackham (13)
Fraserburgh Academy, Fraserburgh

Happiness - Haiku

Up on my tiptoes
Spinning turns across the floor -
Leaping for freedom.

Annette Farquhar (13)
Fraserburgh Academy, Fraserburgh

Sunshine Meadows - Haiku

Rolling, bright meadows -
Flowers blooming, birds whistling
And sunshine gleaming.

Bruce Patterson (14)
Fraserburgh Academy, Fraserburgh

Cherry Blossom - Haiku

Sitting with my friend
By the cherry blossom tree,
In the sunny field.

Vita Katinaite (13)
Fraserburgh Academy, Fraserburgh

Moonlight - Haiku

Hanging in the sky
The moon shines light on the sea
One cold winter's night.

Megan Duthie (13)
Fraserburgh Academy, Fraserburgh

Horses - Haiku

Horses galloping
Excitedly through the fields
Racing through the wind.

Rebecca Tait (13)
Fraserburgh Academy, Fraserburgh

I Don't Care

People snigger
And people shout
Lots of people messing about
In the middle
I stand alone

While other children
Stare and groan
Tears I cry hit the floor
I don't know what to do anymore

People are different
I guess you don't understand

You try and stretch me
Like a rubber band

It's no use
You're just looking for action
Don't expect to find my reaction

Don't care if you don't like me!
For the rest of my life
This is who I'll be

You can keep your thoughts to yourself
I swear it's better for your health

Call me names
And beat me up
Spread round rumours
But
I don't care
I don't care
I don't care.

Hasstie Mirsamadi (12)
Hurworth School, Hurworth

Man's Best Friend

He's always there,
Even when you're down,
Can make you feel happy,
Without making much sound.

A personal friend,
Never judging you,
Will follow you everywhere,
In anything that you do.

Can easily uplift your spirits,
And fill you with joy,
Make you laugh,
Is this his secret ploy?

Makes you feel special,
Sweeps you away,
Trying to have a noisy conversation,
This could go on all day.

Making me giggle,
Licking my face,
I cannot imagine,
Him in a better place.

A wet nose,
A wagging tail,
With my little dog,
Your heart will sail.

Jumping about,
Then onto my knee,
My lovely dog,
Means the whole world to me.

Megan Chown (14)
Hurworth School, Hurworth

Love For Evermore

The first time my eyes fell upon yours
I knew that you were the one
As we walked, our song filled the air
And I knew my heart would never cease to break

Every time your hand clutches mine
I know your love will always be there
Every time you walk by my side
I know that you will never let me down

Each magical moment we're together
My heart begins to pace
Every time you answer the phone
I wish it would become a never-ending race

You're beautiful, so wonderful
Please don't ever change
For you are the one whom I love
And no one can ever replace

I wish you could understand
The way you make me smile
And the way you make me proud
As you walk me to my door

Each day that I wake up
I can only think of you
You make every day special
My only wish would be that they last

The first time that we kissed
I knew that you were the one
That I would never love again
For you would be mine for evermore.

Rachel Dees (14)
Hurworth School, Hurworth

True Life

You look at the world,
And what do you see?
Stupid politics
And rubbish TV.

Boys in tracksuits,
Girls in weird clothes,
Totally orange faces,
So bright it glows.

But look a bit further,
Just over sea,
Where there's real orang-utans
And no MTV.

You'll be shocked,
That I guarantee,
Poor orphan children,
Searching for their tea.

No clothes, no home,
No family, no food,
But loads of good friends
And a great mood.

Wouldn't you rather
Help them out?
Give them something,
Don't just ignore them, you lout.

Pick up the phone
And do them a favour,
Send them some food
So they can taste the flavours.

Nicolle Ward Playford (14)
Hurworth School, Hurworth

Sally Tart

Sally Tart
Comes to school a mess
With dirty hair
Down to her chest

Her coat is too small
Her arms covered in bruises
And even though she tries
She always loses

She lives at 1 Breton Street
And when she comes home,
She gets beat.

She watches TV till early hours,
The smell that comes from her
Overpowers.

The teachers try
To help her out
But all she does
Is scream and shout.

Her parents are just as bad,
Drugs is her mum
And smoking is her dad.

Social Services tried to take her away,
But they just couldn't keep her at bay.

She's got one friend and that is all,
Dreaming,
Thinking happier thoughts.

Stella Whitten (12)
Hurworth School, Hurworth

Heartbreak

From the first time I saw you
I knew our love was true
The way you touched my heart
And told me you loved me too

But then you had to spoil it all
You had to let me fall
I could not breathe late at night
But you didn't care anymore

So why did you have to do this to me?
Why did you have to make me see?
I thought that we could never part
Yet you did it so very easily

I used to feel so in love
But then you finally had enough
How could I have possibly managed
Without an angel guiding me from above

Please, please, please don't go
Please don't leave me all alone
I cannot live without you
Or your huge ego

So when I cry so late at night
And just can't get you out of my sight
I will remember that you forgot about me
And tried to hurt me with all your might
So now I have discovered what love is all about
It's loving somebody without any doubt.

Nikitah Mangat (13)
Hurworth School, Hurworth

They Don't Care

The person I am is who I am,
You cannot change it,
I may not have everything,
Everybody laughs at me,
It feels as if someone keeps slicing through my heart like butter,

It isn't my fault that I am not rich,
I don't have the new gadgets,
Phones, computers, everything else,
So what? I don't care,
I must live without,
This is who I am.

Everybody else thinks that they are the best!
With everything they ask for,
Given to them!
They make fun of me,
I have feelings too!
They don't care,
I get really upset,
They don't care,
Give me a chance
And you will see,
That we are the same, you and me.
Stay with me and I will stay with you friends forever,
And I will be happy.

If they felt the way I feel,
They would want to be like the rest.

Daniel Metcalfe-Evans (12)
Hurworth School, Hurworth

Not Perfect

I'm not perfect,
Just because I'm cool,
I'm not perfect,
No reason to drool.

I'm not perfect,
Because I do drugs,
I'm not perfect,
Because I hang with thugs.

I'm not perfect,
Because I'm fun,
I'm not perfect,
Because I own a gun.

I'm not perfect,
Because I swear,
I'm not perfect,
Because I don't care.

I'm not perfect,
I'm scared of the dark,
I'm not perfect,
I'm not a bright spark.

I sometimes wish,
When I look at the sky,
I'd taken another path,
I don't want to die,
A cool, fun, lonely, imperfect girl.

Rebecca Addison (12)
Hurworth School, Hurworth

A Lonely Shark

I am a shark,
My name is Nasher,
I'm afraid of the dark,
My sister's called Tasha.

I love to play,
Unlike the others,
I get into trouble,
From everyone's mothers.

When the nets float down,
My smile turns into a frown,
The divers keep me awake,
And so does the water snake.

I love everything in the sea,
But fish don't feel the same about me,
They swim away when I come to play,
People think I'm scary.

I wish I could impress Mary,
The shark in my life,
I'd love her to be my wife.

That's enough to say about me,
So go ahead and live life fully,
And remember to look down to see
If you can find me!

A lonely shark in the deep blue sea!

Laura Hill (12)
Hurworth School, Hurworth

Golden Sun

The golden sun
Shines high in the sky
This day's full of fun
And picnics full of pie

The summer sun
A light summer's breeze
Don't look for too long at the sun
As it's likely to make you sneeze

Tiny little daisies
Spring up in the ground
The flowers, they look so pretty
And there are children all around

It's now midday
And still the children play
They watch the butterflies fly up and away
Some hours before the sun fades I say

The sky is blue
The sun sparkles on the dew
Though now the people are plenty
The parks are all empty

The golden sun
Sinks out of view
There is no more fun
Wait until tomorrow, my son.

Amy Jowett (13)
Hurworth School, Hurworth

Grandad's Days

I'm waiting for a miracle,
That's promising to stay away,
So I stay by your side,
In the chair next to where you lay.

Flowers sit on a cabinet,
From family and me,
They try to make this a little better,
But they won't set you free.

You can't talk anymore,
Tell me stories you used to tell,
To me this is torture,
To you a piece of Hell.

I'm trying to figure out,
What you did that was so bad,
But all that ever comes to me,
Is the smile that you had.

I wonder if you'll ever get better,
Or will you stay the same?
Was it just your fault
Or is someone else to blame?

For now I will stay by your side,
Holding your hand so tight,
But I know what will happen,
Once you give up your fight.

Amy Potts (13)
Hurworth School, Hurworth

The Blackout

Tears fall to the ground,
Weeping is the only sound,
Forgotten memories sweep the floor,
Heading towards the open door.

The hairs on his arm stand on end,
As his frightful message begins to send,
Alert as a mother with her newborn cubs,
Shuffling around as though his feet were in tubs.

He can see his reflection wherever he looks,
Around the room are lots of books,
Surrounded by a clinging grey cloud,
Darkness pressing on his ears sounding loud.

Peaceful silence, dark night,
Snuggling down, oh so tight,
Lonely thoughts cascade down,
Giving him a fierce frown.

The sound is magnified, at a huge rate,
It rests on his shoulders, like a large weight,
All on his own, without company,
How long can he stay there? We'll soon see.

Tears fall to the ground,
Weeping is the only sound,
Forgotten memories sweep the floor,
Heading towards the now closed door.

Rachel Gunnell (13)
Hurworth School, Hurworth

Goodbye

Every time I look in your eyes
I suddenly feel mesmerised
You are my whole world
And I know that this is true love
The way you never let me down
When I need you, you are around
The first time that we kissed
I knew you'd be the only one
That I would ever love
You're the best I've ever had
And when I hear our song play
It reminds me of what I feel every day
The magic I feel when we touch
It's like a sudden rush of love
When our hands are intertwined
I know that everything's gonna be alright
When the day is done
When it's time to say goodbye
My whole world will crumble
I'll cry and cry and cry
So I'm asking you now
To never leave
And to never ever
Say goodbye.

Michaela Mullett (14)
Hurworth School, Hurworth

Nature

N atural beauty, not fake and unreal
A lmost all plants have beautiful flowers
T rees so tall, some nearly sixty feet tall
U sually some flowers are all colours of the rainbow
R eds, yellows, greens and blues
E ven pinks, purples and oranges too.

Alanna Stevenson (13)
Hurworth School, Hurworth

Angels

Her time has come,
Her time has run out,
The clock has stopped,
She begins to shout.
She doesn't want to go,
But life's not fair,
God guides her to Heaven,
Her memories share.
She gets blessed
And her loved ones pray,
They'll never forget her,
That's what they say.
A new life will begin,
Up in the sky,
An afterlife will start,
She will soar and fly.
A new grave will be placed,
In which to remember her,
Her name is engraved,
She'll never be a blur.
She is put to sleep,
The clock stays on seven,
I say goodbye and farewell,
As she takes the stairs up to Heaven.

Emily Ralphs (12)
Hurworth School, Hurworth

Who?

Who are you to tell me who I am?
Who are you to push me around?
Who are you to call me names?
Who are you to think you are the best?

I am me
Because I want to be,
And I am me
Because I want to be free.

Who are you to rip my heart out,
And then put it back in again?
Who are you to pick on me because I get good results?
Who are you to find somebody to blame
And copy my work in vain
And tell the teacher it was me?

I am me
Because I like who I am,
I am me
Because I am happy.

You will never pick on me again
Or find someone to blame
Or hurt my feelings
You will stop.

Kelsey Holmes (12)
Hurworth School, Hurworth

Best Friends

Sometimes all you need is a best friend,
Someone who you know will always be there,
Someone who will love you and care,
Someone who gives you the best memories,
Someone who's silly through assemblies,
So basically best friends are like bras -
Close to the heart and always there for support!

Rebecca Evans (13)
Hurworth School, Hurworth

My Friend

My friend, a girl
My friend twirls
My friend, a dancer

My friend, crazy
My friend, bright
My friend eats Weetabix all through the night

My friend walks
My friend talks
My friend listens to bouncing balls!

My friend turns
My friend learns
My friend eats cheesy swirls

My friend's shy
My friend cries
My friend, a big, big lie

My friend, often sad
My friend, quite mad
My friend, sometimes very, very bad

My friend eats
My friend sleeps
My friend steps, up to Heaven she goes.

Leonie Butler (12)
Hurworth School, Hurworth

Why?

I hate it when I feel that way.
Ya no,
Where those feelings come tumbling out of you.
Some make me cry, also depressed,
Some make me smile, also happy.

I keep getting that feeling of déjà vu,
Ya no,
Where those thoughts come tumbling out of you.
My family made me happy,
But now they are gone,
I know we are still together because we still belong.

I keep getting the same dreams as I used to,
Ya no,
When my grandad Bobby was here.
He got taken into hospital and said his last words
'I love you, Abbey.'
I replied, 'I love you too.'

I hate to think of my grandma Sylvia,
Ya no,
The one I never met.
My mam told me she was a lovely woman,
But I can't get her favourite song out of my head.

Abbey Noble (14)
Hurworth School, Hurworth

My Grandad

You're the best grandad
And that's all you need to know
Our love for each other
Has helped us to grow.

We've been through some tough times
But we've made it through
The only one I ever loved was you.

You helped me through my anger
When the world turned tough
You helped me see happiness
When the skies were all grey.

You were the rainbow
At the end of a storm
You held my hand
When I knew we might fall
Every heartache
You see me through it all.

When life drags me down
When there is nowhere to turn
You'll be there to protect me
My guide you'll always be.

Emma Gill (15)
Hurworth School, Hurworth

Cats, Cats, Cats

Sly escape artist through the night,
Loveable and purry when wanting food,
Small, cuddly on the outside,
Sly, sneaky and full of mischief on the inside,
Sharp, white paws, small, pointy ears,
Sharp gnashers, beady eyes,
Twitching nose, long, dagger-like whiskers,
All signs of a cunning hunter!

Ross Carpenter (12)
Hurworth School, Hurworth

I'm A Penguin

I'm a penguin
My world is ice
My new world is not nice
I want to be free
I'm a penguin
I want to go home
I'm a penguin
I feel alone
I'm a penguin
I hate this prison
I'm a penguin
And now I'm being risen
Onto show
I'm a penguin
And I always feel low
I'm a penguin
All I ask for is to go home
To my family

I'm a penguin
My world is ice
My new world is
Not nice!

Amelia Roberts (12)
Hurworth School, Hurworth

Why I Play Golf

I play golf because it is fun,
I sometimes do it whilst eating a bun!
I play golf because I am good,
I like the way the clubs used to be made of wood!

I play golf because I enjoy it,
There is usually a lot of wildlife (well, a tiny bit!)
I play golf because it is sensational,
That's why I wouldn't mind being a professional!

Jonny Dye (14)
Hurworth School, Hurworth

Help

In class,
At lunch,
At home,
At break,
Everywhere,
I worry.

Where are they now?
What will they do this time?
How far will I run?

I could change,
Be one of them,
I could run
And not come back,
I could stand up
And rebel.

But I will just carry on,
I will keep the hope,
Of a free life,
I just need some help.
Help,
Help me.

Robyn Wilkinson (12)
Hurworth School, Hurworth

Cats

Fierce, vicious teeth stare at you,
From inside large, powerful jaws,
Cute, big eyes deceive you,
Big, fat paws with long, sharp claws,
Sneaky, fluffy tail
And a mischievous playfulness.

Cats are cunning,
Fierce and ferocious!

Tom Currie (13)
Hurworth School, Hurworth

Everything

Jelly beans, runner beans
Green beans, kidney beans
But we all love *baked beans!*

Love, hate, it's all part of the heart,
The way I remember it is by putting it in a chart.

I love my dog Blu,
I think she loves me too,
But sometimes she is mad
And a bit of a loopy lou.

Cricket is my favourite sport,
It keeps me really fit,
Sometimes I get tired,
Or maybe just a bit.

Green is a nice colour,
It stays in my head,
Red is a nasty colour,
It reminds me of people who are dead.

Boiling sun,
It gives me a tan,
It also can feel like you're sizzling in a pan.

Lucy Charlton (13)
Hurworth School, Hurworth

Emotions

Bitter as a lemon
Sweet as a plum
These emotions inside
That you'll deny.

Rage, sad and even resentful
Always making yourself presentable
Romantic, nostalgic, passion and love
That fill your brain and make you content.

Rachele Bellu (13)
Hurworth School, Hurworth

My Boxer Dog

Waking up ready
For the day ahead
Ready to socialise
Ready to play
Her big paws smack down
Hard on the ground
Try to see her
In her older age
But cannot be found
Fit and fast
Ready to run
Greedy, she should weigh a ton
So slim, hard to believe
All that bouncing
Causes the fat to leave
Meeting with other dogs
Is hard to handle
Their leads always tangle
When the night arrives
She decides to hibernate
Away from the world
She finds the silence great.

Jodie Walker (13)
Hurworth School, Hurworth

Silent Dog

Silently watching through the night,
Big eyes staring, waiting for the moment to pounce,
Ears twitching for the slightest sound,
Silence . . . his time has come.

Slowly, quietly, his furry paw goes up,
A jump of the strong back legs and he is up,
Creeping forwards step by step,
The job is done as he lies down and settles on the bed.

Jordan Robson (13)
Hurworth School, Hurworth

Please!

Please don't abandon me
Please come with me,
Give me a chance
And you will see!

I will help you
I will love you,
I will care for you
So please come with me!

We can play in the park
We can play poker
In the dark!

We can dance
In the street
While my mum makes up tea,
We can laugh together
While caring for each other!

You can sing
I can bang a drum!
We can show the world
That we're meant to be!

Ashleigh Martin (12)
Hurworth School, Hurworth

Pepper

A cat is a loyal creature
He has magnificent marble eyes
Cats are cuddly and furry
But don't be fooled
They are really fast.
They only sleep when they want
When awake they pounce, have fun
I will love my cat forever
That will never change.

Emily Clayton (12)
Hurworth School, Hurworth

Random Things I Like To Do

I like playing football
I think it is fun
I'm a defender because I'm tall
But I hate to run

I don't like tennis
You'd be lucky to get a scratch
And I'm a bit of a menace
Game, set, match

I'd like to play a game
I always beat my mate
But it's not the same
When I have to wait

I'd like to go to sea
Just to see the fishes
At the age of twenty-three
A genie will grant me some wishes

I watch the telly
I can be lazy
When I broke my telly
It really made me crazy!

Dylan Bradford (14)
Hurworth School, Hurworth

I Am A Monkey!

I am a monkey
I swing from tree to tree all day.
I live in a cage alone
Where no one wants to play.
I like to climb ropes
And hang from my feet.
I like to eat nuts
But a banana's my treat!

Callum Brentley (11)
Hurworth School, Hurworth

Endlessness

The wind blowing in my hair,
The sand collapsing beneath the horse's hooves,
The sea lapping calmly,
Not far from my mare.

Shadows move, following us along the beach,
The sun just setting, deactivating my speech,
The horse's beautiful body,
Supple and steady.

The cliffs in the distance,
And the clouds waving goodnight,
My heart still beating,
The floor never meeting her hooves.

I don't know another feeling this happy,
I don't know another person as happy as me,
I am trapped in a bubble,
But I like being trapped.

It's endless,
The happiness, the beach, the galloping,
I wish it could go on forever,
Because it's endless.

Lucy Baker (13)
Hurworth School, Hurworth

Dogs

They bark, they play until the end of day,
They sleep, some weep in the silent night,
They eat lots of meat.
They're rough and tough, though some are scruffs,
Some are cute, but worth a lot of loot.
Some are noisy as a bell
And as loud as an echo in a well.
They think their dog meat is a treat!

Denver Griffiths (13)
Hurworth School, Hurworth

Daydreamer

I am at it again,
Blank, wide-eyed,
Staring into space,
There's no surprise!

Tapping my pen,
I search around,
See my fellow pupils,
Not making a sound.

An idea comes,
A great supernova,
I think it through,
It passes over.

Tapping my pen,
I search around,
See my fellow pupils,
Not making a sound.

Oh no, how quick!
Only ten minutes to go.
Heads are raising,
Try not to be slow!

Jenny Hall (14)
Hurworth School, Hurworth

My Friends

My friend Jake
He likes footballs
Oh my goodness
He scores another goal.

My friend James
He's great in goal
Oh my gosh
He's the next god.

My friend Mitchell
He does boxing
You get KO'd
When you hear the ding.

My friend Harry
Is hyper and scary
Did I mention
He dances like a fairy?

This is my crew
They are the best
No others to compare
In the north east.

Ben Potts (13)
Hurworth School, Hurworth

I'm Sick Of Bullies!

I'm sick of bullies pushing me around,
I wish they would just shut up and stop being loud.
I want the bullies to be found,
I don't like them pushing me around.

They always seem to get their way,
No matter what I have to say.
They call me names like 'stupid' and 'gay',
They make me sad every school day.

They think they're really cool,
They make everybody drool,
Especially when they make me look like a fool,
This is every day at school.

I really don't care what they say,
I just want to make them pay,
But I hate the leader they call Faye,
I mostly want to make her pay.

I want to stop all this mess,
I wish they would all just confess.
I want to tell the teachers,
But I'm not good at making speeches.

Kimberley Doyle (12)
Hurworth School, Hurworth

Indian Summer

The scent of summer in the air,
The cool, calm breeze blows through my hair,
Running through meadows without a care,
But that would be too fair.

The sky fills with clouds of rain,
A river rages down a country lane,
Quivering hand with pinprick pain,
Hopes of summer wax and wane.

The blue sky's trapped inside my head,
The golden sun, long since dead,
But I heard the birds as they fled,
'Watch the skies,' the bluebirds said.

So I sat and watched for countless days,
'Watch the skies,' the bluebirds said,
And finally, the first fleeting rays,
An Indian summer, so patience pays.

The sun shines, the sun shines through golden leaves,
Dappling fields of golden sheaves,
Shadows cast by conker trees,
The sun sets over silken seas.

Liberty Firby Fisk (13)
Hurworth School, Hurworth

War, War

War, war
Brings bloodshed
And death
Death, death
Brings sadness
And fear
Fear, fear
Brings anger
And hate
Hate, hate
Brings weapons
And imprisonment
Imprisonment, imprisonment
Brings torture
And innocence
Innocence, innocence
Brings mercy
But hate

Hate, hate
Brings
War.

Andrew Hancock (12)
Hurworth School, Hurworth

Daddy's Lil' Princess

Daddy, do you love me?
Would you hold me in your arms?

Do you want to buy me prezzies
And lift me way up high?

When school is over,
I need to be with you.

I love you, Daddy,
And I miss you so much too!

Jasmine Harrison (12)
Hurworth School, Hurworth

Lonely

In the playground
All alone
Girls walking past
With a big, fancy comb
Mirrors in hands
Make-up splashed
My hair's on end
Not all dyed and flashed!

In the house
All alone

Mum's moved out
Dad's not at home
Brother cries all the time
All Dad cares about is cheap, smelly wine!

In the world
All alone
People think all I do is moan, moan, moan
But there's a happy side to me
Just let me into your world
And then you'll see!

Mollie Turnbull (12)
Hurworth School, Hurworth

Summer

Summer is the time for fun,
Road trips and holidays, it's time for the sun,
The beach is exciting,
Warm and inviting,
Summer is the time for fun.

Summer is the time for fun,
Road trips and holidays, it's time for the sun,
Suntans and lying on the ground,
Shorts and bikinis all around,
Summer is the time for fun.

Summer is the time for fun,
Road trips and holidays, it's time for the sun,
Sleepovers and parties, swimming in the pools,
Kids going crazy, acting like fools,
Summer is the time for fun.

Summer is the time for fun,
Road trips and holidays, it's time for the sun,
Barbecues and sunglasses,
School's out, no more classes,
Summer is the time for fun.

Gemma Waters (14)
Hurworth School, Hurworth

Bullied

I hate being bullied
So annoying, so hard
They think they're boss
But they clearly are not
It's just their loss

They punch, they pound
Around and around
Over and over again
Like a dripping tap
All over again

Call me whatever you like
Chav, nerd, gay and dumb
They say, 'I'm not scared'
And when you say
'I'm telling'
They say, 'Don't grass!'

They're soft inside
You can make them love you
But if you get it wrong
They can mug you.

Fraser Watson (12)
Hurworth School, Hurworth

Eternal Peace

Like a feather,
Floating in the wind,
Gradually fading away,
Slowly twisting and turning,
Away with the scent,
This feather will glide,
Spiralling down to its destiny,
Awaiting God to take it in His hands,
To show it the way to go,
Leading it to the heavens,
Where this feather will be put to sleep,
On the ground down below,
Mournings of the passed away soul,
Will forever make its mark,
By the church,
A new gravestone lies,
Rest in peace,
Engraved on the rock,
Relaxation,
Relief,
And eternal peace.

Amy Younger (12)
Hurworth School, Hurworth

What Is Love In Your Eyes?

Have you ever felt it?
A love for someone,

So deep, so real,
Then they go and break you,
Like a dry twig under the mighty old oak.

I hate living without you,
I miss you,
Like the deserts miss the rain,
A knife being driven into my heart,
My heart cracked in two.

Why, oh why?
Why did you dump me?
I'll never be the same without you,
So why don't you come back to me?
My love, my heart, you took all that away.

If only you could feel my pain,
You'd surely see,
My heart is broken,
And you'd come back to me.

James Lapping (12)
Hurworth School, Hurworth

The Worst Place In The World

I was with my family one minute,
They were gone the next.
I do not know what to do with myself,
I am in the worst place in the world.

I scratched,
I clawed,
But they tricked me
And took me away.

Now people stare at me,
Laugh at me,
And scare me.

All I do is hide in a corner,
If you have not realised already
Where I am,
Well, I am in a zoo.

I am a cub,
Scared,
Lonely
And I want my family back.

Jessica Kelly (12)
Hurworth School, Hurworth

Bullies Aren't Clever

I'm quiet,
I'm clever,
I get good grades.
People think that I'm insane,
I'm stupid, silly,
Quite absurd,
Sit and answer every word.

I stand and listen to your whispers,
You giggle loudly like two little sisters.
All the rumours going round,
You'd think I never hear a sound.

Cuts, bruises and black eyes,
I'm sick of all their stupid lies.
They say that I'm the teacher's pet,
As if it is a great big threat.

But then one day I got them back,
Went and gave them a slap.
Now that we are all friends,
If I'm picked on, it all mends.

Jennifer Howell (12)
Hurworth School, Hurworth

The Wild Zoo

I am the owner of a wild zoo,
I have a sheep and a cow and the cow goes moo.
The moo calls the horse and the horse gets cold,
So I wrap him up warm before he gets old.
Oh dear, the zebra escaped with the snake,
So I rounded them up with a 2-ton rake.
Then the panda took the rake off me,
And then he ran off, jumping wildly in glee.
Oh dear, oh dear, this isn't going well,
Oh, what is that stink, oh what is that smell?
Eww, oh eww, it looks like some elephant poo,
I think I need to design an animal loo.
Oops, all my animals have escaped from the wild zoo,
By now all the animals have probably caught the flu.
Hmm, I think I see a lion ready to pounce,
But if he lands on a trampoline he'll go bounce.
Ah, here we are, they are all coming back
And look, the chickens have eggs that I'll put in a sack.
Why don't you join me for tea tonight, it's roast beef?
All the animals are back, oh what a relief.

Callum Stein (12)
Hurworth School, Hurworth

If I Could

If I could rule the world, I'd have a clean up day,
If I could rule the world, I'd make sure people were on good pay,
If I could rule the world, I'd have it fair,
If I could rule the world, I'd make more people care.

If I could fly, I'd see the planes,
If I could fly, I'd see the lion's mane,
If I could fly, I'd see the trees,
If I could fly, I'd feel the breeze.

If I did all these things, people would want to be my friend,
Unlike now simply because all these words don't mend.

Ben Liddle (12)
Hurworth School, Hurworth

The World To Me

As I stare into the world around me,
A world of pain, hate and loneliness,
I think of myself and my life,
As I know I feel this way too,
It makes me shout in my head and it burns,
Burns like a hot flame trying to burst out,
But I keep it in, as my friends shout if I don't
And they would laugh at me and ignore me.
So, at a price, the nightmares are let loose,
They feel so real that I scream,
Scream into my pillow, ignoring the real world
And I wake up sad, lonely and scared.
It has replaced my happiness,
The love and hate I have always felt,
With cruel, dark, depressing thoughts,
That confuse and kill me inside.
But I know you will never understand,
Understand me,
Understand my pain,
Understand my life.

Rebecca Tunstall (13)
Hurworth School, Hurworth

One Dark Night!

One dark night,
The clouds shone bright
Up in the deep blue sky.

Up, up high,
Deep and brightly in the sky,
People fly to the moon in a space rocket
That's taller than you.

One dark night,
The birds fly high,
Up in the starry, blue sky.

Dannielle Mason (11)
Hurworth School, Hurworth

My Grandad

My grandad, he's the best
And please just trust me
When I say,
He's better than the rest

No one could ever replace
Our friendship,
It's as if we're joined
At the hip

He really means the world
To me,
That's why I make him
A cuppa tea

I love him more than anyone,
I dread the day when he'll be gone

He's been there
Through thick and thin,
Who needs boys
When I've got him?

Hannah Sharp (14)
Hurworth School, Hurworth

She Wouldn't Let Me!

I really wanted my picture taken with my friend,
She wouldn't let me!
I wanted to go down the big, red slide,
She wouldn't let me!
I wanted to go to the shop with my mum,
She wouldn't let me!
I wanted to go to my friend's house,
She wouldn't let me!
I needed to go to the toilet,
She wouldn't let me!
I wanted to play with Louise,
She wouldn't let me!
I wanted to shout at her,
She wouldn't let me!
I cried and asked for a tissue,
She wouldn't let me!
I loved my family and friends,
She wouldn't let me!

Oh why not? Why wouldn't she let me?

Amy Donlan (12)
Hurworth School, Hurworth

What's The Point?

What's the point in calling me names?
What's the point in giving me the blame?
What's the point in being a fighter?
What's the point in carrying a lighter?
What's the point in laughing because of my above grade?
Do you know how it feels?
It's like you are cutting me with an invisible blade.

I don't care what you call me,
I am who I am, take or leave it.
Love me or hate me,
The point is, words will never hurt me.

Lauren Riley (12)
Hurworth School, Hurworth

One Summer Morning

It all began one summer morning,
That summer morning . . .

My head was spinning round and round,
My feet no longer felt the ground;

My wondering heart began to pace,
When I first saw your beautiful face;

You were my one true desire,
For it was you who lit my fire;

Forever and ever I longed for you,
But still I know it won't be true;

There's already a man who's in your life,
Whose hope it is you'll be his wife;

I may not be able to steal your heart,
But my passion for you will never break apart . . .

It all began one summer morning,
That summer morning.

Matthew Allenby (14)
Hurworth School, Hurworth

Heaven And Hell

Is there anything after death,
Or is it just another body less?
Are there big, fluffy clouds with a beam of sun,
Or is it painful and your body goes numb?

Is there a place where all the angels live
And do they present you with a gift to give?
Is there evil and spirits around,
Or is it silent with no sound?

Or is there just nothing?
No clouds, no frowns and no ground . . .
Nothing!

Olivia Naisbitt (14)
Hurworth School, Hurworth

Hate

Hate, hate
Your happiness cured
Your fate . . . to compensate
For our world.

Burn it
Higher and higher
Light the match
Start the fire

Level this place
Until there's nothing left
And take them
With it.

Hatred, rage
Destruction, plague
Level this place until
There is nothing left

And take us with it.

Jack Baglee (14)
Hurworth School, Hurworth

Death

Death is peaceful, easy
Life is harder.
Death is a road,
A never-ending road.
Life is the traveller,
And our soul shows the way.

Our bodies die,
And our soul lives on.
Life, death, two opposites.
Life is preventable,
And death is inevitable.

Alexandra Barlow (13)
Hurworth School, Hurworth

I May Not Be!

I may not be as pretty
I may not be as tall
I may not be as smart
But at least I have a heart

I may not be a bully
I may not be interesting
I may not super hate
But at least I am not fake

I may not be as popular
I may not be a smoker
I may not be a great friend
But my friendship is real to the end

I may not be so cool
I may not be a rebel
I may not be who you want me to be
But as long as I am happy with me
There is nothing you can do.

Zita Lofthouse (11)
Hurworth School, Hurworth

Ice-Cold

You icily kiss me and it poisons me cold
Then shadowed lies start to unfold
Your eyes are as empty as the midnight sky
Only starry lies light them up inside

Scared and heartbroken I cry and flee
Stood here in silence, on a cliff, black surrounds me,
Rays shine on me from the silver, violet moon,
I will get my revenge on you soon

Falling through the air I start to slip away
Now I see you have got your own way
I was tormented in my own hurtful past
But now I can say that I am free at last

Leaving you my best guess
Your love was a lie, truthless as a myth
My heart is now a horrific, mushy mess
Don't fall in love, jump off a cliff
It hurts less.

Rebekah Probert (14)
Hurworth School, Hurworth

The Treat Of Summer

The cool breeze whistling through the trees,
The soft, rippling sound of the waves lapping onto the shore,
The silky, golden sand sinking between my toes and fingers

Summer is like a present to all of us,
A treat for getting through the cold winter.

The freezing snow falling onto the ground, growing higher and higher,
Feeling as if it's the end of the world,
People hurrying to supermarkets to stock up food for the week,
Lying in bed with heaps of blankets and quilts piled up on top of you
And yet still feeling cold!

Then summer comes around the corner,
Children's laughter filling the air,
Sunbeams shining on your face,
The cooling ice creams cooling you down like a breath of fresh air,
The heavenly smell of BBQs drifting through the air,
This is the treat of summer.

Hayley McNulty (13)
Hurworth School, Hurworth

England!

England, England, come on now
Quickly win and we'll have a row.
Row, row, we're gonna have a fight
We are going to wake up with a sore head from last night.

'Kabanga, kabanga!' we're supposed to shout
Not going to anyway, we'll just sing out.
And cry for England, hoping we will win
Our cure anyway is just to sing.

We're gonna win, we're gonna win
We're gonna win it all,
But if we lose we're all gonna fall
Down in misery, upset for England's loss
So come on England, win for us.

'Goal! Goal!' We're going for the win
We're gonna crash out in a recycle bin.
Girls, football and fighting is what we do best,
Let's get down to business and we'll let you do the rest.

Matthew Gallagher (14)
Hurworth School, Hurworth

Mistakes

Mistakes are made
We're only human
But it's the price I paid
It's understood in too many ways
I left it blank
Without notice and too many says

Regrets are hard to undo
To untie the knot
And make do
The past is the present
Running seems way too long
I wish that you were gone

Once or twice
I was always given a chance
But never given advice
My life is a nightmare
But you only stop and stare.

Lauren MacLintock (14)
Hurworth School, Hurworth

Fair Share Of Sadness

We've all had our fair share of sadness
Whatever that may be,
Perhaps a loved one's passed away
Leaving only memory.

Perhaps a friend has moved away
Or a dog is on cloud nine,
The only way you'll get over yourself
Is someone telling you that you'll be fine.

So when you're feeling down
Look to a friend, mum or wife,
You know how the old song goes
'Always look on the bright side of life!'

Christopher Mason Howard (11)
Hurworth School, Hurworth

Trio Of Crayolas

My early childhood dream
As I sat under the table
With orange, red and blue.

I was a poor 'un so had but three colours
My lovely little trio of sticks
Of orange, red and blue.

Pages of small child's waxy work
Brushing off the coloured shavings
Of orange, red and blue.

'I'll stick them up,' my mum would chorus
Those energy bursts of scribble
With orange, red and blue.

As I grew up my Crayolas shrank
No more waxy work
And no more scribbles
Of orange, red or blue.

Amelia Crow (14)
Hurworth School, Hurworth

The City

The city went on for miles and miles
Different buildings in all different styles

Mosques, temples, churches and pubs
Men in nice suits and men dressed as thugs

Some people use cars
Some people use bikes

Some people have parties
Long into the night

I can understand the parties
The pubs and the bikes

But I can't understand why there are so many lights!

Andrew Baker (13)
Hurworth School, Hurworth

Honour Among Pirates

Pirates sail upon the seas
Singing the old 'Hey Ho'
Thunderous cannons that tremble knees
And give a mighty blow.

A fair maiden sleeps below the deck
Kidnapped and held for ransom
A monkey with gold round his neck
Gold stolen from some.

Pirates sail upon the seas
And honour the 'Pirates' Code'
'Parlay' might get annoying
but that's a pirate's load!

Honour is found among pirates,
But a few go against the grain
Captains have respect for others
But others can be a pain!

Victoria Monk (14)
Hurworth School, Hurworth

The Story Of The Hobo

There he stands, all alone
Not enough money to buy a home
Smoking a cigarette with his bare hands
People laughing at him as he stands

As the guy sits in the cold
The face is ageing, but he's not old
Money being thrown left, right and centre
This is the hobo to remember

Wearing raggy, horrible clothes
The weather is telling, as he is cold
Playing with his fingers, bored to hell
And that is the story of the hobo to tell.

Jordan Harland (14)
Hurworth School, Hurworth

Ice Cream

Ice cream, ice cream
Yummy, cold ice cream
Delicious, cold ice cream
So yummy, cold ice cream

Different fruity flavours
So sweet and so sour
Yummy, cold ice cream
Delicious, fruity ice cream

So perfect on a warm day
Not too cool on a cold day
When the sun's out and proud
And the kids are running around

So there it is
Yummy, cold ice cream
Delicious, fruity ice cream
So yummy, cold ice cream.

Amy Thubron (14)
Hurworth School, Hurworth

Bubbles

I emptied my bubble bath into the tub,
Determined to get myself thoroughly scrubbed.
The bottle had said 'Only one cap or two',
So I poured in the lot to see what it would do!

That still didn't seem quite enough to get clean,
So I followed it up with another fifteen.
Then three bars of soap and a dozen shampoo,
And two broken bath bombs to finish my brew!

I'll cut to the chase, this did not turn out well,
As the burbling, foaming bath bubbles did swell!
It wasn't all bad, I was clean and smelled sweet,
But outside, my soapsuds had buried the street!

Danny Howell (13)
Hurworth School, Hurworth

Love

Love is like a dream
You never know how you will feel
It keeps you strong and alive
It makes you want to survive.

Love is like a dream
You never know when it'll come to an end
You spend your days waiting for the one
To love them on and on.

Life can be hard sometimes
But when you think of your special one
You bound back up with a smile on your face
And keep on going to win the race.

You tell them now much you love them
They say, 'I love you too.'
Remember those special memories together
Those long walks in the sunny weather.

Adele French (14)
Hurworth School, Hurworth

I Am A Dog

I am a dog
I want to be free
Even though
I love my family.

I love walks
So does my brother
But the saddest day of our lives
Was when we got taken from our mother.

This is my life
My owner has the key
Me and my brother
Wish we could be free!

Nathan Hill (12)
Hurworth School, Hurworth

A Wolf In The Park

Is there a wolf,
A wolf in the park?
A wolf that walks when it gets dark,
Is there a wolf in the park?

Is there a wolf,
A wolf in the park?
From his hidden den when the day sleeps,
Is there a wolf in the park?

Is there a wolf,
Whose nightly tracks,
Circle the park fence, zigzag back?
Is there a wolf in the park?

Is there a wolf,
Who rode his way
Between the closed café?
Is there a wolf in the park?

James Mason (12)
Hurworth School, Hurworth

Holiday

Flying high and the excitement begins,
No school for a week,
Let the holiday start with a tie-in,
What more could we seek?

Relaxing, swimming, enjoying,
Spending every minute in the sun,
And end up swimming half the day,
Oh really this is fun.

What a unique place,
Eating lots, Is where the fun is best,
But now we need to pack the case,
Holiday, please don't close.

Daniel Ireland (13)
Hurworth School, Hurworth

On Athletics

Feel the speed, flow past your body,
Through your hair and between your fingers,
Dust from the track rises up in the air -
Floats around and lingers

Javelins fly into the air and the crowd begins to stare,
The javelins land - the people stand and they're
All cheering loud and proud

People of speed and people of strength,
The scores we read and measure distance or length
And every throw and step we take,
Reminds us of honour at stake,
Runners of track and bikers of pedals -
Going all out for glory and medals.

An age-old art that keeps countries together
And events that should last forever - this is
Athletics.

Thomas Clelland (13)
Hurworth School, Hurworth

Balance

The stars shine brightly in the sky,
The moon beams down from up high,
Black holes and dark matter consume space,
But the world goes on at its pace.

Nature brings beauty to our world,
Humans wait upon leaders' words,
Nature fights a war against pollution,
Whilst people search desperately for a solution.

Balance is kept through nature and the stars,
But pollution undermines them 'damn those cars',
If we lose nature to logging and farming,
Balance will be lost as well as humanity.

James Conner (14)
Hurworth School, Hurworth

The Joys Of Maths

I love numbers,
1, 2 and 3,
Sometimes in the lesson,
Algebra is the key.

My teacher is the best,
He's always very helpful,
When I'm in that room,
It's never very dull.

Although I hate homework,
He tries to make it easy,
And at least I'm not in trouble,
Just because I spoke!

Now it's time to go,
I'm sad to say goodbye,
I've thoroughly enjoyed this,
But I'll see you next time!

Oliver Clelland (13)
Hurworth School, Hurworth

Cat The Dog

Always a cat
Never a dog
Stuck inside
This mind fog

This was our land
Always had been
But now it's been taken over
By this cat-eating machine

But I'm not a cat
I cried
Looking around
I sighed

Running away from madness
Jumping over my log
I only wanted less
As I am Cat the dog!

Simon Metcalfe (14)
Hurworth School, Hurworth

Spring

Spring is inviting,
Warm and exciting,
Happy and jolly,
As we say bye to the holly.

Spring is crazy,
With a newborn baby,
At every corner you turn,
There's so much more for us to learn.

Baby lambs and otter dams,
Pregnant sheep,
And a little cheep
From all the baby chicks.

Sun is high in the sky,
Without the rain, it must be shy!
Early morning, bright day . . .
Well, that's spring, what can I say?

Becky Ward (13)
Hurworth School, Hurworth

Close

Friends are close
Enemies are closer
But never put your enemies
First before your family.

Some friends are distant
Some friends are close
Trying to keep them all close
Can slash through reality.

You and me were close once
Now we are nothing but memories
Memories I wish continued
Memories I wish were real.

Maybe one day this could happen
Maybe one day this could come true
Until that day comes, I will be waiting
Until that day comes, I shall be planning.

James Reese (14)
Hurworth School, Hurworth

Life

Life is everlasting,
It can be like a dream,
Daydreaming about anything,
Every second is a minute it seems.

Life passes by fast or slow,
Like it has a mind of its own,
As it has its own little show,
At the end of the day some people may moan.

Life can be sweet or sour,
It can be nice or harsh upon you,
It can pass by in days or hours,
It's up to you what you do.

Life can be sparse or it can flourish,
Death can end that spark of life,
But it can give life in many numbers,
But in the end it's up to you what you do in life.

Ryan Horner (13)
Hurworth School, Hurworth

Summer Day

Lying still
Sunbathing
BBQ
Green grass
Sky so blue
Eyes glistening
Summer heat
Waves crash
At my feet
Slowing down
Sparking starts
Wondering what
Lives on Mars
Summer day
Comes to an end
Hanging out
With good friends.

Emma Glarvey (14)
Hurworth School, Hurworth

I Am Who I Am!

I am who I am,
I won't change!
I love my family,
I love my friends.
I am proud, proud to be me.
I go to school,
I have a laugh,
I work hard, till the sun sets,
I play, I shout.

I don't care if you call me names,
I have confidence in myself!

This is me!
Will you ever accept me for me?

Victoria Speed (11)
Hurworth School, Hurworth

The Never-Ending Worlds

Stars are in the sky,
With the birds and the planes,
They are everywhere,
They are in the universe,
Are they in reverse?
That is the mystery of the world.

We are unsure of what is out there,
Other planets,
Other things,
Will it ever end?
Is there anything?

We rely upon our universe,
For everything we have,
It takes control of the sky,
It is big and mighty,
Too big for the eye.

Rebecca Buchan (14)
Hurworth School, Hurworth

The Weather

Some days it's sunny,
Some days it rains,
Why is the weather always a pain?

It blasts us with heat,
It shelters us in shade,
As the day starts to fade.

People always complain,
About the weather today,
But hey!
People will never be happy,
People will never be sad,
Weather around the world always changes,
And frankly, I'm glad.

Lucy Bramham (14)
Hurworth School, Hurworth

Can't Change The Past

'Never!' she cries,
Tears in her eyes.
As she runs away,
The sky going grey,
Leaving the past behind.

She believes what she believes,
Covered in leaves,
As the trees moult their last.
She thinks of the early past,
All of the fun,
And just one second with that
Gun!

She turns her head in shame,
Knowing she will get the blame.
Her friend,
The end.

Holly Fossitt-Darby (12)
Hurworth School, Hurworth

The Legend Sleeps

In the morning, the legend sleeps,
But in the night, it's awake.
Its name is not a long one.

Its name is Lugia,
It sleeps on the silver seabed
For most of the day and night.

Its body is mostly white,
But it has patches of blue
And nobody's sure if the legend is true.

If you dare come and see,
Don't anger it.
If you come near it, be kind,
If you are true, so it will be.

So sleep well, legend of the sea,
And never cause a storm.

Eloise Baldam (12)
Hurworth School, Hurworth

Music

Music is a brilliant, wonderful thing
A lot of fun and a bit of a sing

Music is happy, music is sad
Music is great, music is bad

Music is the loud screech of a guitar
Music is the excellent voice of a professional singer

Music is the movie soundtrack that sets the scene
It gives the impression if the character is kind or mean

Music it varies from rock 'n' roll
All the way to 60s soul

Music can be very, very fun
Listen to it in the rain or in the sun

Poems are music just like this one
But unfortunately now this poem is done.

Tom Jones (13)
Hurworth School, Hurworth

I Am A Monkey

I am a monkey
I swing from tree to tree
I want to be free!

I live in a cage
In the zoo
All I do is eat and poo!

I am a monkey
I swing from tree to tree
I want to be free

I jump around all over the ground
Can you see this is me?
I want to be free
So can you help me?

Harriott Hall (11)
Hurworth School, Hurworth

Jelly Beans

Some are yellow, some are green
We all like a good jelly bean.

Some are red, some are blue
I like anything that is new.

Some are purple, some are pink
I have eaten them all, at least I think.

Some are orange, some are jade
I wonder how each of them is made.

Some are clear, some are crystal
I make sure I always get a fistful.

Some are white, some are lime
I will get them all in good time.

Some are yellow, some are a bit plain
But despite that I still love them.

Ryan Hamilton (13)
Hurworth School, Hurworth

The Seaside

Waves crash down
As children paddle
Others eat ice cream
Some build castles

People burn whilst others tan
The summer air is breezy
Either way, suncream's the plan
For a perfect day in summer

Frisbees fly by
Little ones amazed
Beach balls blown up
For the summer games

That now sums up a seasidey day!

Sarah Conner (12)
Hurworth School, Hurworth

Life

There are some events,
That make your life,
Like the day you find,
Your amazing wife.

The seasons of spring,
The cold winter dawn,
To the leaves of autumn.

Some things,
Can make your week,
Others?
Can just be bleak.

I'd like to tell you,
That you'll be fine,
But honestly?
Your life's on the line.

Dave Smith (14)
Hurworth School, Hurworth

Swimmers Rule

Swim on a morning
Swim on a night
Jump in the cold lake
Get a big fright

Rule the pool
Swimming's cool
You win, you lose
'Take off your shoes!'

Technique, technique
Six times a week
Fly, back, breast, crawl
They're the strokes, I swim them all

In the pool
Life is cool
Swimmers rule.

Anna Brewster (13)
Hurworth School, Hurworth

Hunter

Lying in the grass, no sound can be heard,
The sound of breathing, is taken away by the morning breeze,
The enemy is in sight,
The rabbit's beady, black eyes stare right at me,
He cannot see me, he cannot hear me,
I am nothing to him,
Just a speck in the distance.
I line up my scope,
The wind will not affect the shot,
Death hangs over the creature by only a thread,
Unaware of the perils he will face, the rabbit doesn't move,
My finger over the trigger,
I breathe in, the sweat rolls down my face,
The rabbit falls gracefully to the floor,
One shot, that's all it takes,
Nature is cruel, but not as cruel as Man.

Nathan Maybrey (13)
Hurworth School, Hurworth

I Believe

I believe England can win the World Cup
I believe that a rocket will go up.
I believe people will stop bullying
I believe the bell will ding.
I believe that God is real
And that everybody is real.
I believe someone could help you
And you could help them too.
I believe the volcanic ash will go
I believe in something special
And every sentence has a capital.
I believe Darlington could win a game
And achieve a lot of fame.

I believe in everything
Do you believe too?

Lee Johnstone (12)
Hurworth School, Hurworth

I Want To Know - What's The Point?

Haven't you ever felt this way?
Where your entire life just seems to shatter in front of you?
Where you want to know - what's the point?
Why try? Why pick yourself up, only to be knocked down again?
This poem is for everyone who feels this way,
So this poem is for everyone,
Nobody goes through life without wondering - what's the point?
It is the feeling the world is against you,
Where you feel yourself melt into a spiralling mess of anxiety,
Pain and frustration.
You will have to go very far to find someone who hasn't felt this way.
If there is a soul in this world lucky enough not to know how it feels,
Let us all meet that person.
The only question I would ask that person is . . .

What's the point?

Thomas Metcalfe-Evans (15)
Hurworth School, Hurworth

Roxy!

My dog, Roxy
So cute, cuddly and crazy,
And a loyal ball of fun!

My dog, Roxy
Is out of control,
And nudges you
With her wet nose!

My dog, Roxy
Is cuddly and mischievous
And is big and skinny too!

My dog, Roxy
A black bundle of evil,
But I love her
All the same!

Sophie Hall (13)
Hurworth School, Hurworth

Guns

Guns, guns,
So dangerous,
Terrorist threatening,
Public giving up,
Gangs bring blood,
Terrorists bring hate,
Thieves bring hand guns,
That hide away,
Terrorists bomb,
Thieves steal,
Gangs fight,
Violence on the streets,
Guns, oh guns,
So strong
And lethal.

Adam Howell (12)
Hurworth School, Hurworth

Wars

War begins with hostility and hatred,
A debate between right and wrong.
Fighting and killing for nothing,
Forgetting the joyful meaning of life.

War is a cruel thing,
That tears families apart.
The long-lost days pass by,
Parents or siblings waiting for news,
Hoping for a miracle . . .

War is a death sentence for all the poor innocents,
Something we can't forget or take back.
What good does it bring?
It cannot mend a broken heart . . .
But it brings an eternity of pain and horrible memories.
War is inhuman and sinful.

Wars end - but lives are lost.
What will you tell your children?
Who was right or wrong?

Alice Mace (13)
Kelso High School, Kelso

The Great Swim

The expectations so high,
The chances so low,
The competition so great,
How fast can I go?

The building is so large,
The pool cleaned to perfection,
I can look in the water,
And see my own reflection.

The tension is rising,
I need to do well,
Can I win this?
I just cannot tell.

The warm-up has started,
The swimmers are piling in,
Practising their swims,
To pull out the win.

The pool as cold as the sea,
And is salty as it too,
I ask my coach, 'Can I pull out the win?'
She says, 'Yes, it's all up to you.'

I stand behind the blocks,
I'm ready to swim,
This is what I've been waiting for,
It's time to begin.

I look on one side of the pool,
And then at the other,
I can get there without any bother,
I just have to be quicker than all the rest.
I can't take it anymore,
This terrible pain in my chest.

I step up to the blocks,
How clean and dry they are,
I wait for the race to start,
There's no backing out now.

The shout is made,
I dive in as quick as a flash,
I may not win,
But I'll give it a bash.

One length out the way,
Now the second,
I look at my opponents,
It's so close to the end,
I hear the commentator scream my name,
I want this more than ever,
I touch the wall and look at the board,
My name's at the top,
I've won by a split second!

Alex Thompson (13)
Kelso High School, Kelso

What A Goal!

I hear the thudding,
They must be near,
The clacking of sticks,
The anticipation of the crowd.

Here we are,
In our shower of red,
Adrenaline pumping
Right through my bones.

They're running, passing, dodging, tackling,
Getting further up the pitch,
Smack! What was that?
Yes! Yes! Yes!

The crowd cheers,
We all run,
A fab hit,
We scored!

The ball loves their goal!
It's not yet visited ours . . .
Oh no!
They're coming, as fierce as ever!

No! We can't get back in time!
It's going, going, going into our goal . . .
She dives . . .

What a superb save!
The zero is still intact!
We're not sharing our goals with them!

The whistle blows,
We've won the match,
Our hockey team,
My favourite team.

Sarah Burton (13)
Kelso High School, Kelso

I Am . . .

I am the rivers,
Tweed and Teviot,
Curving and twisting
My way through the town.

I am the abbey,
A sacred and centuries-
Old building,
Standing tall.

I am the bridges,
Old and new,
Helping people cross
The water.

I am the square,
The centre of the town,
Thousands of feet
Walk across me.

I am the people of Kelso,
Old and young,
Making this town
What it is.

I am all of these things
And more.

I am Kelso.

Maia Lyall (12)
Kelso High School, Kelso

The First Race

The crowd so loud,
The sun so hot,
The other runners ready,
Me completely nervous.
The crowd goes silent,
100 metres in front of me,
The gun ready to fire,
Anticipation on all the runners' faces.
Me, ready to start,
All I can hear is the birds,
But nothing else.
My running spikes tight and ready,
My running number
Pinned onto my T-shirt
And ready.
My first race.
Butterflies kicking in.
'Set.'
Bang!
I'm pulling into 3rd,
Now 2nd,
Now 1st,
I've made it.
I couldn't be happier.
My first race done and dusted.

Daniel Chapman (13)
Kelso High School, Kelso

Dauner Through The Toon

Yonder in the fields,
Wee poppies in the breeze.
The schuil bairns laughing,
The smoking men coughing.
A dae ken whaur am gan,
Anywhaur but here.
I feel all alane,
But I just cannae gae hame.

Me mam sitting at the fire,
Me papa in his rocking chair.
It's as if I'm naewhaur to be seen,
Naebody seems to care.
When I get to the hills,
The wee lassie turns to me.
Wise beyond her years,
She scolds me and me stupidity.

Dauner through the toon,
Whatna way, today?
Richt or left, up or doun?
Meybe I'll stay here.
Until ma dying day,
I stood tall and still up on ye hill.
Naebody ever sees me,
Naebody ever seems to care.

Amelia King (14)
Kelso High School, Kelso

Jimmy

There wis a man,
His name wis Jimmy,
He lived in the Highlands,
The Highlands o' Scotland.

Wi his braw tartan kilt,
An' his sparklin' sporran,
He wis a richt sight wis Jimmy,
Aye, he'd leave ye gawpin'

And ye really really dinnae,
Wannae ha mess'd wi Jimmy,
Cus Jimmy's muckle muckle muscles,
Wid mak ye greet fir mammy,

An' ye'd ne'er see Jimmy,
Wi'oot his whiskey,
Always in his richt hand,
Swiggin' away, aw day,

But Jimmy isn'ae here the day,
Cus Jimmy's kicked the bucket,
After years af crazy living,
His hert just gave in,

There wis a man,
His name wis Jimmy.

Jack Bayram (15)
Kelso High School, Kelso

Bird's Eye View

As I look down on this beautiful town
I see people happy and people sad,
I see people celebrating and people reminiscing
I see people playing and people sitting.

As I look down on this beautiful town
I chime by the hour as people watch -
I see shops changing and people moving
I watch the fairs and festivals all year round.

As I look down on this beautiful town
I see seasons change -
I see the colder autumn and winter
I see the warmer weather of spring and summer.

As I look down on this beautiful town
I see buses departing and later returning,
I see people saying hello and then saying goodbye
I see people ending the day and others just starting.

As I look down on this beautiful town
I see some learning to talk and others learning to walk -
I see a town ever growing
I see a community of joyful people.

As I look down on this beautiful town
I see Kelso, the place where I want to be.

Monica Walker (12)
Kelso High School, Kelso

Scots Writing: Racism

Just as I wis daunering,
Daunering to work,
I hear the auld wifie crooning,
Crooning like a bird.
Cannae no understand me?
Well you're gonnae have tae try
I'll carry oan in my Scots,
For noe ye wull have tae try.
Daunering to work I see a laddie daffing,
Daffing with his lassie friend.
Ilka ilka day
I stand against the muckle tree
Sae I can watch the bonnie sight.
How they'll grow up one day
One day being a mither and fither
Ilka night in the hame sat with the wee bairns
Twae I refleck or maybe three whae minds? No me.
The laddie's bleck, the lassie's white
In towmond 2010
Gie ower tae refleck
Sould it metter o tha colour
Oor a tha same inside.

Sophie Douglas (14)
Kelso High School, Kelso

Aw A Wish That A Coud Gan

Oan yonder muckle mountain
Ah heard the bagpipes caa,
Ah heard the drummers drummin'
Marchin' ay tae war.

Aw, how ah wished that a coud join 'em,
But whit wid ma mither say?
She wouldna be tae happy
Or cheer me oan ma way.

Ma faither wid be prood o' me,
He'd say, 'Aff ye gan me lad.'
He'd ken ah wouldna come hame again,
But he wouldna be tae sad.

But alas ah cannae go
Fur a am much tae young.
The days 'til a can leave ur passin',
But they're takin' much tae lang.

'Til then a will stand upon the mountain
An' listen tae the pipes a pipin'.
Ah'll watch the armies march tae battle
An' imagin' a am fightin'.

Rebecca Mark (14)
Kelso High School, Kelso

The Sea

My waves roll upon the shore,
I shake the pebbles as I roar,
I am the home to a school of fish,
A group of hungry sharks,
And an almighty whale.

I curl up at the tip of my waves,
Ready to crash into the cliff,
I am the paddling pool,
To the kids,
And the view from Heaven.

I sparkle and shimmer,
As the evening sun,
Beats down upon me,
Calm and still I am,
For dangerous I can be.

As a crescent moon appears,
I settle as the sun goes down,
Gazing at the amazing sight,
For nobody can have my astonishing job,
Not even with a fight.

Kate Thomson (12)
Kelso High School, Kelso

The Sock Monster

There is one massive monster
That slips and slides
Around my room every night.
I can't get to sleep
Because of the noise it makes
It steals all of my odd, smelly socks
Out of my drawer at night.
This monster is named
The sock monster.

It is gigantic
With its rotten, yellow teeth
And huge, red eyes
Gazing at me in my sleep.
It leaves lots of green sticky trails
Around my room.
It lives inside my
Gigantic, black wardrobe.

The other night
It ate my cat.
I hope that one night it won't eat me!

Owen Campbell (13)
Kelso High School, Kelso

Ma Wee Friend Robin

As I wis daunderin' alang the road
I seen a wee robin wi' his reid brest
He leuked bale wi the cauld
Shiverin' on his fence post.
The pare wee thing came and sat on ma arm
He started twitterin' away to me
I suddenly started twitterin' back to him.
He got scared an' flew away.
I went daunderin' alang the road again,
But now a wis lonely without ma robin friend.

Rebecca Kerse (14)
Kelso High School, Kelso

Kelso Poem

The cobbled stones lie still on the roads,
While the town centre watches the square
Overseeing the parks.
Watching football, rugby and cricket too.

In the square,
The farmers' market is selling its goods
Nearby, is the old bridge
Which goes over the River Tweed.

The new bridge at the other side of Kelso
With cars rushing over it,
Also stands over the Tweed.

The town celebrations, every year,
St James' fair,
Civic week,
All get the town going.

The town hall clock and flagpole,
Are also important in Kelso,
But overall,
Kelso is a very enjoyable town.

Stuart Briggs (12)
Kelso High School, Kelso

My Granny

My granny is
Caring, loving,
She has white hair,
Blue eyes,
Her favourite colour
Is red, purple, pink,
Blue.

She is always tidy,
In her houses,
She is jolly and unforgettable,
She gets us everything we need.

She likes bingo,
She goes every night,
When she comes home,
She has some chips.
When we went on holiday,
She went to the bingo there.

My granny's name is Elizabeth Kellington.

Ashleigh Revel (14)
Kelso High School, Kelso

Jimmy The Goat

I wis daunerin doon the brae
When I saw a goat named Jimmy
I'd niver seen the like
A goat crooning ower me wumman
I spear him whit for,
And this he replied
I'd love yir wumman
She'd make me muckle meals
She'd make ma days aa richt
So I shoved him doon the brae
And I niver saw him yince mair.

Rory Connochie (14)
Kelso High School, Kelso

A Blood-curdling Nightmare!

Angels, asleep in their stimulating dreams,
No dark thoughts or doubts,
A dark shadow lurks behind them,
Haunted, haunted, haunted.

The demons' dance occurred in the garden,
Moving in and out of the moonlight,
A laughing face in your head,
You are haunted, haunted, haunted.

'Here they come to those who carry my bloodline!'
Words of the Devil spoken to his sons,
A creak of the door, then you know,
You know that you are haunted.

Angels, awake from their stimulating dreams,
Only to find horror and terror,
A laughing face, a demon, a devil,
Haunted . . .
Haunted . . .
Haunted.

Emma Smith (14)
Kelso High School, Kelso

The Sheepdug

'Twas a cauld, lang day,
but still plenty tae dae.
The wee dug was warkin hard,
Takin all o' the sheep tae the yard.
Wha else would dae his wark,
Nae time for any other lark.

Faither fand the dug aneath a tree,
Bleck in colour, we cawed it Bee.
Brought the dug hame . . .
Gave the dug a name . . .
Mither said he was a sheepdug,
We all thought the same.

Rain, snow or hail,
The dug never fails.
He will rin roun efter the sheep,
Roundin them up without a bleat.
Even now, he's getting auld,
He still does the wark, in the cauld.

Rebecca Rogers (14)
Kelso High School, Kelso

A Poem For Kelso

Rugby, football, cricket and golf,
They have done a lot for Kelso.
Rugby has provided Kelso with memorable matches
And disastrous defeats,
As well as the odd flop player.

KCC or Kelso Cricket Club,
A coaching set-up for kids of all ages,
The under 13s and under 15s produce great young players
And the adults fare just as good.

Kelso Football Club down at Woodside every week,
Black, white and red go well together in the shirts.
Too bad the players don't go well together!
And now it's time for golf.

The man calls 'Fore!' You know he's a golfer,
Next door to the golf course is Britain's friendliest racecourse,
The horses go round as the golfer hits down,
And guess what? He hit a hole in one!

Logan Palmer (12)
Kelso High School, Kelso

Walking Through The Town

Yin day I wis a walking,
Through the toon a squawking
Wi cars zoomin' by,
I heard my friend cry,
Archie,
Yer new boots er nae good fer talking.

I did good to reply,
They talked to this guy
As we walked ore the hill,
And I said that's one nil
Ta Archie,
But all he could say was, I.

Archie Lees (14)
Kelso High School, Kelso

Kelso's Big Events Poem

Kelso has two big vehicle events
Every year
One of the two big events is the
Honda Goldwings
The Honda Goldwings are big bikes
Every year the riders dress up their
Bikes with lights
Then they parade around Kelso with
All their lights flashing
The other big event is the Jim Clark Rally
Where lots of people come to see
Rally drivers and cars
From all over the UK
To race in tribute to the F1 driver
Who crashed into a tree and died
Normally the start and the finish are in Kelso
This year the start is in Duns
And the finish is in Kelso.

Kevin Wilson (13)
Kelso High School, Kelso

Poem About Sport Activities In Kelso

There are lots of sport activities in Kelso
Kelso also has lots of pitches and courses to play on
So if you like sports
Kelso is the place to go.

All the sport activities are great fun
There is rugby, football, golf, cricket and many more
There is Poynder and Croft Park to play rugby
Woodside Park to play football
The golf course to play golf and many more.

The sport activities are there for something to do
To keep you fit and healthy
To win medals and trophies
Lastly, just to enjoy it and have great fun.

So if you decide to come to Kelso
You must do at least one sport activity.

Aaron Walker (12)
Kelso High School, Kelso

A Poem About Floors Castle And The Bridges

Floors Castle has 365 windows,
One for every day of the year.
The Duke of Roxburgh lives in Floors Castle.
Floors Castle has a lot of land,
Floors has a lot to do with Civic Week.
Lots of visitors visit Floors Castle every year,
To see around the castle grounds,
Or sometimes even see inside the castle.

The River Tweed runs under the old and new bridges,
The new bridge has a bypass running over it.
The old bridge has two lights from Waterloo Bridge on it.
Hundreds of tourist flock every year
To see the Junction Pool where the Tweed and Teviot meet.
The Tweed eventually runs into the sea at Berwick-upon-Tweed.

Gordon Heatlie (12)
Kelso High School, Kelso

Wee Jimmy

I wis walking roond ti ma pal's hoose
Late yin windy night
And when I tirned the corner
I got such a bloomin fright.
There was a wee man dancing,
Jimmy was his name
He leaped and pas de basqued,
Heiland dancing was his game.
He jumped and hopped and leaped and rocked
And twirled aw ower the toon
He looked up to the stars
And sang ti the moon.
His dancing looked like fun ei ken,
So I joined in masel
And Jimmy and I danced aw night
Until the moon finally fell.

Zoe Young (14)
Kelso High School, Kelso

The Sock Monster

Where are my socks?
Someone has stolen them.
Now they don't match,
I must find out who took my socks.

It's not my family,
They have got their own.
It must . . .
It has to be . . .
The sock monster!

The only way you know he's there
Is if you smell his greasy hair.
He has eyes red as blood,
His hair is curly and dark as mud.
He has teeth sharp as knives,
Great for taking socks' lives.

Ryan Jarvis (13)
Kelso High School, Kelso

The Burgh Standard!

It is now my time to shine
The moment that is only mine
The Kelsea Laddie grips me tight
This is going to be a bonnie sight
We make our way into the square
A crowd of 500 must be there
The music changes, off we go
Lower and lower down I go
A bonnie young lassie meets me there
Tying the ribbon of freedom with care
The ribbon twists, turns and unravels
O, what a lovely sight
Higher and higher I go
'Dae Richt, Fear Nocht' is let out with a roar
I am the Burgh Standard.

Emma Gibson (12)
Kelso High School, Kelso

My Poem

Bullies, bullies, there they are,
Standing there in their non-uniform.

Looking as if they are dead hard,
Making sure that everyone is scared.

I walk closer, almost able to smell
That minty breath, I'm ready for their hurtful words.

I get closer, I can hear them shouting,
They're pouting.

They turn around and see me
And they are glaring at me.

I am trying not to look scared,
I am trying not to care.

I take a closer look,
Looking at me as if I'm a big, fat pud.

They come closer to me,
Drag me by my collar. I'm scared!

They take me into a room,
I struggle because I want to zoom!

I need to get away,
I pull and push to get away.

I see a fist,
I see a slap.

I feel a crunch,
I feel a punch.

They think they have won,
But wait to see what I have done.

I kick, slap, punch and shove,
I ain't gonna show them any love.

Big, small, fat, thin,
It's up to you, don't let them win.

Carrie Eaton (12)
Pensby High School for Girls, Heswall

Child Abuse

In the street, and through the city
Lives a young girl that I pity
It's hard to see a broken heart
But in her eyes she is falling apart
Messy curls and tear-filled eyes
Beneath her skin and behind the lies
Lives a shattered soul of pain
And it repeats again and again

Every day I hear her prayers
As she asks why no one cares
Her tearful cries call out at night
A voice of fear, dread and fright.
Don't make a sound! She's just heard a car
Her daddy is back from Chester's Bar
The screams I hear, I can't explain
As he slams the door and curses her name
This time he's had far too much to drink
And he's so drunk that he can't even think

He grabs her by her tattered shirt
And shouts, 'It's your fault I suffer at work!'
He violently throws her against the door
As he kicks her and hits her and yells at her more
'I'm sorry!' she screams, but it's far too late
His face is twisted with unimaginable hate
Then she calls out a pleading cry
'Oh God, please help me! I'm going to die!'

As he finally leaves her and heads for the door
Her body lies crookedly, sprawled on the floor
Scared, bruised, battered and beat
She's so weak, she can't stand on her feet
Everything's fading, the room's going dark
She's growing her wings, she's leaving her mark
An angel girl with an upturned face
Maybe now she's going to a better place.

Louise Dobbing (14)
Pensby High School for Girls, Heswall

Bessy

Bessy
Well, what can I say?
All the time we spent together
Seems to have gone away
But all the memories that I have will stay with me forever

Bessy
It is so easy to see
How lovely and friendly you were
In my heart you will stay with me
You and your golden fur

Bessy
In the car she was in the front seat
The radio would turn on and she'd nod to the beat
Mum would try to get her down
It never worked and she'd come to town

Bessy
When her food was in sight
She would take off in a flight
Never leaving any, she would eat it all up
And always ate as much as a pup

Bessy
I loved her special ways
A memory was shared with her each and every day
So friendly and fun
She loved lying in the sun

Bessy
Loved to lie in the wrong place
But we would forgive when we saw her face
The face that will stay
As she was great in every way.

Olivia Findlay (14)
Pensby High School for Girls, Heswall

My Cat Fudge

I stand in the garden
I gaze up at the sky
The clouds are grey
The rain falls heavily on the ground
Or is it the tears in which I drown?
My memories come flooding back to me,

The gleaming sun shines through the deepening mist
The shadow of my cat reflects on the ground
As she lies in the garden sunbathing
She is so gentle sleeping softly
I stroke her and she purrs
I tickle her and she purrs again,

When I came home from school she would be waiting
Waiting for her dinner
My cat always ate a lot
Salmon with carrots, that was her favourite
She licked her lips when she was finished
I knew she enjoyed what I gave her,

Her fur was such a lovely colour
Brown with ginger highlights
Her fur used to shine in the sun
Her eyes were big and round
Pools of deep green
Her pride was shown in her eyes.

Here I stand on my front lawn
Planting a rose -
In memory of my cat
I love to sit here on my front lawn
Remembering all the good times
The good times I had with my cat - Fudge.

Megan Gillen (14)
Pensby High School for Girls, Heswall

Soulless Passion

Inspired by 'Twilight' by Stephenie Meyer)

They're cold but warm,
Beautiful but feared,
They're lonely but loved,
Liked but jeered.

Two immortal enemies,
United by a human,
A werewolf and a vampire,
Hatred runs through them.

No one can live up
To the standard that they set,
It is a romance,
You will never forget.

The desire for her blood,
The hunger for his love,
The need for a friend.

His soulless passion,
Grows stronger day by day,
So he can fight the urge,
To make her his prey.

The Cullens are
So fast and smooth,
Yet strong and elegant,
In the way they move.

She looks into
His dazzling golden eyes,
And sees the real him,
Not his deep disguise.

Megan Rimmer (13)
Pensby High School for Girls, Heswall

Searching For The Heart

I'm looking, I'm searching,
And will the piece of my heart,
Ever find the other half?

I'm looking high, I'm looking low,
Will it always be lonely?
Will I always be lonely?

Searching for the heart,
Can it be this hard?
I'm losing patience,
I need to find it soon.

I know it won't be too long,
Good things are occurring,
Could he be the one?
Am I in luck?

There has always only been one,
Can I move on?
I'm going to be strong,
Even if I am wrong.

You only get one shot,
Try and make it right,
Once it's gone,
It's gone forever.

Searching for the heart,
It can be hard,
Be strong, be patient,
It won't be far.

Lucy Barker (14)
Pensby High School for Girls, Heswall

Standing Alone

Standing alone, along a grey path,
It's roaring and speeding fast,
When I see bright, burning eyes,
I'll start to remember my past . . .

Can I think? Can I feel?
Do they think I cannot hear?
I wish the bruises would fade away,
So I can disappear.

Should I be intimidated by my own classmates?
Because I know that they'll be waiting beyond the school gates.

I cannot go inside for lunch, I know they will be there,
I'm last out of class so they can't follow, could this really be fair?

My mother grounded me this week because I stole her money,
To replace torn books and folders. To you, is this funny?

I went off to school this morning, wearing a white T-shirt,
After school it's soaked, see-through, red and covered in dirt.

I try to run, to hide, to feel that wherever I may run,
That I can cry without the laughter of the friends that find this fun.

Friends? You ask. Friends, I said. The ones who laughed with glee?
Or perhaps the people who I thought I trusted who shall either join or flee.

Standing alone, along a grey path,
It's roaring, speeding fast,
When I see bright, burning eyes,
My pain . . . finally won't last.

Emma Carroll (14)
Pensby High School for Girls, Heswall

No Answer

Flowers, sunshine,
The bright, silver stars too,
These are the things that remind me of you.

Your warm, bright smile
That could brighten the day,
And a loving embrace to chase fears away.

I know you're still here,
But my heart tells me you're gone,
That this is your shell and your spirit's moved on.

Where are you now?
Are you happy or sad?
Is this new life you have, the same, good or bad?

Where you are now
Is the sun in the sky?
Do people wear smiles and the birds sing as they fly?

Or is it all dark,
With no moon or stars,
Nothing around, no streetlights or cars?

I know you are here,
That I can't forget,
But if I ask you a question, no answer will I get.

It hurts to see you this way,
And makes me want to cry,
For you told us long ago, that you would rather die.

Amber Bryce (14)
Pensby High School for Girls, Heswall

My Family

Well, there is my lovely big family,
We all live happily.
Then there's my grandma,
Who's obsessed with camels.
Then there's also my daddy,
Who is a number one Everton fan
Which inspired me to follow.

I love that I have a big family,
We all look out for each other.
Also the fact I only have one brother.
I love my mum,
Because she has always been there since I was born,
Because my dad wasn't.

I have four sisters,
They don't all live with me but I still see them.
We all look after each other.
They make me feel like I'm all wrapped up in a blanket,
When they leave I just think about the good times we had.

My grandad sadly passed away two years ago,
But he will forever stay in my thoughts.
He came down and saw us every other week,
He now has a tree on a golf course.

Even though I kick and scream,
I know you're really not that mean.
We are like a big sandwich all squashed together!

Anna Willis (13)
Pensby High School for Girls, Heswall

The Happy Ending

Those girls are always mean to her,
They push her around and pull her hair,
Is this the way to treat someone
Just because they're not number one?

They pick and prod and poke at every chance they get,
Nothing's ever right on her, no standards ever met,
They never really understood,
They always pushed her in the mud.

Some people just don't understand,
She really needs a helping hand,
She goes home and cries all night,
Sits alone full of fright.

Will anyone help her
Or will you forget about her without a care?
She always was so understated,
Always judged and isolated.

Then someone helped her back to the ground,
Then the bullies made no more sound.

She soon learned that life was worth living,
All about the happiness, joy and giving.
Now her life's on track,
There's no going back.

Won't let anyone bring her down,
Upon her face won't be a frown.

Jessica Flaherty (13)
Pensby High School for Girls, Heswall

The One-Way Friendship

Whenever you need me, you know I'll be there
When I need you, I know you won't care
The money I lend, you never give back
Like the friendship, we never had.

She is pretty, even I can see
But she's not pretty on the inside, unlike me
I know she is popular, but I wonder why,
Everybody knows your friendship's a lie.

We all have talents, we all have aims
But unlike you, we don't play games
Most good friends count on each other,
Not with us, why do I bother?

I tell you things, I wouldn't tell anyone
Arrive tomorrow, and you've told everyone,
I always truly depended on you
But you treat me like the dirt on your shoe.

I know I'm not everything, I know that well
I'm hurt inside, no one can tell
You don't have to like me, you don't have to share
All I want is someone to care.

It's only recently I took into account
How badly you treat me, I want to scream and shout
Our friendship's over now but this time it's not you,
For once, it's me, it's me, it's me.

Katie Williams (13)
Pensby High School for Girls, Heswall

Better Than A Best Friend!

I love how they do everything for me
They have been there since the start

Whenever I need them they are right there
I love everything about them and how they care

Life without, one word -
Unthinkable

I could never thank them enough
My mum is amazing, in fact she's more than that
She's my best friend!

She's the one who tells me to stand up for myself
She's the one who tells me what's wrong and right
She's the one who tells me I look beautiful at night
She's the one . . . I couldn't ask for a better friend

Whenever I feel like there isn't a care in the world
I look to them
And notice I'm wrong
I could never live without them

There are two words that completely equal this poem
And they are

My parents!

Whenever I need them
They are right there!

Courtney Leigh Brown (14)
Pensby High School for Girls, Heswall

It Hurts

Waiting for the time to come,
Waiting for the girl to run,
She puts her head down when she walks past the beasts,
Her little arms shaking as she tries to feast.

She says to her mum, 'I am ill.'
'Don't be silly, dear, you can take this pill.'
'But Mum, I am, I don't want to go to the death place.'
Her bag on her back, she walks with a slow pace.

Help me die,
I just can't survive,
I don't like this feeling,
I'm just revealing.

I have a little heart,
But not so little brain,
They think the words don't hurt,
They think the fists don't bother.

Those beasts aren't real, they just can't see,
The pain they give to 2 or 3.
When you are a bully,
You're a bully for life,
Don't go down that road,
Because it's not nice.

Milly Costello (14)
Pensby High School for Girls, Heswall

She Thinks She's It

Look at them just standing there,
Like a pack of wolves,
Glaring when young cubs walk past,
They are 'it' and they know they're 'it'.

Why do they do it?
Looking me up and down,
Masquerading themselves with lacquer,
They're not even allowed to wear it!

They're the teacher's pets,
Popular ones,
Ones with boyfriends,
And then . . .

There's me,
Standing alone,
No friends,
And no one to talk to.

Why can't I be like them?
In the mainstream,
I want to be wanted,
And I want to be needed.

I want to be them.

Jocelyn-Faye Cottrill (14)
Pensby High School for Girls, Heswall

Summer Days

Long days at the beach with sunny skies,
Going to the park, seeing colourful butterflies.
Music, movies and late nights,
Going on holiday and seeing the sights.

Those water fights are so much fun,
In the hot, electric sun.
Trying to make daisy chains,
Gazing up at passing planes.

Barbecues with family and friends,
Checking out the latest trends.
Eating vanilla ice creams
And having lovely daydreams.

Wearing massive sunshades,
Drinking icy lemonade.
Taking long, refreshing walks,
Whilst remembering those late-night talks.

Wearing shorts and vest tops,
Going into different shops.
Going camping or going away,
It's all fun on a summer's day.

Hannah Brisco (14)
Pensby High School for Girls, Heswall

Run Away

It's a lie,
The only love I share is with 'Ben and Jerry',
I miss you hugging and kissing me,
Being there when I need someone,
Being in a room with loads of people
And still no one to talk to.
It's like you have gone because I can't find you,
You've run to another planet,
Please come back, I miss you.

Millie Palfreyman (14)
Pensby High School for Girls, Heswall

Notice Me

I know what I can see
I know what I want to be
But when I count to three
I know you won't agree

I try to make you notice me
But I know you just don't see
I try to be like you
I just wish you knew

I try to be bad
But I know this just makes me sad
I just want you to notice me
Why can't you see?

I may be different than everyone
I don't know what I've become
I think about these days in the sun
And oh, what fun!

I realise now I don't have to be like you
And that is true
Now you notice me, but
I don't have to notice you.

Aimee Dodd (13)
Pensby High School for Girls, Heswall

My Wreck And My Ship

My life is a wreck
My heart is a ship
Yet we sail so swiftly
As I am soundly asleep

The wind on my face
The rain in my hair
Leads me closer and closer
So that I will soon be there

My life is a wreck
My heart is a ship
Yet we sail so swiftly
As I am soundly asleep

The wind in the sails
The rain on the boat
The engine isn't running
I am alone

My life is the land
My heart is the sea
As I set foot on Earth
I am now free.

Anne-Alicia Guignaud (11)
Pensby High School for Girls, Heswall

The Sad And Lonely Dog

I'm hungry and feeling sad,
My owner neglects me, he is angry and mad.
My fur is dirty, tattered and knotted,
My sores are infected with flesh that has rotted.

A pat, a stroke, a loving hand, someone who cares,
I don't deserve the way I live,
I have so much love to give.

I yap and bark in the rain,
The singing bird really knows my pain.
I wait for days and days
For someone to just come and play.

I am tied up outside
Nowhere to hide,
Feeling so empty inside.
Someone comes to untie me,
I might, once again be free.

They take me to a place where I will be cleaned up,
I look like a cute little pup.
Then I am put in some sort of cage, they lock me in,
Then I can see them hold up a needle with a tiny pin . . .

Sera Davies (14)
Pensby High School for Girls, Heswall

I'm Losing You!

Sometimes I'm angry,
Sometimes I'm mad,
Sometimes I'm happy
And sometimes I'm sad.
Sometimes I laugh,
Sometimes I cry,
But sometimes I feel like
I need to die!

I jump off a bridge,
And break my spine,
Because I know you'll,
Never be mine!

I see you in my dreams,
I see you in my mind,
All I keep on saying is,
That this love is blind!

I see you with her
And it is breaking my heart,
Jealousy runs through my veins
And it's tearing me apart!

Shelleyy Kangurr (14)
Pensby High School for Girls, Heswall

The Dark, Lonely Corner

As I sit in the dark, lonely corner,
As I turn my head to the left,
As I see another child in tears,
As I look up at a dark, gloomy figure,
As I lose my strength to cry.

As children watch me helplessly,
As I fall to my death,
As my head smacks to the floor,
Adding another bruise or two,
As mysterious laughs come from above.

As I push myself up with my last bit of strength,
As I walk back to my dark, lonely corner,
As I watch other children get the same abuse,
As I am afraid to call out,
As I look over and see children in tiny, shabby cells.

As I shut my eyes,
As children squeal in pain,
As I wait for the new day,
To hit me in the face.

Rachael Holden (12)
Pensby High School for Girls, Heswall

Be Your Own Person

Be your own person
Don't follow the crowd
Don't be all for the fashion
Difference is allowed
Speak what you see
And not what others hear
But don't reveal the secrets
Of a friend or peer
Don't hide behind the band
Don't shy away
Take your stand
Reveal your way
Ignore simple ridicule
But report sharper spite
Don't be afraid
To back away from a fight
Be your own person
As I am me
I am my own person
And always will be.

Catherine Entwistle (12)
Pensby High School for Girls, Heswall

Racism

Racism and discrimination lead to life devastation,
Whatever race, black or white, we all have the same right,
The right to laugh,
The right to cry,
The right to smile,
The right to sigh.
One name is all it takes to take the smile and laugh away,
But one nice word will make their day.
Maybe you should say:
Your hair is nice,
I like your style,
You should be proud,
I like your smile.
Listen guys, we're all the same and life is just a big, huge game,
Just different colours and different names.
If it wasn't for that, no one would be in love,
Have best friends or be original.
I don't want that, I like it the way it is.
Please, just think what you say . . .
Before you go and say it!

Melissa Pearson (14)
Pensby High School for Girls, Heswall

Lads

You act like you're hard around your friends
You laugh at people who you don't know
You make people feel like they're two feet small.
You skit at them
You say things to people to make them cry
You make me feel like you don't care
You make me feel empty inside
You show off with them all the time
You don't think about anyone else but yourself.
But you're not always like that
When it's me and you,
You make me feel special
You take an interest
You listen to me
You make my wishes come true.
You make me laugh
You care about me
You love me.
You act like my world is your world.
I wish it was always this way.

Eden Halligan (13)
Pensby High School for Girls, Heswall

Fear Of The Mind

For every mind there is always a fear
A horror so clouded, dark and unclear
Clawing away at emotions on high
Snapping and fighting, refusing to die.
A cold, distant thought, so painfully real
All my happiness it would willingly steal
It plays to my mind till I can bear no more
Destroying the thoughts I ought to adore.

Hopes and dreams are pushed aside
Along with the things I try to hide,
The fear I bear knows not the real me
It is too focused on misery to see.
It grows ever stronger, leaving me weak
Its dark potential menacingly unique.

When I try to unmask my fear
I usually find that the message is clear,
I should not fear something as strongly as this
For dreams and laughter surely exist.

Sophie O'Brien (13)
Pensby High School for Girls, Heswall

The Bully

I look over to my right, she is standing there.
Why does she pick on me? It really isn't fair.

I stay where I am, trying to hide,
Many scared thoughts going through my mind.

Another victim is looking up at her now.
He's half the size of her, she's as big as a cow.

How I feel sorry for him as she makes him cry.
If she did that to me, I think I would die!

I finally feel happy as she lets him run away,
But I know it will be my turn at the end of the day.

Elena Davies (11)
Pensby High School for Girls, Heswall

I Love Music

Dance, hip hop, R'n'B
The music I listen to is what makes me.
Rock, punk and rap too
We can listen to it, just me and you.

Sometimes I like to lie on my bed,
Listening to the words spinning in my head.
I could listen all day long
To that catchy, addictive, same old song.

Looking up to the rainy skies
Slow, cold music brings tears to my eyes.
But then comes along the summer sun
This calls for music that can bring on the fun.

In my room dancing around
Wrapped up in this musical sound.
Music is a drug that can amend
Hoping that my supply will never end.

Lauren Thomas (14)
Pensby High School for Girls, Heswall

Saying Goodbye

As we travel through the sky,
I think of a way to say goodbye.
As I fly past the moon and stars,
My experience is getting more bizarre.

Now I can see a planet or two,
They start to remind me of me and you.
Mars, Jupiter, Venus as well,
I'm really sorry I've put you through hell.

I wish you could be with me until the end,
I wish you still wanted to be my friend.
I'm sorry if I hurt you, you know I truly am,
I've never had a friend like you; you're as sweet as jam.

Phoebe Knight (14)
Pensby High School for Girls, Heswall

Stop Animal Cruelty

The dog said . . .

I'm sitting here wagging my tail,
Ready for the long night trail,
My owner's face long and frail,
I'm left abandoned on the midnight rail.

The cat said . . .

I sit at the door,
Tapping my claws,
Hoping for someone to open the door.

The horse said . . .

I stand here all alone,
Waiting for my owner to come home,
I haven't been washed,
I haven't been fed,
I haven't even had a chance to live a long and happy life.

Fiona Cook (12)
Pensby High School for Girls, Heswall

Alone In A Corner

Today again I sat in my lonely corner,
My life couldn't get any worse,
Taking my money, thinking it's funny,
It's like my life is a curse.

Tomorrow has more to come,
Hitting, punching, slapping me,
Shouting abuse like there is no tomorrow,
I wish they would just leave me be.

Every night I walk home,
Followed by my enemies,
I feel like screaming out, 'Help!'
Soon these'll be bad memories.

Shannon Gateley (14)
Pensby High School for Girls, Heswall

The Intimidation Game

As soon as I hear the door slam,
I know they're home,
Heavy footsteps pound up the stairs,
Screaming voices shout my name,
Maybe they won't hurt me today,
Maybe they'll forget,
I try to phone for help,
They have blocked my phone,
I try to scrape the paint off the windows,
Only for it to be repainted,
I do my homework for it to be ripped up,
Why would they do this?
If they knew they didn't want me,
Why did they become parents?
Wait. Something just happened downstairs.
What was it?
Silence.

Elizabeth Frost (14)
Pensby High School for Girls, Heswall

Darkness

The darkness of the night, I ran into alone
Everything around me frozen, all into stone.
With no one by my side, darkness will rule again.
The blackness of my thoughts, echoing in my brain.

Realising again. The coldness is sinking in.
All I loved means nothing now, coldness sinking in.
I know the time is nearing again, bearing with the thought,
Though I can't surrender now, so onwards I fought.

The darkness inside, now tearing into my soul,
My final tears of life, dripping, filling the bowl.
The creatures of death come, my shoulders they jump on,
Stealing love from my heart, all emotions are gone.

Rachel Meyer (12)
Pensby High School for Girls, Heswall

Fight

The air is clear, not a cloud in sight,
But there is grey in the distance of an oncoming fight.
Thunder crashes, absorbing the light,
Loud and clear, shaking the once peaceful land.
Lightning bright, brief flashes of hate,
The clouds clear, the sun returns,
But boiling heat quickly gobbles the happiness that was to return,
As if being thrown into a boiling pan.

The air is clear, not a cloud in sight,
But then once again swords clash.
There is no good or bad, only each side,
Red eyes glaring from both sides.
Why is there such madness?
Thunder growing louder until everyone hides themselves,
I feel like darkness shrouds me,
When my friend has a fight.

Jessica Harrison (11)
Pensby High School for Girls, Heswall

Suffering In Silence

It's such an evil glare
When you give me that stare
When you give me that nudge it makes me blush
I only need one final push
You don't care how I feel
My wounds will never heal
They say it's all in my head
All of what you said
You stand there proud and tall
Trying to knock down my safety wall
I never let out a single sound
You constantly knock me to the ground
Sticks and stones will break my bones . . .

. . . words will *always* hurt me!

Olivia McIvor (13)
Pensby High School for Girls, Heswall

Shooting Star

I was lucky to have you
Even though it wasn't as long as I wanted
I think of the laughs we had together
I think of the memories we had
I think of all the ice creams
And our walks through Park Gate
But now they're all just memories
Like a shooting star they went away
Now my life feels like an hourglass
It drags and each day is like a grain of sand
The day that he was gone
The day that my life changed
The day my soul went away
That moment I found out my heart dropped
I felt alone, I wondered how I could do it on my own
The day that my dad died was the day I was no longer whole.

Victoria Daley (14)
Pensby High School for Girls, Heswall

Friends For Life

What did I do?
What did I say?
Why do I seem to be in your way?
Friends till the end
That's what I thought
Whether you were right or whether you were wrong
I stood by you, we were friends all along
We have had good times
None are bad
We help each other
When we are sad
You're a needle in a haystack
True friends are hard to find
That's why I'm glad to call you mine.

Jessica Wade (14)
Pensby High School for Girls, Heswall

Forever And A Day

Now those days have all gone away
But in my heart is where they will stay
Even though you're gone, you will always be in my heart
All the memories we shared will never part
I remember the days I spent with you
Fun and laughter with just us two
You weren't only a grampa, you were a friend as well
When I was upset and lonely you could always tell
Love and affection you always gave
Will remain with me beyond the grave
The warmth inside when you are in my mind
Your love and happiness wasn't hard to find
Everything about you will stay with me forever and a day
Even though you're gone all our memories will stay
I look up to the sky and know you're there
And you are cherished and loved everywhere.

Anya Clarke (13)
Pensby High School for Girls, Heswall

Lyrical Poem!

I wish you were here
With me today
To make my tears
Go away

To make me laugh
Until I cry
And the fun we have together
Will make time fly by

To help with my homework
And make me nice tea
I hoped that you would always
Be here for me.

Jennifer Rule (14)
Pensby High School for Girls, Heswall

Digital Update - The Seven Stages Of Humans
(Inspired by 'As You Like It' by Shakespeare)

All the world's a screen
And all the people merely pixels
They have their off and on buttons
And every pixel has many roles
Their roles being seven ages
At first the morning television
Consisting of children's shows
And the news
Then the mid-morning television
Made up of chat shows
And house finders
Then the midday television
Antiques shows and political
Shows galore
Then the afternoon television
Primarily aimed at a
Child audience, consisting
Of cartoons and game shows
Then dinner time television
The enigmatic drama shows
Filled with action and adventure
Satisfying people's appetites
Then the pre-watershed television
Sad soaps, serious stories on
Politics and crime
Finally the after-watershed television
Adult programmes not for kids
The off button is pressed
The screen goes off.

Craig Barclay (14)
Stonelaw High School, Rutherglen

Internet Era Storybook

(Inspired by 'As You Like It' by Shakespeare)

All the world's a storybook
And all the people merely tales.
They have their beginning and end and life and death
And every character has many roles.
Their roles being seven ages.
At first the infant baby crawling by itself, having nothing to worry about. He's happy, joyful.
Then he's no longer the infant who barely talks nor walks.
Then the schoolboy who moans to school,
At times cheerful, at times he finds things hard.
He wanders to school, talking to his friends,
Enjoying life, staying strong whilst growing.
Now the teenager, skipping classes, getting into trouble
And then fooling around, staying out day till night.
And then the freedom. For themselves.
A big leap for a man and making choices on their own.
Working hours. Providing and hunting for money.
Finding new things and making a name.
Now in the middle age,
Becoming a manager,
Living life to its fullest.
Enjoying money each day and living in a luxury house.
Finding love, two bonds of partnership.
And then finally becoming old,
Just like an infant.
Weak, tired, not doing things on your own.
Sometimes you may think back on times that you had and shared,
Wishing you were young again.

Edwina Atiso (14)
Stonelaw High School, Rutherglen

The Seven Ages Of Man - Updated

(Inspired by 'As You Like It' by Shakespeare)

All the world's a man's head
And all the people merely hairs
They are grown and cut off
And every hair has many purposes
Their purposes being seven ages . . .
At first the wisp on the baby footballer
Laughing and shouting as they kick a ball into 2 foot high goals
Then the spike of the cheery schoolboy
Running and jumping all over the place
Eating sweets until they throw up
Now the dyed hair of the grumpy teenager
Mumping and moaning at the smallest task
Choosing which social group to be in
Then the conforming hair of young adult
Unemployed, single and partying every second night
Spending more time in the Job Centre than their home
After this, the greying, middle-aged man, making lots of cash
Contrasting his time between his boring job and his bouncing family
He shows off his flashy Mercedes and his new Dell laptop
To his old school friends
Next the whitening OAP
Wishing their family would come and visit
Moaning about everything from the price of digestives
To the prime minister
Now the final age, wispy then baldness
The razor's had its way
There's no more hair.

Gordon Wynne (13)
Stonelaw High School, Rutherglen

The Seven Ages Of Man - Updated

(Inspired by 'As You Like It' by Shakespeare)

All the world's a camera
And all the people merely pictures
They can all be 'printed and deleted'
And every picture captures a role
The role being seven ages.

At first the chubby, dribbling, hairless
Baby, chewing Mum's car keys.

Then the snapshot of a scared schoolboy,
Wandering the school yard looking for friends.

Now the tabloids teenager,
Only caring about booze and girls.

The picture seems less colourful as he moves out,
Worrying what he will do once he matures
Buying a car and paying the bills.

Middle age, a sepia, luxurious colour,
Making his own cameras now,
Living in luxury with many kids in his way.

Next the picture turns black as the pension comes in
And bingo is the way.
It seems not yesterday he was partying away.

Now the picture fades and the printing has stopped,
The camera has run out of batteries and someone else's life begins.

Steven Mulligan (14)
Stonelaw High School, Rutherglen

The Seven Ages Of Man - Updated

(Inspired by 'As You Like It' by Shakespeare)

All the world's a road
And all the people are drivers
Some have fast cars, some have slow cars
And every driver has many roles
Their roles being seven ages . . .

At first the toddlers in their big, red push cars
And their beloved teddies playing the part of the passenger
Then the snotty schoolboy
Thinking he's cool on his BMX
Down at the BMX track every day after school
Now the boy racer
In his cheaply modified car
Impressing the ladies on a Saturday night
And now the mature adult
One has a high flying job driving his Ferrari
Or Lamborghini
The other working 9 to 5 driving his cheap
Hatchback
Finally the OAP
On the bus with his pass, picking up his pension
And all of his pills to keep him happy
Then the final age
All their cars break down
Then they can't go anywhere.

Fraser Doonan (13)
Stonelaw High School, Rutherglen

The Holiday Era
(Inspired by 'As You Like It' by Shakespeare)

The entire world is a beach
And all the people merely grains of sand
They have their 'high tides' and 'low tides'
And every grain has many roles
Their roles being seven ages . . .
At first the dribbling baby,
Stumbling about in a pile of toys
Then the naughty schoolboy
Bored out of his mind in class
Running home with his cut knee
Now the teenager
An expert in wait-behinds and suspensions
Taking an energy drink
After being at a friend's for a night
And now the home leaver, unhappy in a job
Feeling weaker every day, hardly surviving
Now in the middle age, high up in business
Spending all of his money on cars and drink
Next the OAP
Complaining about his pension
Comparing prices before his final purchase
Now the final age
The waves roll in
The sand is gone.

Morven Bell (13)
Stonelaw High School, Rutherglen

The Seven Ages Of Man - Updated
(Inspired by 'As You Like It' by Shakespeare)

All the world's an Xbox
And all the people merely players
They have their inserts and ejects
And every player has many roles
Their roles being seven ages
At first the newbie
The newbie playing with his V-tech
Then the Game Cube
Making gestures to the other players
A moody player screaming down at the TV
Now the PlayStation
Specialising in very different tactics and getting the win
Taking too many energy juices
After an 'all nighter'
And now the PlayStation 2, facing improvements
Living in his room, just surviving on game play
Now the Xbox, new programming in the system
The casual look with its green and black colour
Splashing his games on different times each night after work
Next he plays chess
Challenging other people
Complaining about tea
Now reading, he turns the page
The story is done.

Alistair Moore (13)
Stonelaw High School, Rutherglen

The Ways Of Nature

(Inspired by 'As You Like It' by Shakespeare)

All the world's a flower
And all the people merely petals
Blossom in the spring and die in winter
And every petal has a purpose
Their purpose being seven ages
First a sapling
Getting its nutrients from the gardener's hand
Then a bud
Trying to blossom to see golden sun
Now a full blossomed flower
Showing off its beauty
Bragging in the wind to its less coloured cousins
Then the flower that's fighting the wind
But is getting weaker every day
Losing its bright colours
Gaining brown leaves
Watching life fade away
Now a hunchbacked weed
Looking down to the petals it has lost
Finally a decayed stalk turning back into dust
Dissolving into the dirty soil
Waiting to be seen again.

Sarah Malorie Ali (13)
Stonelaw High School, Rutherglen

Digital Discovery

(Inspired by 'As You Like It' by Shakespeare)

The entire world's a television,
And all the people are merely pixels,
They have their digital age and their analogue age.
And every pixel has many roles,
Their roles being seven ages.
The plastic toy enthusiast,
That dribbles down their property,
Then the Xbox-addicted schoolboy,
Shooting his foes online,
Now the taunting teenager,
Mocking people for their misfortune,
Then comes the so-called grown man,
Worried at the sight of a frying pan,
The middle-aged man, crisis and all,
Only thing he's good at is kicking a ball,
The OAP,
Finding it hard to walk down the hall,
Now the final age,
The pixel is burnt out,
The screen goes blank.

Jack Fell (13)
Stonelaw High School, Rutherglen

The Seven Ages Of Man - Updated

(Inspired by 'As You Like It' by Shakespeare)

All the world's a board game,
And all the people merely players.
Each has their beginning and end
And each has many turns.
Their turn being seven goes . . .
At first the beginning,
Getting a quick start,
Then the anxious turn,
Attempting to catch up.
Now to being a rebel
And cheating all the way.
Then comes the serious one,
Trying to win at all costs
And here comes the loser,
Time to make or break.
The restless one comes next,
Complaining about everything there is.
And now we are back to the start,
Ready to begin the game, again and again.

Amber Mohammed (13)
Stonelaw High School, Rutherglen

Jealousy In Love

Music strikes as a fuel for love,
We understand each other better than the heavens above.
Now don't get stressed dear,
Don't get jealous,
I'll turn around and notice I'm being rebellious.
For him I'd do anything but don't get stressed dear,
Don't get jealous.
I'll turn around to notice I've lost everyone.
My stubbornness, my stupidity,
Now I've noticed the toxicity
Of love.

Amy Barlow
The Elton High School, Bury

Grateful Apology

As I grew up, I was told,
To always say sorry even if inside you're stone cold.

Later on though, a teacher told me,
'If you don't mean it, don't say sorry.'

What do the adults expect me to do
When they don't give me one message about something
But they give me two?

'Actions speak louder than words'.
Guess what this one is telling me?
Don't even bother saying sorry.

Now I don't know how to do the right thing
And believe me, it hurts more than a jellyfish sting.

'Lessons are learnt from saying sorry'.
This is not one I'm trying to get rid of in a hurry.

Now that has made me realise what to do,
When I've said sorry, I will also say thank you.

Qurat-Ul-Ayn Fatima (14)
The Elton High School, Bury

What Does It Mean To Me?

Why is there world hunger?
What does it mean to me?
Why are people living in poverty?
They should have a suitable home,
They shouldn't be starving!
What does it mean to me?
My family and friends are the world to me.
I have pets, a suitable home,
I guess I'm lucky.
Some people don't have this as often you may see.
You can tell that all of this means something to me.

Chloe Hunt (13)
The Elton High School, Bury

Gone And Come Back

Mum she went and there was the girl
Alone with one dark life.

Cold and small she lay, with someone
Coming close, a spark of joy and a
Shine of a shoe!

Maybe a message for her, maybe a
Ghost walking by, music in the air and
Closer and closer she came.

It was her, was it? She knew who she
Was, her arms opening wide, the
Joy of her face shone like a star.

She gave her a hug, her life was
Luxury and tears ran down her
Face. Then her life was good
Again and Mum no longer had
Any pain.

Charlotte Paterson (13)
The Elton High School, Bury

Back In Your Day

Being held in the limelight
Apparently it wasn't always this bad
Being told we are not right
Old folk saying, 'Back in my day'
Old folk not understanding
That now their time has passed
Old folk keep demanding
That their time was meant to last
Being disliked by those that don't know me
Being restricted by those that don't own me
Being told we are doomed to fail at anything we try
The youth of today being moulded, moulded like clay
Forever in another's shadow, wishing you were someone else.

Thomas Critchley (14)
The Elton High School, Bury

Rabbits

Fluffy, cute and really small,
They answer to your every call.
They stay in a little hutch,
Softness in every touch.
Eyes as cute as can be,
Hopping with ultimate glee.
White, black and grey fur,
In the dark the foxes lure.
In the hutch the rabbits lay,
Nice and cosy in their hay.
Food and water all prepared,
Not as if they really cared.
Veg fed to them as a treat,
Ruby has the red eyes,
Missy has the brown,
But to me they both wear the crown.

Alisha Wroe (13)
The Elton High School, Bury

Jaiden

My cousin, Jaiden, is such a cutie
I could eat him up in-between brown bread
He smells so sweet, it's almost quite fruity
Wherever he is, he'll always be fed
I only see him one day of each week
He comes running with open arms and laughs
I love him so much, I want to keep him
When he is older I will teach him maths
We have a draught excluder he thinks is a snake
His favourite toy is Thomas the train
On special occasions we have a cake
We don't let him play outside in the rain
That special little boy is such a star
He can't say Charlie yet, so calls me Char.

Charlie Dawson (13)
The Elton High School, Bury

I Can't Write Poems!

I'm not very good at writing rhymes,
No super ideas pop into my head,
Although I try at it all the time,
It's almost as if my brain has gone dead.

I get no ideas from my best mate,
Also my imagination has gone,
Then I thought, so far this poem was great,
So I've decided it will carry on.

I could write about a lot of good days,
Like when we were on the scorching hot beach,
Or when we were in a castle and got chased,
Or I might write a few lines about each.

Now I've decided that poems are like friends,
And I will make this one come to an end.

Luke Richardson (12)
The Elton High School, Bury

Daydreaming For Love

The sun blazes across a deep blue sky,
It brings a brilliant smile to my face
And a very happy glint to my eye.
Lying in a field, in an open space,
Breathing in the freshest, sweet summer air.
My mind wanders to where it always goes,
I see her face, brown eyes, pale and red hair
And I think, surely she already knows
That I love her dearly with all my heart
And that we are meant to be together?
Hopefully, we shall never grow apart.
So as I lie here in gorgeous weather,
Mind wandering in the middle of May,
I hope to goodness she'll love me back one day.

Billy Nuttall (13)
The Elton High School, Bury

I Am Me And Me Is Mine

I am me and me is mine!
I love my M8s, I don't like crime!
I am me and me is mine!
I don't care but I don't mind.
I am me and me is mine!
You can call me whatever you want
But I don't care, you say it's for fun.
I am me and me is mine!
Mi 'n' Chloe, Livi, Abz 'n' Jen.
BFFs right till the end.
Me is me and me is mine!
OMG just leave us alone.
But I have my M8s to lol wiv me,
To laugh it off and help me be!

Leah Nicholson (12)
The Elton High School, Bury

My Name Is Sophie Lou

My name is Sophie Lou
There's lots of things I like to do
Including rounders and basketball
And even shopping at the mall.
My brother's called Nate and my mum is Shell
When we go out we get on quite well.
Gary is my dad
He's a tad mad.
I go to Elton and live in Bury
My favourite meal is chicken curry.
All these facts I have written are true
I dedicate them especially to you.
My name is Sophie Lou!

Sophie Young (14)
The Elton High School, Bury

What I Am

I am not a musician, I just like to listen to music.
I am not soft, I just don't fight.
I am not poor, I just don't have designer clothes.
I am not a bookworm, I like to read books.
I am not unloveable, I just haven't found the right person.
I am not stressy, I just keep my anger concealed.
I am not weird, I just like different stuff.
I am not closed up, I am free,
Free to express myself amongst other people.
I like what I like and hate what I hate.
It's what I am.

Chloe Hutchinson (14)
The Elton High School, Bury

People Change

BFFs till the end?
BFFs 4eva on end?
Side by side, come on then,
Erm, but no . . .
People change but M8s don't
People change friend by friend
People change in every way
But what happened?
What went wrong?
People change but I don't!

Lucy Pilling (12)
The Elton High School, Bury

I Love . . .

I love my bed, it keeps me warm at night,
I love cuddles, when they are so close and tight.
I love football, it's my favourite sport to play,
I love friends, I listen to what they say.
I love singing, even though I'm not very good,
I love 'Twilight' with vampires and all the blood.

I love my family, they're always there for me,
I love chocolate, I'm sure you'll all agree.
I love holidays, especially to Spain,
I love watching telly, though sometimes it can be lame.
I love my best friend, I'm always there for her,
I love my cat, she's so cute when she purrs.

As you can see, I love a lot of things,
However, there is nothing I love more
Than all my friends and family.

Lisa Hale (13)
UCE Academy, Ellesmere Port

Holiday!

I am waiting for my holiday,
It's going to be as fun as playing with my friends!
It is not far away,
I am counting all the days,
I am counting day by day,
I am going to go on holiday,
I am going to go to Spain,
I am going to enjoy my holiday,
Hope it doesn't rain.
When it ends,
I'll still enjoy my life,
Even if it sprinkles down with rain,
If it does, when will it end?

Jake Morris (12)
UCE Academy, Ellesmere Port

Fireworks

Love is like a firework,
You set it up then light it
And wait till it goes off.
When it does,
It's a beautiful sight to see.
But when it goes out,
You feel depressed
And that no one loves you anymore.
But every year that firework
Will go up into the sky
And back down again.
You're never alone,
So never feel that way!

Zoë Bell (12)
UCE Academy, Ellesmere Port

Friends

How did we even become friends?
How do we know our friendship will never end?
We laugh, we joke,
We have water fights and get soaked.
We have our fall-outs,
We can always find a way with no doubt.
Friends are forever
And we will always stick together.
When we are bored and have nought to do,
We had snow and made an igloo.
We are all such good friends,
We hope our friendship will never end.

Shannon Witkiss (14)
UCE Academy, Ellesmere Port

My House!

My house is a quiet house until I come home,
Telly on, music playing, talking on the phone.
Mum and Dad think elephants have moved in
When I'm dancing in my room,
I like it nice and tidy, but I'd never pick up a broom!
I love my cats, they think they are the queen,
All they do is eat, sleep and clean.
I love my house, it's my special place,
It's like chocolate-coated strawberries
And chocolate-coated dreams.

Amy Clough (14)
UCE Academy, Ellesmere Port

Triumphant

To conquer your fears
With your head held high
And face adversity like a raging bull
To come out on top
To get a strike in life
To feel like you won
To get the high score
To be on top of the world
To feel triumphant.

Alex Gee (12)
UCE Academy, Ellesmere Port

Family

I love my family,
They're caring and kind,
They are always on my mind.
They think I'm crazy,
They think I'm lazy,
But they love me all the same.

Leila Rennie (13)
UCE Academy, Ellesmere Port

That's Not The Point

Their stomachs turned,
Their hearts burned
When they saw.
They tried to ignore,
They were only desperate,
But that's not the point.
Well, it now comes to the end.
Just be safe,
Just like the others . . .

Connor Antill (12)
UCE Academy, Ellesmere Port

Love

Happy face, jumping around
The pretty face in the sunset.
They can see a man and a dog
They are kissing under the sunset.
Walking happily and holding hands
And singing a song.
Phoning everyone up to say
They are going to be together forever!

Roxy Williams (12)
UCE Academy, Ellesmere Port

Love

Happy, smiley face
Bright red face
Wearing pinkish dress
Skipping along
Using a lovely voice
Sitting in red cushioned room
Speaking on the phone for hours
Telling each other how they love one another.

Karolina Dobler (12)
UCE Academy, Ellesmere Port

The Straightener Poem

My straighteners are broke, it's not fair
That means I have to go to school with frizzy hair
I know it's a mess, I have to confess
They're great tools, but sometimes break the rules
I love my straighteners, they're so cool
People who don't straighten their hair are just complete fools
I've got new straighteners, they're even better than my last pair
Now I can go to school with nice straight hair.

Hayley Rice (14)
UCE Academy, Ellesmere Port

Love

Happy face
Brown hair and red eyes
Pink and red dress
Walks poshly
Speaks slowly
In the bedroom
Looking at the bed and the table
Kissing.

Sophie O'Rourke
UCE Academy, Ellesmere Port

Bike

On my bike I go to the skatepark,
On my bike I go really far.
Up and down in the air all day,
Land a new trick, I say hooray.
Land a tuck no-hander, what a trick!
That was super quick.
Maybe one day I'll be a pro,
I hope no one will say no.

Ashley Dutton (12)
UCE Academy, Ellesmere Port

BMX Poem

BMXing is my life
Every time I pull a trick
I think it is pretty sick.
I like to ride for fun
But only in the sun.
I never ride in the rain
Because if you slide it's a lot of pain.

James Cunningham (12)
UCE Academy, Ellesmere Port

Love!

I walked down the streets like a leaf
Flowed down the stream!

As I walked towards the house
My heart raced like a car raced around the track.

They tried to ignore what they saw!
Would that be the end or around the bend?

Rebekka Clarkson (11)
UCE Academy, Ellesmere Port

Friends

Friends are there for you all the time,
They will always be there,
Even when you caused crime.
Keep them close, don't let them go,
Care for them and they will love you
From head to toe.

Jade Hughes (13)
UCE Academy, Ellesmere Port

Distant Voices

Every gunshot,
Every man down,
A world of peace shall not be restored.
Fighting for our country,
Filled with pride and fright,
Death shall not be his fatal last sight.

Devils' gunshots firing into a million heads,
Families knowing that their loved ones are dead,
Trenches are flooding helplessly,
Unconscious at a fellow's breast,
Twenty thousand soldiers,
Bullets in their chests.

Love and tranquillity conquers all,
But not for evermore . . .

As the adrenaline-hungry soldier
Marches through the sludge and shotguns,
He stands, softly turning back.
Shells.
Proudly waving the English flag.
Soaring and blasting his way to victory.
The breathing air tastes like unforgiven souls.
People at home, sat with empty plates.

The mechanism of life is struck
By the selfishness of others.
The sound of ringing in the sergeant's ear.
The sound of crying - mercy unforgiven.
Mercy! Mercy!

Cry o baby, cry, set my head on aching for the blasts
That build the walls of home,
Never home, hungry for war, hungry for death.
The leaver's head on stake . . . 'dulce et decorum est'
The point of life, the point of death.

Declan Baxter (12) & Leah Whitehead
Verdin High School, Winsford

The Bonny Dug Of Carlisle

The bonny dug of Carlisle
Walked a mile to see his bonny owner,
There's still a gad place
To put a bonny dug on the land,
The dug is a bonny gold colour,
The dug cannot get a puny if he wants one,
The dug helps at the scale with the pupils,
The dug lies on the rug in the hosse,
The dug chews his bone all day and all night,
The dug was a hero,
The last day of the dug's life, he said guidbye,
The dug died at a guid age,
The owner was a sad man when the dug died.

Eli Anderson (13)
Waid Academy, Anstruther

Skateboarding Is . . .

Skateboarding is cool, skateboarding is fun,
It's hotter and better than a hot cross bun.

When I pull a 360 I really know,
I'm in the air and for a moment I glow.

When I'm skatin' around I feel real ace,
But if I make a wrong move I'm on me face.

Peter Ramsden (14)
Windlestone School, Ferryhill

The Way You Make Me Feel
(Dedicated to Arron H)

Sometimes at night, when I look to the sky,
I start thinking of you and I wonder why.

Why do I love you? I think and smile,
Because I know that my list could run on for miles.

The whisper of your voice, the warmth of your touch,
So many little things that make me love you so much.

The way you support me and help me with my emotions,
The way you care and show so much devotion.

The way your kiss fills me with desire,
And how you hold me with the warmth of a blazing fire.

The way your eyes shine when you look at me,
Lost with you forever is where I want to be.

The way you make me feel when you're by my side,
A sense of competition and overflowing pride.

The dreams that I dream, that all involve you,
The possibilities I see and the things we could do.

How you finish a puzzle that lies within my heart,
Deep in my soul you are the most important part.

I could go on for days telling you what I feel,
But all you need to know is that my love for you is real.

Lauren Stephens (14)
Windlestone School, Ferryhill

Young Writers Information

We hope you have enjoyed reading this book - and that you will continue to enjoy it in the coming years.

If you like reading and writing poetry drop us a line, or give us a call, and we'll send you a free information pack.

Alternatively if you would like to order further copies of this book or any of our other titles, then please give us a call or log onto our website at www.youngwriters.co.uk.

Young Writers Information
Remus House
Coltsfoot Drive
Peterborough
PE2 9JX
(01733) 890066